ALPHA NUMBER CHART

1	2	3	4	5	6	7	8	9
A	B	C	D	E	F	G	H	I
J	K	L	M	N	O	P	Q	R
S	T	U	V	W	X	Y	Z	

HOT NUMBERS ™

HOT NUMBERS™

How to Use Numerology to Discover What Makes Your Lover, Boss, Friends, Family, and <u>You</u> Really Tick!

Jean Simpson

GRAMERCY BOOKS
NEW YORK

For Dr. Frank Richelieu,
who taught me to focus
on the HOT side of life.

As your life is what you make of it, numbers are guidelines to a life that you can create by living up to the positive messages in your numbers.

This 1998 edition is published by Gramercy Books®, an imprint of Random House Value Publishing, Inc., by arrangement with Crown Publishers, Inc., 201 East 50th Street, New York, NY 10022.

Gramercy Books® and colophon are registered trademarks of Random House Value Publishing, Inc.

HOT NUMBERS™, logo and design are trademarks of Jean Simpson.

Printed in the United States of America

Random House
New York • Toronto • London • Sydney • Auckland
http://www.randomhouse.com/

Library of Congress Cataloging-in-Publication Data

Simpson, Jean, 1942-
    Hot numbers: how to use numerology to discover what makes your love, boss, friends, family, and you really tick! / Jean Simpson.
        p. cm.
    Originally published: New York : Crown, c1986.
    ISBN 0-517-20276-X
    1. Numerology.   I. Title.
BF1623.P9S546 1998
133.3'35--dc21   97-50247
                                                                    CIP

CONTENTS

NAME NUMBER RELATIONSHIPS

LESSON NUMBERS

PERSONAL YEAR NUMBERS

INTRODUCTION

I was twenty-six years old when I met my first numerologist. Helena "held court" in the Beverly Wilshire Hotel in Beverly Hills. She sat at the front of the huge ballroom giving readings to one person at a time while her other clients waited patiently in the back.

I didn't know what to expect, but I could hardly wait for my turn. Finally I sat in the chair facing her.

She began by asking for my full name, exactly as it appears on my birth certificate, and my birthday. With only that information, a pencil, and a piece of paper, she quickly figured out "my numbers."

Helena said many things that amazed me during that first encounter. I was struck by the accuracy of her comments and touched by the experience, which left me feeling very special. She told me, "You have a gift for teaching, and your mission in life is to inspire others." For a long time after that first reading, I felt wonderful.

Like most of us, I love hearing about myself, especially when the message is uplifting. Every four months, like clockwork, I was back in that chair opposite her. The numbers were always right.

My self-confidence grew each time she emphasized my strengths. Encouraged, I realized that the numbers would become a very important part of my life. I wanted to know how Helena knew what she knew, and I begged her to tell me.

After dozens of readings, she sent me a birthday card with the promise that she would teach me the basics of numerology. I was ecstatic!

Months of intense study prepared me for the fascinating part—practicing. For the next several years, I asked anyone and everyone for their name and birthday. I was so intrigued by the numbers that I seriously began to consider numerology as my life's work. I was determined to simplify the numbers so I could share my new knowledge with others.

A new door opened in my professional career as a numerologist when I did numbers for a talented palmist named Spencer. "You know," he said, "you're very good. Have you ever thought of doing numbers for people at parties?"

I was flattered when he invited me to do numbers for some of his clients the following weekend. The very first reading I did was for a businessman, Michael. "Gosh!" I said. "You're in the middle

1

of a major job change. You're about to launch an extremely profitable business venture."

He chuckled. "I know. Today I gave my notice at the studio. I'm opening up my own personal management firm on Monday. I've rented the most expensive office I could find on the Sunset Strip, and I don't know how I'm going to pay for it."

"Don't worry," I said. "You're going to be a huge success." His numbers had shown me that he was going to be financially secure within six months. He's still my client and his business has skyrocketed.

I read numbers for five hours that night and wasn't even tired when I got home. The feedback from the clients was fantastic. They were amazed at the accuracy of my readings. So was I!

From that night on I was in business. An entertainment agent contacted me, began booking more parties, and scheduled me for lectures on cruise ships. Along the way, I attracted my own clientele. After the *Star* named me "one of the nation's ten most accurate psychics" the phone never stopped ringing. I appeared on "A.M. Los Angeles" and other top local radio and television shows. The response was incredible. Talk show hosts and audiences were amazed at how quickly I figured out their numbers and could tell them something positive about themselves and their futures.

With each reading, the numbers gradually took on new meanings for me. I have developed my own unique system, called HOT NUMBERS.™ I emphasize only the positive, or the HOT side of the numbers. Given hope and encouragement, people can use their numbers to take more control over their own lives.

HOW TO USE THIS BOOK

If you know your name, your birthday, and can add the numbers between 1 and 9, you can figure out your HOT NUMBERS. Your numbers have been carrying messages for you from the day you were born. They are powerful tools you can use to discover what roads to take, and when to take them.

The three most important numbers in my system are the NAME NUMBER, which reflects your character and personality traits; the LESSON NUMBER, which tells you what you need to learn in order to fulfill your potential; and the PERSONAL YEAR NUMBER, which indicates where you are, where you have been, and where you are headed.

YOUR NAME NUMBER

You have no idea how special your own name really is until you unlock its secrets with HOT NUMBERS. The NAME NUMBER reveals the story of your life. It affects how you will write, produce, direct, and perform in the play called "Life." Your NAME NUMBER tells whether you want to play the lead on center stage, or cast yourself in a variety of supporting roles. Will the director's chair have *your* name on it, or will you look to others for your cues?

If you have a NAME #7, your idea of fun might be an evening in a motel room filled with kinky toys. If you are a NAME #4, your urge for variety may be satisfied simply by changing sides in your bed at home.

People with a NAME #5 may run off to buy this month's newest diet book and then celebrate their resolve with one last hot fudge sundae. A NAME #8 might be expected to climb daily onto her doctor's scale and record the caloric content of every morsel she's eaten, along with the specific location where it was consumed.

WHAT NAME DO YOU USE? Your name, *exactly* as it appears on your birth certificate, gives you your NAME NUMBER. What about mistakes? If rumor has it that the doctor was drunk when he wrote your name, or the secretary at the Office of Vital Statistics left out or added letters, your birth certificate name is *still* the name to use. My experiences have proven that the birth certificate name, no matter how different it may be from the name you have used throughout your life, will give you the most accurate reading of your numbers.

3

Sometimes finding out what is written on your birth certificate comes as a surprise. Most of us don't look at this document until we apply for our passports. One woman discovered that there was no name on her birth certificate; only the words BABY GIRL appeared where her given name should have been written. I told her that BABY GIRL was the name she should use to figure out her NAME NUMBER. She tried to persuade me that her "real" name, the one she had used as a child, would be more accurate. Instead of arguing with her, I suggested doing her numbers both ways so she could decide for herself which name provided a more accurate reading. She agreed. Sure enough, when I explained the meanings of each NAME NUMBER, the description based on the number for BABY GIRL most accurately described her.

ARE YOU ADOPTED?

If you are adopted, and if you do not know the name on your birth certificate, you have several options. Try to have your records opened to determine the name, even if it was used only for the brief period before your adoption. If that fails, work with the name you have used most of your life. It may not be as accurate as the actual birth certificate name, but it will have great value.

Interestingly enough, some people find that the name on a newly discovered birth certificate and the name they have been using often add up to the same number.

IF YOU ARE JR., II, III, OR IV

If you have been named for someone else and carry a Jr. or Roman numeral after your name, add your NAME NUMBER with and without the title. Judge for yourself which version best describes you. Generally, I find that your name without the Jr., II, III, or IV is the most accurate.

IS YOUR NAME WRITTEN IN A FOREIGN ALPHABET?

Use the American version of your name, spelling it the way it sounds in English. Realize that it may not be 100 percent accurate.

WERE YOU FOUND UNDER A ROCK?

Is your birth certificate missing or nonexistent? Use the name given to you as a child, assuming it would have been used on your birth certificate.

WERE YOU GIVEN ADDITIONAL NAMES WHEN YOU WERE BAPTIZED?

If you have a baptismal certificate, don't use the name on it unless it carries the same name as your birth certificate.

WHAT ABOUT EXTRA NAMES? Some cultures routinely use additional "middle names." Take singer Vikki Carr, for example. Her birth certificate reads: FLORENCIA BISENTA DE CASILLAS MARTINEZ CARDONA.

Even if she runs out of space on the paper, she has to use the whole enchilada to get an accurate calculation for her HOT NUMBERS!

NAMES AND NUMBERS Numerology is based on mathematics. Pythagoras, the father of mathematics, theorized that every letter in the alphabet has a corresponding number. The number for each letter is determined by its place in the alphabet. Since A is the first letter, A is 1. B, the second letter, is 2, C is 3, etcetera. When you come to the letters with numbers that are made up of two digits, add the numbers together, and reduce them to a single digit. For example, J is the tenth letter of the alphabet. Add 1 + 0, which equals 1. J is 1. K is the eleventh letter of the alphabet. Add 1 + 1, which equals 2, and K is 2. Use the same method of adding and reducing every letter all the way up to Z, which is the twenty-sixth letter. Add 2 + 6, which equals 8. And that's all the arithmetic you need to know to figure out your HOT NUMBERS.

ALPHA NUMBER CHART

1	2	3	4	5	6	7	8	9
A	B	C	D	E	F	G	H	I
J	K	L	M	N	O	P	Q	R
S	T	U	V	W	X	Y	Z	

For handy reference, this important chart also appears at the end of this book and on the endpapers in front and back. You will need to refer to it often.

Now I'm going to reduce you to a number!

HOW TO FIND YOUR NAME NUMBER Write your complete name on a blank piece of paper. Allow enough space to write the corresponding number under each letter.

For an example, let's start with a name I know best, mine. JEAN MARIE WAMSER appears on my birth certificate.

J E A N   M A R I E   W A M S E R

Step 1   Below each letter write down the corresponding numbers from the ALPHA NUMBER CHART.

J	E	A	N		M	A	R	I	E		W	A	M	S	E	R
1	5	1	5		4	1	9	9	5		5	1	4	1	5	9

Step 2   Add the numbers of one name at a time. Start with the first name, JEAN. Add the numbers using the HOT NUMBERS method. Add $1 + 5 + 1 + 5$, which equals 12. Reduce the 12 to a single digit by adding $1 + 2$, which equals 3. Your calculations should look like this:

$$J \quad E \quad A \quad N$$
$$1 \quad 5 \quad 1 \quad 5$$
$$(1 + 5 + 1 + 5) =$$
$$12$$
$$(1 + 2) =$$
$$\textbf{3}$$

Step 3 Add the middle name, MARIE. Add the numbers $4 + 1 + 9 + 9 + 5$, which equals 28. Next, add $2 + 8$, which equals 10. Reduce 10 to a single digit by adding $1 + 0$, which equals 1. You've got it! MARIE adds to 1.

$$M \quad A \quad R \quad I \quad E$$
$$4 \quad 1 \quad 9 \quad 9 \quad 5$$
$$(4 + 1 + 9 + 9 + 5) =$$
$$28$$
$$(2 + 8) =$$
$$10$$
$$(1 + 0) =$$
$$\mathbf{1}$$

Step 4 Add the last name, WAMSER. Follow the same procedure: $5 + 1 + 4 + 1 + 5 + 9$, which equals 25. Reduce 25 to a single digit by adding $2 + 5$, which equals 7. WAMSER adds to 7.

$$W \quad A \quad M \quad S \quad E \quad R$$
$$5 \quad 1 \quad 4 \quad 1 \quad 5 \quad 9$$
$$(5 + 1 + 4 + 1 + 5 + 9) =$$
$$25$$
$$(2 + 5) =$$
$$\mathbf{7}$$

Step 5 Add the totals of each of the three names to get the NAME NUMBER. Since JEAN equals 3, MARIE equals 1, and WAMSER equals 7, add 3 + 1 + 7, which equals 11. Reduce 11 to a single digit by adding 1 + 1, which equals 2. The NAME NUMBER for JEAN MARIE WAMSER is 2.

J	E	A	N		M	A	R	I	E		W	A	M	S	E	R
1	5	1	5		4	1	9	9	5		5	1	4	1	5	9

$$(1 + 5 + 1 + 5) = \qquad (4 + 1 + 9 + 9 + 5) = \qquad (5 + 1 + 4 + 1 + 5 + 9) =$$

$$12 \qquad\qquad 28 \qquad\qquad 25$$

$$(1 + 2) = \qquad (2 + 8) = \qquad (2 + 5) =$$

$$10$$

$$(1 + 0) =$$

$$3 \qquad + \qquad 1 \qquad + \qquad 7 =$$

$$11$$

$$(1 + 1) =$$

$$\mathbf{2}$$

SHORTCUT SLASH METHOD

This shortcut method uses a slash to show the reduction of two digits to a single digit.

When you compare the example of the original method to the example of the shortcut slash method you can see that the slash (/) replaces the written addition.

Original Method

J	E	A	N
1	5	1	5

$$(1 + 5 + 1 + 5) =$$

$$12$$

$$(1 + 2) =$$

$$\mathbf{3}$$

Shortcut Slash Method

J	E	A	N
1	5	1	5

$$12/\mathbf{3}$$

Here's another name using the shortcut slash method. Let's find the NAME NUMBER for DON SCOTT ROGERS.

Step 1 Write the full name as it appears on the birth certificate, and place the corresponding number under each letter.

D O N   S C O T T   R O G E R S
4 6 5   1 3 6 2 2   9 6 7 5 9 1

Step 2 Start with the first name, DON. Add the numbers using the HOT NUMBERS method. DON adds to 6. Your calculations should look like this:

D O N

4 6 5

15/**6**

Step 3 Add the middle name, SCOTT. Add the numbers and reduce to a single digit. Your result will be 5.

S C O T T

1 3 6 2 2

14/**5**

Step 4 Add the last name, ROGERS. Following the same procedure, keep adding the numbers and reduce them to a single digit. ROGERS adds to 1.

R O G E R S

9 6 7 5 9 1

37/10/**1**

Step 5   Now find the NAME NUMBER by adding the totals of the first, middle, and last names. DON equals 6, SCOTT equals 5, and ROGERS equals 1. The NAME NUMBER for DON SCOTT ROGERS is 3.

D	O	N		S	C	O	T	T		R	O	G	E	R	S
4	6	5		1	3	6	2	2		9	6	7	5	9	1

15/6	14/5	37/10/1
6	5	1

$$12/\mathbf{3}$$

To reduce your margin of error, I have taught you how to add the sums of the corresponding numbers of the first, middle, and last names *separately* to find your NAME NUMBER.

However, you will arrive at the same NAME NUMBER if you add the corresponding numbers of every letter in the first, middle, and last names *all together*. Using the HOT NUMBERS method, reduce the sum to a single digit.

Let's use the name on my birth certificate as an example, JEAN MARIE WAMSER. I have placed the corresponding number under each letter. When added together, the sum is 65. $(6 + 5) = 11$ $(1 + 1) = 2$. My NAME NUMBER is 2.

The calculations look like this:

J	E	A	N		M	A	R	I	E		W	A	M	S	E	R
1	5	1	5		4	1	9	9	5		5	1	4	1	5	9

$$(1+5+1+5 + 4+1+9+9+5 + 5+1+4+1+5+9) =$$

$$65$$

$$(6 + 5) =$$

$$11$$

$$(1 + 1) =$$

$$\mathbf{2}$$

If you check the figures on page 8, you will see that when I added the sums of the corresponding numbers in the first, middle, and last names *separately*, I arrived at a NAME #2 also.

No matter how the corresponding numbers are added, the result is the same. One method may be used to check the other.

Here's a brief overview of the actual meanings of NAME NUMBERS, just to whet your appetite. Full descriptions are provided in the NAME NUMBERS section beginning on page 37.

NAME NUMBER MEANINGS

1 A leader with a pioneering spirit, strength, independence, and determination.

2 A diplomat and peacemaker who is sensitive to the feelings of others as well as his own.

3 A master with words, forever youthful, who juggles many projects, and becomes more self-confident with age.

4 A practical, hard worker who is patient and good with details.

5 A freedom-loving traveler who thrives on variety and change, and is able to do many things at one time.

6 A harmonizer who values a peaceful home and family, loves nice things, and takes responsibilities seriously.

7 An analyzer who wisely takes time alone to read, write, and see the forest—in spite of the trees.

8 An organizer who attains power and success when in control of his own destiny.

9 A humanitarian, lover of art, music, or travel, who gives generously and requires appreciation.

WITHIN YOUR NAME NUMBER Now that you have read the descriptions of some of the NAME NUMBERS, you may have some questions.

You may be wondering why some of the characteristics in your NAME NUMBER description don't fit you perfectly.

You may also be wondering why some people with the same NAME NUMBER are so different.

I have the answers to those questions.

Within your NAME NUMBER are your PERSONALITY NUMBER and HEART NUMBER. They are not as important as your NAME NUMBER, but they are necessary because they describe you more fully.

Think of yourself and your NAME NUMBER as a package. In my HOT NUMBERS method, there are nine different kinds of packages, numbered 1 through 9.

The first thing people notice about your package is the outer wrapping. This outer wrapping is called your PERSONALITY NUMBER. Some packages are flashy with red ribbon and bells, while others are simply tied up with a cord.

A group of packages with the same NAME NUMBER may look different because of their distinctive wrappings. People with the same NAME NUMBER may appear different because of their unique personalities.

Hidden inside your NAME NUMBER package is your HEART NUMBER. It represents the innermost thoughts, feelings, desires, and talents that motivate you. Some hearts beat softly inside their packages, others sound like jungle drums.

Just as a group of packages with the same NAME NUMBER may have different wrappings, so they may have different contents. People with the same NAME NUMBER may have different PERSONALITY NUMBERS and different HEART NUMBERS.

So, in order to understand your NAME NUMBER fully, it is essential to know your PERSONALITY NUMBER and HEART NUMBER. Although the NAME NUMBER is the most important, the PERSONALITY NUMBER and HEART NUMBER are two parts that make up the whole.

HOW TO FIND YOUR PERSONALITY NUMBER Your PERSONALITY NUMBER is found by adding the numbers that correspond to the CONSONANTS in your name. Consonants are all the letters in the alphabet *except* for a, e, i, o, and u.

Let's figure out the PERSONALITY NUMBER of my own name: JEAN MARIE WAMSER.

Step 1 Write the corresponding numbers from the ALPHA NUMBER CHART *below* each consonant, and leave blank the space below each vowel.

J	E	A	N		M	A	R	I	E		W	A	M	S	E	R
1			5		4		9				5		4	1		9

Step 2 To make things as easy as possible, add one name at a time. Start with the first name, JEAN. Add the corresponding numbers of the consonants J and N, using the HOT NUMBERS method. Add $1 + 5$, which equals 6. Your calculations should look like this:

$$
\begin{array}{cccc}
J & E & A & N \\
1 & & & 5 \\
(1 & + & & 5) = \\
& & 6 &
\end{array}
$$

Step 3 Now add the corresponding numbers of the consonants, M and R, in the middle name, MARIE. Add $4 + 9$, which equals 13. Reduce 13 to a single digit by adding $1 + 3$, which equals 4. You've got it! Your calculations should look like this:

$$
\begin{array}{cccc}
M & A & R & I & E \\
4 & & 9 & & \\
(4 & + & 9) = & & \\
& 13 & & & \\
(1 + 3) = & & & & \\
4 & & & &
\end{array}
$$

Step 4 Now add the corresponding numbers of the consonants, W, M, S, and R, in the last name, WAMSER. Using the HOT NUMBERS method, add $5 + 4 + 1 + 9$, which equals 19. Add $1 + 9$, which equals 10. Reduce 10 to a single digit by adding $1 + 0$, which equals 1. Your calculations should look like this:

$$
\begin{array}{cccccc}
\text{W} & \text{A} & \text{M} & \text{S} & \text{E} & \text{R} \\
5 & & 4 & 1 & & 9 \\
(5 & + & 4 + 1 & + & & 9) = \\
& & 19 & & & \\
& & (1 + 9) = & & & \\
& & 10 & & & \\
& & (1 + 0) = & & & \\
& & \mathbf{1} & & &
\end{array}
$$

Step 5 Now add the single digits of the sums of the consonants in the first, middle, and last names to find the PERSONALITY NUMBER for JEAN MARIE WAMSER.

The consonants in JEAN equal 6, the consonants in MARIE equal 4, and the consonants in WAMSER equal 1. Add $6 + 4 + 1$, which equals 11. Using the HOT NUMBERS method, reduce 11 to a single digit by adding $1 + 1$, which equals 2. The PERSONALITY NUMBER for JEAN MARIE WAMSER is 2. Your calculations should look like this:

$$
\begin{array}{lll}
\text{J E A N} & \text{M A R I E} & \text{W A M S E R} \\
1 \quad\quad 5 & 4 \quad 9 & 5 \quad 4 \; 1 \quad 9 \\
(1 \;+\; 5) = & (4 \;+\; 9) = & (5 \;+\; 4 + 1 \;+\; 9) = \\
 & 13 & 19 \\
 & (1 + 3) = & (1 + 9) = \\
 & & 10 \\
 & & (1 + 0) = \\
6 \quad\quad + & 4 \quad\quad + & 1 = \\
\end{array}
$$

$$
\begin{array}{c}
11 \\
(1 + 1) = \\
\mathbf{2}
\end{array}
$$

Now let's find the PERSONALITY NUMBER for DON SCOTT ROGERS using the Shortcut Slash Method.

Step 1 Write the full name exactly as it appears on his birth certificate. Then refer to the ALPHA NUMBER CHART and write the corresponding numbers *below* each consonant, leaving blank the spaces below the vowels, a, e, i, o, and u.

```
D O N      S C O T T      R O G E R S
4   5      1 3   2 2      9   7   9 1
```

Step 2 Start with the first name, DON. Add the corresponding numbers of the consonants together using the HOT NUMBERS method. The consonants in DON add to 9. Your calculations should look like this:

```
        D O N
        4   5
          9
```

Step 3 Now add the corresponding numbers of the consonants in the middle name SCOTT, using the HOT NUMBERS method. The consonants in SCOTT add to 8. Your calculations should look like this:

```
        S C O T T
        1 3   2 2
            8
```

Step 4   Now add the corresponding numbers of the consonants in the last name, ROGERS. Keep adding the numbers and reduce them to a single digit. The consonants in ROGERS add to 8. Your calculations should look like this:

$$\begin{array}{ccccc} \text{R} & \text{O} & \text{G} & \text{E} & \text{R} & \text{S} \\ 9 & & 7 & & 9 & 1 \end{array}$$

$$26/\mathbf{8}$$

Step 5   Find the PERSONALITY NUMBER by adding the single digits of the sums of the consonants in the first, middle, and last names. The consonants in DON equal 9, in SCOTT equal 8, and in ROGERS equal 8. Reduce to a single digit. The PERSONALITY NUMBER for DON SCOTT ROGERS is 7. Your calculations should look like this:

$$\begin{array}{ccccccccccc} \text{D} & \text{O} & \text{N} & & \text{S} & \text{C} & \text{O} & \text{T} & \text{T} & & \text{R} & \text{O} & \text{G} & \text{E} & \text{R} & \text{S} \\ 4 & & 5 & & 1 & 3 & & 2 & 2 & & 9 & & 7 & & 9 & 1 \\ & 9 & & & & & 8 & & & & & & 26/8 \end{array}$$

$$25/\mathbf{7}$$

Here is a brief overview of the meanings of the PERSONALITY NUMBERS. Full descriptions are provided in the PERSONALITY NUMBERS section beginning on page 125.

PERSONALITY NUMBER MEANINGS
(Others perceive you as . . .)

1 Daring, independent, original, strong-willed, and competitive.

2 Receptive, sensitive, sympathetic, cooperative, and diplomatic.

3 Friendly, optimistic, talkative, lighthearted, and entertaining.

4 Disciplined, practical, hard-working, reliable, and loyal.

5 Alert, multifaceted, active, adventurous, and up-to-date.

6 Loving, adaptable, supportive, responsible, and fair.

7 Reserved, poised, discriminating, analytical, and trustworthy.

8 Self-sufficient, organized, efficient, powerful, and successful.

9 Gracious, generous, helpful, charitable, and influential.

HOW TO FIND YOUR HEART NUMBER Your HEART NUMBER is found
by adding the corresponding numbers of the VOWELS in your
name. Vowels are a, e, i, o, and u. Let's use my name once again,
JEAN MARIE WAMSER.

Step 1 Write the corresponding numbers from the ALPHA NUM-
BER CHART *above* each vowel, leaving blank the spaces above the
consonants. Only a, e, i, o, and u have numbers above them.

```
  5 1        1      9 5        1        5
J E A N    M A R I E    W A M S E R
```

Step 2 To make things as easy as possible, add one name at a
time. Start with the first name, JEAN. Add the corresponding
numbers of the vowels, E and A, using the HOT NUMBERS method.
Add 5 + 1, which equals 6. Your calculations should look like
this:

$$6$$
$$(5 + 1) =$$
```
      5 1
  J E A N
```

Step 3 Add the corresponding numbers of the vowels, A, I, E, in
the middle name, MARIE. Add 1 + 9 + 5, which equals 15. Reduce 15 to a single digit by adding 1 + 5, which equals 6. Your
calculations should look like this:

$$6$$
$$(1 + 5) =$$
$$15$$
$$(1 \quad + \quad 9 + 5) =$$
```
   1      9 5
  M A R I E
```

Step 4 Now add the corresponding numbers of the vowels, A and E, in the last name, WAMSER. Add 1 + 5, which equals 6. You are becoming a master at adding the HOT NUMBERS way. Your calculations should look like this:

6

(1   +   5)=

1   5

W   A   M   S   E   R

Step 5 Now add the single digits of the sums of the vowels in the first, middle, and last names to find the HEART NUMBER for JEAN MARIE WAMSER. The vowels in JEAN equal 6, the vowels in MARIE equal 6, and the vowels in WAMSER equal 6. Add 6 + 6 + 6, which equals 18. Using the HOT NUMBERS method, reduce 18 to a single digit by adding 1 + 8. The HEART NUMBER for JEAN MARIE WAMSER is 9. Your calculations should look like this:

9

(1+8) =

18

6   +   6   +   6 =

(1+5) =

15

(5 + 1) =   (1 + 9+5) =   (1   +   5) =

5   1   1   9 5   1   5

J E A N   M A R I E   W A M S E R

Let's figure the HEART NUMBER for DON SCOTT ROGERS using the Shortcut Slash Method.

Step 1   Write the full name exactly as it appears on his birth certificate. Referring to the ALPHA NUMBER CHART, write the corresponding numbers *above* each vowel, a, e, i, o, u. Leave blank the space above each consonant.

```
   6              6           6     5
D O N     S C O T T     R O G E R S
```

Step 2   Start with the first name, DON. There is only one vowel, O, and its corresponding number is 6.

```
      6
   D O N
```

Step 3   There is also only one vowel, O in the middle name, SCOTT. Its corresponding number is 6.

```
      6
   S C O T T
```

Step 4   Add the corresponding numbers of the vowels in the last name, ROGERS. The vowels, O and E, add to 11. Reduce to 2. Your calculations should look like this:

```
       11/2
     6     5
   R O G E R S
```

Step 5 Now find the HEART NUMBER for DON SCOTT ROGERS by adding the single digits of the sums of the vowels in the first, middle, and last names: 6 + 6 + 2 = 14. Reduce to a single digit. The HEART NUMBER for DON SCOTT ROGERS is 5. Your calculations should look like this:

14/5

6		6		11/2	
6		6		6	5
D O N		S C O T T		R O G E R S	

Here is a brief overview of the meanings of the HEART NUMBERS. Full descriptions are provided in the HEART NUMBERS section beginning on page 131.

HEART NUMBER MEANINGS
(Your inner feelings and talents motivate you to . . .)

1   Lead and direct using your own original ideas.

2   Cooperate and please others using your sensitivity and diplomatic skills.

3   Express your optimism and creative ability.

4   Make sacrifices to gain tangible results with practical plans.

5   Seek adventure and to travel in the fast lane.

6   Create a harmonious and peaceful atmosphere.

7   Spend time alone to search for the truth and contemplate the quiet side of life.

8   Take charge and organize your efforts to acquire money, power, and success.

9   Share your knowledge and compassion to benefit the world.

A NEAT TRICK Have you discovered that when you add your PERSONALITY NUMBER and HEART NUMBER you get your NAME NUMBER?

That's proof that the outer wrapping, the PERSONALITY NUMBER, and the inner contents, the HEART NUMBER, add together to make the entire package, the NAME NUMBER.

For instance, my PERSONALITY NUMBER is 2 and my HEART NUMBER is 9. Add the 2 of my PERSONALITY NUMBER to the 9 of my HEART NUMBER, and you get 11. Reduce 11 to a single digit and you get 2, my NAME NUMBER.

The NAME NUMBER of DON SCOTT ROGERS is 3. His PERSONALITY NUMBER is 7 and his HEART NUMBER is 5. Add 7 + 5, which equals 12. Reduce 12 to a single digit and you get 3, his NAME NUMBER.

Now that you understand the entire concept of the NAME NUMBER, you are ready to learn your next important number, your LESSON NUMBER.

YOUR LESSON NUMBER

To understand your LESSON NUMBER, you will need the answers to these questions.

WHAT ARE YOUR LESSONS? Points along a road. Think of a trip you are planning by car. Road map in hand, you are in New York, singing "California, Here I Come!" Each stop along the route is a dot on the map. Those dots represent lessons you must learn to reach your goal, and are the personal characteristics and abilities you should develop in order to meet your greatest opportunities in life.

WHEN AND HOW DO I LEARN MY LESSONS? It's up to you! Lessons are not always fun and some of us tend to put off learning them. Think of your lessons as exercise. If you want a gorgeous body, you'll have to work on it. No one can do it for you. You may not like to exercise, but it takes a little sweat to learn your lesson and to live up to the HOT side of your numbers. Choose the gym or the sport and plan your own schedule. The options are open to you. You may even decide to avoid the whole matter. Some people learn their lessons early. Others learn their lessons late in life.

To discover your LESSON NUMBER and the opportunity it holds, you need one simple formula.

22

HOW TO FIND YOUR LESSON NUMBER Using the HOT NUMBERS method, add and reduce:

The MONTH + the DAY + the YEAR you were born.

To find the MONTH number, refer to the chart below:

January	1	May	5	September	9
February	2	June	6	October	10/1
March	3	July	7	November	11/2
April	4	August	8	December	12/3

Notice that October, November, and December have two digits, which have been reduced to single digits. For example: November is 11; $(1 + 1) = 2$, December is 12; $(1 + 2) = 3$.

Let's find Brooke's LESSON NUMBER. She was born July 19, 1969.

$$
\begin{array}{ccc}
\text{July} & 19 & 1969 \\
7 & (1 + 9) = & (1 + 9 + 6 + 9) = \\
& 10 & 25 \\
& (1 + 0) = & (2 + 5) = \\
7 \; + & 1 \quad + & 7 = \\
& 15 & \\
& (1 + 5) = & \\
& \mathbf{6} &
\end{array}
$$

Michael was born on December 29, 1961. Using the Shortcut Slash Method, let's find his LESSON NUMBER.

$$
\begin{array}{ccc}
\text{December} & 29 & 1961 \\
12/3 & 29/11/2 & 17/8 \\
3 & 2 & 8 \\
& 13/\mathbf{4} &
\end{array}
$$

Here is a brief overview of the meanings of the LESSON NUMBERS. Full descriptions are provided in the LESSON NUMBERS section beginning on page 301.

LESSON NUMBER MEANINGS

1   Learn to stand up for yourself in a nice way. Be strong and independent.

2   Learn to cooperate. Be a diplomat, work with others, and don't take things personally.

3   Learn to socialize and use words. Do things creatively and develop self-confidence.

4   Learn to work with details and be patient. Be practical and finish what you start.

5   Learn to be flexible and welcome change. Be more spontaneous and do things on the spur of the moment.

6   Learn to be a harmonizer. If others argue, smooth things over. Be loving and responsible.

7   Learn to be alone, without being lonely. Analyze and get to know the quiet, mystical side of life.

8   Learn to be organized, handle money, and balance your emotions. Tend to health, diet, and exercise.

9   Learn to reach out to others and be concerned for their welfare. Give without expecting to receive.

YOUR PERSONAL YEAR NUMBER

Your PERSONAL YEAR NUMBER instantly reveals where you are, where you've been, and where you're going. It provides the answer to the question most frequently asked: "What should I do now?"

A nine-year cycle regulates the PERSONAL YEARS. If you are in a PERSONAL YEAR #1 this year, you will be in a PERSONAL YEAR #2 after your next birthday. And so the cycle continues through #9, when it starts all over again in a PERSONAL YEAR #1.

My HOT NUMBERS system is unique. Unlike other numerologists, who calculate the PERSONAL YEARS from January 1, I find it more accurate to use your birthday as the beginning date of the PERSONAL YEAR.

There is a rhythm to life based on the nine-year cycle. Knowing your PERSONAL YEAR NUMBER and its meaning gives you a sense of where you belong in the scheme of things. The PERSONAL YEAR NUMBER sheds a light like a beacon on the tides of life. You'll know when to anchor, when to set sail, and most important, when your ship is coming in.

HOW TO FIND YOUR PERSONAL YEAR NUMBER Using the HOT NUMBERS method, add and reduce:

Birth MONTH + Birth DAY + YEAR of your last birthday

Stop and think about that. Your birth *month,* your birth *day,* and the *year of your last birthday.*

Assume that today is June 6, 1990. In what year did you have your last birthday? If you were born between January 1 and today, June 6, you have already had your birthday this year. So the year you had your last birthday is 1990. If your birthday is between June 7 and December 31, you have not yet had your birthday this year. The year you had your last birthday is 1989.

Let me show you an example. Let's still pretend that today is June 6, 1990, and we are figuring the PERSONAL YEAR NUMBER for Ann, whose birthday is May 6. Here is my step-by-step method:

Step 1   Ann's birthday is May 6.

Step 2   Today's date is June 6, 1990.

Step 3   Has Ann had her birthday yet this year? Yes, she has. Her birthday was a month ago today on May 6. So, the year Ann had her last birthday is 1990.

Step 4   Now let's find Ann's PERSONAL YEAR NUMBER by adding and reducing her:

Birth MONTH + Birth DAY + YEAR of her last birthday

$$
\begin{array}{ccc}
\text{May} & 6 & 1990 \\
5 & 6 & 19/10/1 \\
5 \; + & 6 \; + & 1 = \\
& 12/\mathbf{3} &
\end{array}
$$

Step 5   Ann is in a PERSONAL YEAR #3.

Let's do another one. Bob's birthday is December 31. Let's still pretend today's date is June 6, 1990. What PERSONAL YEAR is Bob in? Here is the step-by-step method:

Step 1 Bob was born December 31.

Step 2 Today is June 6, 1990.

Step 3 Analyze: Has Bob had his birthday yet this year? No, he won't have his birthday for another six months, so we need to go back to the year he had his last birthday. You're right. Bob had his last birthday in 1989.

Step 4 Now let's find Bob's PERSONAL YEAR NUMBER by adding and reducing his:

Birth MONTH + Birth DAY + YEAR of his last birthday

$$
\begin{array}{ccc}
\text{December} & 31 & 1989 \\
12/3 & 4 & 27/9 \\
3 \quad + & 4 \quad + & 9 = \\
& 16/\mathbf{7} &
\end{array}
$$

Step 5 Bob is in a PERSONAL YEAR #7.

Figure your PERSONAL YEAR NUMBER and consult the chart that follows for a brief overview of the PERSONAL YEAR NUMBER meanings. Full descriptions are provided in the PERSONAL YEAR NUMBERS section beginning on page 305.

PERSONAL YEAR NUMBER MEANINGS

1   This is the new beginning you have been waiting for; the slate has been wiped clean for a fresh start. The seeds you plant now will determine your future harvest.

2   Togetherness and partnership are on your mind. Don't be too sensitive or take things personally. This may be a waiting time. Study something of interest.

3   A year to socialize, create, communicate, and reap the seeds you have sown. There will be many small things to do and you may be scattered. A period of expansion, so watch your waistline!

4   A year of hard work and possible feelings of restriction or boredom. Keep your nose to the grindstone and build a firm foundation for the future.

5   Keep your suitcase packed, and expect the unexpected. A year of fun, freedom, sex, change, and travel. Get out of the rut and enjoy yourself!

6   A year centered around love, home, family, responsibilities, and adjustments. You may beautify yourself or your surroundings. Be a magnet and attract people.

7   Take time for yourself this year. Curl up with a good book or commune with nature. Think about where you've been, and where you are going in life. Analyze.

8   Hit it on all cylinders! A time for money, power, success, health, and diet. Get organized. Balance yourself mentally and physically.

9   This is a good year to weed your garden and discard things that are no longer useful. Share and think of others. If a door closes, look for a new one to open next year.

YOUR PERSONAL MONTH NUMBER

You have twelve PERSONAL MONTHS in the course of your PERSONAL YEAR.

Your PERSONAL MONTH NUMBER reflects how your feelings and your circumstances change during the year and helps you understand the direction your life is taking month by month. PERSONAL MONTH NUMBERS provide answers to questions such as when should I go on vacation? or when should I start a new project?

Each PERSONAL MONTH begins and ends on the calendar day of your birthday. My birthday is on August 23, so my PERSONAL MONTHS all begin and end on the 23rd.

If you are born on the 29th, 30th, or 31st of any month, use the last day of the months that don't have 29, 30, or 31 days.

Before you figure your twelve PERSONAL MONTH NUMBERS, you need to know two things:

1. Your PERSONAL YEAR NUMBER. Add and reduce:

   Birth MONTH + Birth DAY + YEAR of your last birthday.

2. The CORRESPONDING NUMBERS for each of the twelve calendar months:

January	1	May	5	September	9
February	2	June	6	October	10/1
March	3	July	7	November	11/2
April	4	August	8	December	12/3

The double digit numbers of October, November, and December have been reduced to a single digit. For example, October is the 10th month: $(1 + 0) = 1$. November is the 11th month: $(1 + 1) = 2$. December is the 12th month: $(1 + 2) = 3$.

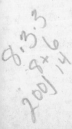
8.3.3
8×6
200/14

HOW TO FIND YOUR PERSONAL MONTH NUMBER Using the HOT NUMBERS method, add and reduce:

The MONTH in question + Your PERSONAL YEAR NUMBER

Let's use my birthday as an example. I was born on August 23 and I am currently in a PERSONAL YEAR #5.

First, make a vertical list of my twelve PERSONAL MONTHS, which begin on my birthday and last until the same day one month later. Place the corresponding number for each calendar month in the space below each month. Then, add the number corresponding to each month to my PERSONAL YEAR NUMBER.

Here is my list:

August 23 to September 23
8   + 5 PERSONAL YEAR = 13/4 PERSONAL MONTH
September 23 to October 23
9   + 5 PERSONAL YEAR = 14/5 PERSONAL MONTH
October 23 to November 23
10/1   + 5 PERSONAL YEAR =   6 PERSONAL MONTH
November 23 to December 23
11/2   + 5 PERSONAL YEAR =   7 PERSONAL MONTH
December 23 to January 23
12/3   + 5 PERSONAL YEAR =   8 PERSONAL MONTH
January 23 to February 23
1   + 5 PERSONAL YEAR =   6 PERSONAL MONTH
February 23 to March 23
2   + 5 PERSONAL YEAR =   7 PERSONAL MONTH
March 23 to April 23
3   + 5 PERSONAL YEAR =   8 PERSONAL MONTH
April 23 to May 23
4   + 5 PERSONAL YEAR =   9 PERSONAL MONTH
May 23 to June 23
5   + 5 PERSONAL YEAR = 10/1 PERSONAL MONTH
June 23 to July 23
6   + 5 PERSONAL YEAR = 11/2 PERSONAL MONTH
July 23 to August 23
7   + 5 PERSONAL YEAR = 12/3 PERSONAL MONTH

Figure your PERSONAL MONTH NUMBERS and consult the chart that follows for a brief overview of the PERSONAL MONTH NUMBER meanings. Full descriptions are provided in the PERSONAL MONTH NUMBERS section beginning on page 311.

PERSONAL MONTH NUMBER MEANINGS

1   A time to be actively independent and plan something new.

2   A time for togetherness, patience, and gathering facts.

3   A time to use words, be creative, and entertain.

4   A time to rest, be practical, and do the things you have neglected.

5   A time to have fun, keep your suitcase packed, and expect the unexpected.

6   A time to adjust, be loving, and responsible.

7   A time to analyze your goals and reflect on your progress.

8   A time to organize your act and take it on the road.

9   A time to complete projects, reach out to other people, and travel.

YOUR PERSONAL DAY NUMBER

You have 365 PERSONAL DAYS during your PERSONAL YEAR. Knowing your PERSONAL DAY NUMBER will help you to plan the right activity for the right day. Your PERSONAL DAY NUMBER is useful for deciding what day to get married, when to schedule a root canal, when to plan a party, and so on.

HOW TO FIND YOUR PERSONAL DAY NUMBER Using the HOT NUMBERS method, add and reduce:

MONTH in question + DAY in question + PERSONAL YEAR NUMBER

To find the corresponding number of the months, refer to this chart:

January	1	May	5	September	9
February	2	June	6	October	10/1
March	3	July	7	November	11/2
April	4	August	8	December	12/3

The double digit numbers of October, November, and December have been reduced to a single digit. For example, October is the 10th month: $(1 + 0) = 1$. November is the 11th month: $(1 + 1) = 2$. December is the 12th month: $(1 + 2) = 3$.

Let's figure my PERSONAL DAY NUMBER for January 4 during my PERSONAL YEAR #3. My calculation would look this this:

January   4

$1 + 4 + 3$ PERSONAL YEAR $= 8$ PERSONAL DAY

Let's suppose you want to know what kind of a PERSONAL DAY to expect on August 15 and you are in a PERSONAL YEAR #9. Your calculation would look like this:

August   15

$(1 + 5) =$

$8 + 6 + 9$ PERSONAL YEAR $= 23/5$ PERSONAL DAY

Consult the chart that follows for a brief overview of PERSONAL DAY NUMBER meanings. Full descriptions are provided in the PERSONAL DAY NUMBERS section beginning on page 315.

PERSONAL DAY NUMBER MEANINGS

1	Go for it!
2	Sit on it!
3	Express it!
4	Work on it!
5	Chase it!
6	Love it!
7	Think about it!
8	Organize it!
9	Share it!

HOT SHEET

Now that you know your own HOT NUMBERS, let me introduce you to the HOT SHEET.

The HOT SHEET will help you keep track of all the numbers that you figure for yourself and your friends.

At the top of the HOT SHEET, there is a place to write the name currently used by each of your HOT NUMBERS. The person you know today as Beth Wilson may be Mary Elizabeth Kornfelder on her birth certificate. And given current statistics, she may not be Beth Wilson the next time you see her.

There is a place for every HOT NUMBER. I've used my own HOT NUMBERS in this example. Fill in the blank HOT SHEET with your own HOT NUMBERS.

HOT SHEET

JEAN SIMPSON
CURRENT NAME

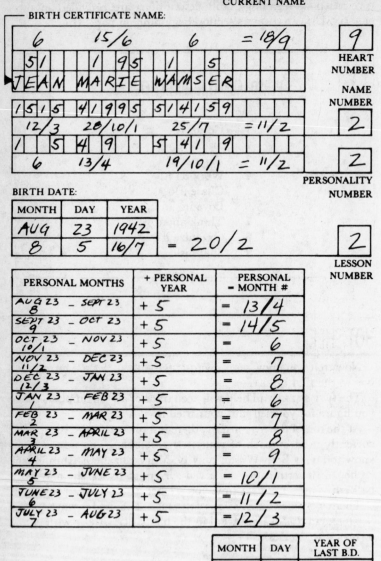

BIRTH CERTIFICATE NAME:

6	15/6	6	= 18/9	**9**

HEART NUMBER

| 5 1 | | 1 | 9 5 | 1 | 5 | |

J E A N   M A R I E   W A M S E R

NAME NUMBER

| 1 5 5 | 4 | 9 9 5 | 5 4 | 5 9 | |

| 12/3 | 20/10/1 | 25/7 | = 11/2 | **2** |

| 1 | 5 | 4 | 9 | | 5 | 4 | | 9 | |

| 6 | 13/4 | 19/10/1 | = 11/2 | **2** |

PERSONALITY NUMBER

BIRTH DATE:

MONTH	DAY	YEAR
AUG	23	1942
8	5	16/7

= 20/2   **2**

LESSON NUMBER

PERSONAL MONTHS	+ PERSONAL YEAR	PERSONAL – MONTH #
AUG 23 – SEPT 23 8	+ 5	= 13/4
SEPT 23 – OCT 23 9	+ 5	= 14/5
OCT 23 – NOV 23 10/1	+ 5	= 6
NOV 23 – DEC 23 11/2	+ 5	= 7
DEC 23 – JAN 23 12/3	+ 5	= 8
JAN 23 – FEB 23 1	+ 5	= 6
FEB 23 – MAR 23 2	+ 5	= 7
MAR 23 – APRIL 23 3	+ 5	= 8
APRIL 23 – MAY 23 4	+ 5	= 9
MAY 23 – JUNE 23 5	+ 5	= 10/1
JUNE 23 – JULY 23 6	+ 5	= 11/2
JULY 23 – AUG 23 7	+ 5	= 12/3

DATE OF LAST BIRTHDAY:

MONTH	DAY	YEAR OF LAST B.D.
AUG	23	1990
8	5	19/1

14/5

CURRENT PERSONAL YEAR NUMBER

HOT SHEET

CURRENT NAME

BIRTH CERTIFICATE NAME:

HEART
NUMBER

NAME
NUMBER

PERSONALITY
NUMBER

BIRTH DATE:

MONTH	DAY	YEAR

=

LESSON
NUMBER

PERSONAL MONTHS	+ PERSONAL YEAR	PERSONAL – MONTH #
–	+	=
–	+	=
–	+	=
–	+	=
–	+	=
–	+	=
–	+	=
–	+	=
–	+	=
–	+	=
–	+	=
–	+	=

DATE OF LAST BIRTHDAY:

MONTH	DAY	YEAR OF LAST B.D.

CURRENT PERSONAL YEAR NUMBER

HOW TO USE WHAT YOU'VE LEARNED

Now you have all the information you need to figure HOT NUM-BERS and understand their meanings.

So far you have:

1. calculated HOT NUMBERS for your NAME, PERSONALITY, HEART, LESSON, PERSONAL YEAR, PERSONAL MONTH, and PERSONAL DAY.

2. filled in your own HOT SHEET.

The next steps are to read about:

3. your NAME NUMBER.

4. your PERSONALITY NUMBER.

5. your HEART NUMBER.

6. your NAME, PERSONALITY, and HEART NUMBER COMBINA-TION.

7. NAME NUMBER RELATIONSHIPS after you have calculated HOT NUMBERS for important people in your life.

8. your LESSON NUMBER.

9. your current PERSONAL YEAR NUMBER.

10. your current PERSONAL MONTH NUMBER.

11. your current PERSONAL DAY NUMBER.

Have fun and may all of your NUMBERS be HOT!

NAME NUMBERS

Your NAME NUMBER is determined by the full name on your birth certificate and describes how you play your role in life. Instructions for calculating your NAME NUMBER begin on page 6.

THE NAME #1 MAN

The #1 MAN is a strong, self-confident leader. Decisive by nature, he moves quickly toward his goal with a no-nonsense approach. It's obvious that his pioneering spirit gives him the courage to explore new fields.

Capable of original thinking, he believes in the superiority of his ideas. He's also a good debater, with the tenacity to maintain his own opinion regardless of what others think.

Single-minded and persistent, he's determined to succeed and proud of his accomplishments. The #1 MAN is a trendsetter who enjoys the attention he attracts when he's the first on the block to own the latest gadgets. From the satellite dish on his roof to the latest software for his computer, he enjoys his state-of-the-art possessions.

HOME

Whether he owns a palatial estate or a custom-made tent, the #1 MAN is king of his castle. His home is his haven, a place where he can retreat from the outside world. An unlisted phone number, answering service, or electronic gate gives #1 the solitude he needs to generate creative new ideas.

When #1 host plans a party, it's a major production requiring a staff to prepare it; he presides over the grand affair as if he did all the work himself. Although the #1 MAN enjoys entertaining, houseguests who stay longer than three days or drop in unexpectedly are not his style.

FRIEND

Loyal to those he likes, a #1 MAN chooses his friends regardless of their station in life. He gives them his all, including his opinions, for which he expects to be admired.

Too busy to entertain out-of-town VIPs? Call upon your #1 FRIEND to mastermind the entire evening. From the limo to the restaurant to the front-row seats, you can rely on him to impress your guests. Just make sure to pay the bill and give him all the credit.

You'll know when your forthright #1 FRIEND wants to be

alone; he will tell you. Respect his need for privacy and prepare for the next flurry of activity generated by this innovative man.

LOVER

The passionate #1 MAN approaches sex with intensity and determination—he wants what he wants when he wants it.

Expect him to initiate love-making with take-charge bravado. From the boardroom to the bedroom, #1 likes to be on top. Allow him to have his way, or at least let him think that it's his idea when you're on top.

If you enjoy excitement and adventure, he's the man for you. Inventive and daring, #1 is "try"-sexual; he'll make love anywhere once—in the kitchen, on the dining-room table, or in his office. Not even the impending arrival of the cleaning crew will deter your dynamo lover.

FATHER

A proud #1 FATHER sets high standards for his children and expects them to excel at whatever they do. To help them compete effectively for first place, he'll provide nothing but the best for his budding achievers—the latest computer or private lessons with a tennis pro.

An original thinker in his own right, he respects and encourages individuality in each of his children. He listens when they express their opinions and considers their side of the story in matters of discipline.

A first-class father, #1 will choose opening-day ceremonies, premier performances, front-row center seats for family outings.

BUSINESS

Nonstop drive and ambition propel the #1 MAN into positions of leadership. Whether he's a CEO or a maverick entrepreneur, his self-reliance and ability to make shrewd decisions explain his stellar career.

His peers consider him a pioneer in his field because he has the courage to be progressive in the face of popular opposition. A nonconformist, he frequently finds new solutions to old problems.

Back him all the way if he wants to launch a business with his innovative product or service. But understand that an equal partnership will not satisfy #1; he needs at least 51 percent.

BOSS

A decisive #1 BOSS is clearly in control; he wastes no time defining priorities and setting his goals.

He goes after what he wants and expects you to help him get it. Creating the initial plan is his forte; filling in the details should be yours. Tenacious and compulsive in his work habits, he demands the same commitment from his employees.

If his memos seem terse or he raises his voice, don't take offense; at least you always know where you stand with a #1 BOSS. Even though he likes his ideas best, you can influence him by appealing to his sense of logic. He is fair to subordinates who carry out his orders and give him the respect he knows he deserves.

EMPLOYEE

The independent #1 EMPLOYEE loves to be in charge. A natural leader, he uses innovative methods to direct a project efficiently. Because he requires little supervision, it's wise to define areas of responsibility for your #1 EMPLOYEE and allow him the freedom to implement his own approach.

He's great at brainstorming; encourage him to participate in product development. Or, if you have stock that's gathering dust on the shelf, count on him to find that new market.

Give your #1 star employee top billing whenever possible, or resign yourself to the fact that he'll move on quickly in his meteoric rise to the top.

HEALTH, DIET, EXERCISE

Mind made up, the #1 MAN is a very determined dieter; he doesn't stop until he reaches his goal. If he seeks the help of a nutritionist, she's in for a challenge; he will state his likes and dislikes loudly and clearly.

Exercise becomes a competitive game with daring overtones. In the morning he leaves his handball partners panting; after a quick lunch, he's ready to hike to the highest precipice.

If you are sick, he'll hire the most renowned specialist. On the rare occasion that he is sick, be at his beck and call—this is one time he doesn't want to be alone. Muster all the patience you can when you care for demanding #1. Heaven help you if he has a bell or buzzer at his fingertips!

TRAVEL

If you're planning a trip with this trailblazer, don't expect him to join a guided tour. And never mind the jet set's current watering hole; his favorite destination is "offbeat" and "unknown." He'll advise you to pack your running shoes, yet is perfectly happy to go on alone if you need to take a break.

The impulsive #1 MAN likes adventure on the spur of the moment. Give him the fastest, most direct route, a first-class seat, and he'll be content. Be ready to do it his way, because he'll find a means to get wherever he wants to go—even if it requires chartering a plane or renting a rubber raft.

Never hesitate to accept his invitation for an evening of slides. Far from the usual home movies, his presentations are always professional. You won't fall asleep—he won't let you!

GIFTS

If you're tempted to give him a surprise party—don't! The #1 MAN likes to be in control. Ask him to make up the guest list and choose the restaurant, and let him select the menu and order the wine.

In selecting a gift for your #1 MAN, listen for clues in his conversation; he has definite tastes. Even though he's hard to buy for, he would be pleased with a subscription to an entertainment or travel magazine, or a coffee-table edition of famous firsts. But to be on the safe side, give him a gift certificate so he can choose a gift from his favorite high-quality store.

THE NAME #1 WOMAN

The #1 WOMAN is a trendsetting pioneer with the confidence and enthusiasm to project her innovative ideas. Regal in her bearing, she is a strong leader who can hold her own in any group.

The self-sufficient #1 WOMAN is a law unto herself; she'd rather give directions than take them. She is quick to make up her mind, and not likely to change it; nor does she hesitate to state her opinions in open debate.

Goal-oriented, she moves decisively to accomplish tasks in an efficient manner. Determined to succeed, she aims to be the first with the best. She enjoys competition, and when her persistence pays off, she expects to be recognized for her achievements.

HOME

While she may not surround herself with a moat, the #1 WOMAN enjoys her privacy. Respect her schedule and call before you drop in; she doesn't appreciate surprises.

When she's in the mood for company, the #1 WOMAN plans and presides over original parties. Even if she has enlisted the help of a caterer, she will choose her favorite foods, have them served in her own dishes, and then take all the credit. After all, she made the decisions!

Queen of her castle, the #1 WOMAN refuses to be influenced by current trends. She has eclectic tastes and mixes styles according to her own rules.

FRIEND

She's discriminating in her choice of friends, so consider yourself fortunate if she chooses you. Although she may not always ask for your opinion, she's happy to offer hers, which will never be less than candid.

When you decide to follow her plan for redoing the front of your house, make sure to hang a brass plaque honoring your #1 FRIEND.

And remember, she likes to take charge. Defer to her when she announces last-minute plans to take you to her latest restaurant find. Suppress that urge to speak up when she orders for you—she just wants you to have the best—and compliment her novel choices. Next time she feels like company, you'll be at the top of her list.

LOVER

Passionate and aggressive, the #1 WOMAN won't hesitate to make the first move. She's direct and to the point, so don't beat around the bush. She is not impressed by an old line; if you can't be original in your approach, at least be honest and sincere in your flattery.

Her creativity becomes daring when she wants to make love on the veranda while the neighbors are having a garden party. And don't be surprised when she christens your new car with a rendez-vous in the front seat. You suspected it, but now you know: she won't take a back seat to anyone!

Lavish her with attention, and never say no. A #1 WOMAN in love is a HOT NUMBER.

MOTHER

The proud #1 MOTHER expects excellence in her children, whether they are playing the flute or running a race. She encourages even their slightest interests if she thinks her children will succeed.

Because she values individuality, she doesn't compare her children to one another. Rarely swayed by the opinions of others, she believes in her children and stands up for them.

A #1 MOM takes charge and expects her children to follow her directions. In return, they will have every advantage she can provide. She's an innovative parent, willing to implement her creative ideas for birthday parties and weekend outings. Count on her to dream up something more original than Pin the Tail on the Donkey.

Even though it's hard to change her mind, she will listen to reason before handing out the punishment. She views minor rebellions as her children's way of asserting themselves.

BUSINESS

Her love of challenge and competition makes the #1 WOMAN ideally suited to the business world. Even if she starts at the bottom of the ladder, she will climb to the top; she is ambitious, goal-oriented, and determined to succeed.

She is capable of working independently or she can be in charge, directing others to carry out her original ideas. A #1 WOMAN often operates her own business.

She's respected for her ability to make decisions and stand by them in the face of opposition. Her progressive vision enables her to initiate new concepts or improve existing systems with innovative methods.

BOSS

Once a decisive #1 BOSS charts her course, nothing will deter her from achieving a successful result. She generates enough original ideas to keep a large staff busy executing the details. Her directions are loud and clear: she wants you to work as hard as she does.

If you disagree and want to change her mind, appeal to her sense of logic. Presented with the facts, she will reach a new conclusion and think it was her idea.

Get ready to produce; she wants it yesterday. And when she says jump, salute and ask how high. When you turn out work she can show with pride, she won't forget to praise your efforts.

EMPLOYEE

Count on her to give you an honest assessment of any situation, whether you ask for it or not. You can't beat her, so you might as well use her.

An individualist, #1 works best alone or in charge of a team, so give her the freedom to exercise her ingenuity and leave the nit-picky details to someone else.

She'll improve any program with her ability to identify key problems and implement creative solutions. A #1 EMPLOYEE has the self-confidence to compete effectively under the most demanding circumstances. She won't stop until she has met your deadline and accomplished her goal.

As long as you respect her by providing challenging assignments and the recognition she deserves, the #1 EMPLOYEE will continue to use her initiative in your behalf.

HEALTH, DIET, EXERCISE

The #1 WOMAN has the determination and persistence to succeed in a weight-loss program. She doesn't rely on standard diets or the support of a diet counselor or group. The reducing regimen she has designed is as unique as she is, and her willpower has no equal. When everyone else at the table orders dessert, she'll be the one who abstains.

To keep in shape, the #1 WOMAN devises the most effective fitness program; but for recreation, she competes in her best sport and plays to win.

She makes a willing, efficient nurse when friends or family are sick, as long as the doctor listens to her diagnosis and lets her prescribe her special brand of treatment. As a patient, #1 expects immediate attention to her specific requests.

TRAVEL

First-class and fast-paced describes the itinerary of the #1 WOMAN. Warning: if you ask her how to see Europe, she'll tell you to improvise exactly the way she does, taking advantage of the offbeat and unique. Even though she hates prescribed tours, she'll insist that you repeat her latest adventure down to the smallest detail.

While the self-assured #1 WOMAN can travel alone, she enjoys an agreeable companion who is willing to follow her lead and do the unusual.

GIFTS

Flatter the #1 WOMAN with a gift that represents quality and reflects her sophisticated tastes. She states her preferences so often that you should already know who her favorite designers are. But, if you can't find exactly what she wants, give her a gift certificate from a store that meets her high standards.

To pay tribute on a special occasion, set the stage and crown her queen for the day. Instead of arranging a surprise, let her command the performance.

THE NAME #1 CHILD

The #1 BABY asserts himself (or herself) the moment he arrives. When he cries, he wants action!

He is an independent tyke. Expect him to toddle off to his first day of nursery school without a backward glance. A natural leader, he can marshal the troops at school and leave a timid teacher quaking in her boots. The competitive #1 CHILD wants first place in line, the title of team captain, and top spot on the honor roll. If he (or she) finds himself in second place, give him a quick pat on the back to renew his determination. Remember, even though he is born with self-confidence, he is sensitive to criticism.

Respect his need for privacy. Give him his own room and time to be alone. Though he can entertain himself, he likes to have a best friend. When the #1 CHILD opens his first lemonade stand, he's already hired an assistant.

Don't be surprised when he wants to pursue unusual hobbies; he'll be the first kid on the block to train boa constrictors or tinker with a chemistry set. Resist your protective urges when he jumps off the top of the jungle gym; he always lands on his feet.

He's good at making decisions, but he's also good at changing his mind, as long as he think it's his idea. Encourage his strength and uniqueness; what may seem willful and stubborn to others, you recognize as determination and a pioneering spirit. The things he does which cause you to gray prematurely are also the keys to his success.

THE NAME #2 MAN

The #2 MAN is a born listener. He's tuned in to all frequencies, even the static. Fortunately, he comes equipped with patience and understanding. He has the power to inspire others, and people naturally gravitate to him.

Valued for his tact and intuition, the #2 MAN is often given jobs requiring his diplomatic skills. Insightful and aware of all the options, he occasionally has difficulty making decisions. Knowing how carefully he considers his opinions, people frequently ask for his advice.

The tolerant #2 MAN harbors few prejudices. Although he may be conservative, he accepts the unconventional in others.

A #2 MAN is like a walking Yellow Pages and an encyclopedia. His resources for the weird and wonderful are endless, and his open mind overflows with an astounding collection of facts. He's an avid student, and an even more enthusiastic teacher. To him, half the fun of learning is being able to share his knowledge.

He is by no means a loner; however, when too many people require his attention, a #2 may seek time alone to renew his energy.

HOME

The #2 MAN's home is a gathering spot for his friends, loved ones, and prized possessions. He is a consummate collector of people and things. He's the kind of man who owns an array of original sculpture or a vast assortment of classical tapes, and fills his home with exotic plant specimens.

Consider yourself fortunate to receive an invitation to one of his parties; he's famous for his creative menus. An inspired cook, the #2 MAN's meal is superb and various in cuisine and theme. Occasionally he may rely on the neighborhood gourmet deli, but when he goes to the trouble of seeding the cucumbers, be sure to notice and admire his skill. In return, he'll make sure you have met at least one new friend or business contact before the memorable evening is over.

FRIEND

A #2 FRIEND is a friend for all reasons: if you need to talk, he'll listen; if you need advice, he'll give it; if you need a shoulder to cry on, his will be the strongest, softest, and most waterproof. He's a social creature and genuinely likes the company of his friends.

The #2 FRIEND derives great pleasure from helping his friends. He's the one who can assemble the mail-order jungle gym when the directions are missing.

When you are feeling playful, resist the impulse to tease him. He can't take being the brunt of a joke. Don't risk hurting his feelings; you need him too much to lose him.

LOVER

The idealistic #2 MAN is happiest when he's in love with another sensitive soul. He responds to his lover like a knight in shining armor; his courtly manners and thoughtful gestures are designed to win a fair maiden's heart.

Because he's so intuitive, he can sweet-talk his love to fever pitch without so much as a single touch.

In bed, your wish is his command; he hates to say no. And since he's as good a teacher as he is a student, staying after school may soon be one of your favorite indoor sports.

His eye for detail makes an evening with him a romantic fantasy, right down to the scented candles and satin sheets. Considerate and sentimental, your #2 LOVER will always call the next day to say "I love you." On the anniversary of your first trip together to the shore, he will order the same wine you had the first time and give you a seashell.

Although he's understanding if you are late for a date or too tired to make love, he won't accept a lie. Respect his sensitive side and settle little problems tactfully and truthfully.

FATHER

Patient and understanding #2 makes a divine Dad. He listens to both sides of the story and he'll be fair provided he is told the truth.

Children love him because he can be a kid for a day, setting aside his gourmet taste for French food in exchange for pizza or hot dogs. There is always room for friends to come along, as long as they keep the noise down to a dull roar.

A #2 FATHER is a perpetual student who loves to help with research projects. If the encyclopedia he bought isn't adequate, he'll move the term paper research to the public library. He also shares his hobbies and encourages his children to pursue their own interests.

BUSINESS

Check out a successful partnership and you're likely to find a #2 MAN. His ability to synchronize his skills with others makes him ideally suited to a business duo. Competition takes a back seat to cooperation in this #2 MAN's book—in fact, he wrote the company arbitration policy.

His talent for research is a great asset in business; once he gathers the facts, he considers them carefully before making a decision. Although the #2 BUSINESSMAN is persuasive and sensitive to his clients' needs, don't expect him to drive a hard bargain. On the other hand, he won't claw his way to the top over your dead body!

BOSS

A #2 BOSS appreciates his employees and shows it. Because you want to please him, you may set your alarm clock early so you can put in an extra hour. Don't hesitate to ask him questions. He loves to teach and will do more than give you a pat answer.

If you make a mistake, admit to it and show that you have learned from the experience; he'll reward your honesty. Need a day off? Ask him. He is sensitive to the needs of others, and knows that a happy employee is a productive one. But don't take his generosity for granted; he runs a business, after all!

EMPLOYEE

Your resourceful #2 EMPLOYEE is just the man to succeed with a special assignment requiring detailed organization. Don't overlook his obvious talent for planning major entertainment events: trust him with a dinner, a cocktail party, or a grand opening.

If you are gone for an hour or a week, he'll run the office smoothly. You won't lose any business, and you may gain a satisfied client or two in your absence.

He's a true diplomat who will listen carefully to both sides of a problem, then come up with a carefully worded solution that will make everyone happy.

Repay his loyalty with praise and a healthy bonus when an exceptional task is complete.

HEALTH, DIET, EXERCISE

Diet is a familiar word to the #2 MAN, who loves to indulge. In his book, anything worth doing is worth overdoing. So if you are curious about the latest diet, he can recite menus and calorie counts chapter and verse. However, he's a bit vague when you ask him how much weight he's lost.

On the subject of exercise, he'll expound enthusiastically on the ambiance of his spa or the endurance of his jogging partner. Press him, and he may admit they meet for breakfast and jog across the parking lot.

When you are sick, there is no more considerate an attendant than generous #2. He often sacrifices his energy to his friends and family. To maintain his health, he needs to take time off to recharge his batteries.

TRAVEL

Considerate and adaptable, a #2 MAN makes a great traveling companion. Whether he finds himself in a lavish villa or in a cut-rate motel, he'll be content as long as he has a companion to share the trip.

He's resourceful and finds adventure around every corner.

Leave the itinerary and travel arrangements to him; his diplomacy and tact will open the most unlikely doors.

Be prepared for the unusual. After you have had your bath, you'll be glad you bought those marvelous rugs at the dusty bazaar. And with pictures to prove it, you can regale your friends with the story about riding the spitting camels.

If you are meeting his plane, bring the station wagon; although he may have departed with only one suitcase, he'll return with three more filled with trinkets for friends.

GIFTS

The generous #2 MAN is more a giver than a receiver. However, he secretly loves receiving gifts for the thought they represent, rather than for what they cost.

Before you add to one of his collections, consider a gift that will help him organize or display what he already owns. He would also appreciate an offer to help him catalog his slides or mount his pictures; he enjoys working with a partner.

He is a sponge when it comes to absorbing new information—give him a reference book or a new biography. With any gift, include a personal note; he'll be touched that you recognize him for being special.

THE NAME #2 WOMAN

A peacemaker, the #2 WOMAN is a great diplomat with a natural sense of protocol. So good is she at sensing the emotions and moods of those around her, you'd swear she is equipped with radar. Although she intuitively knows just the right words to uplift your spirits, she is also an expert at facilitating a mutually satisfactory agreement between two parties.

The symbol of 2 affects her life: partnership and cooperation are vital to her happiness. Doing two things at once is easy for her; and she can always see two sides of any question. Faced with many options, she often has difficulty making a decision.

She possesses extraordinary powers of observation, particularly for details. A perpetual student, she gathers knowledge from life as well as from books. Using her patience and uncanny ability to simplify the most complicated concept, the #2 WOMAN makes an effective teacher.

There is an indefinable presence and elegance about her; she's a lady with style. With an aesthetic sensibility, she enjoys refined music; a honky-tonk piano in a noisy bar would unnerve her. Romantic by nature, she prefers a movie with a tender love story to a blood-and-guts Western.

She is extremely sensitive and can often be hurt by an innocent remark. Ignore her too long and she wilts. If you look up and find her missing, chances are she's just recharging her batteries.

A #2 WOMAN is patient and cooperative long after most people lose their cool, but there is a limit to her patience. Don't push her too far; she'll come out swinging.

HOME

From the moment the #2 WOMAN opens her front door, you'll feel at home because she puts people at ease.

If you've been invited for dinner, don't be surprised if your favorite food is on the menu. Watching her cook is fascinating; she is able to talk on the phone, whip up a soufflé, and catch up on all of your latest news at the same time.

She may rush at the last minute to get herself ready, but the table is set for a meal that looks as good as it tastes. If you like something, don't bother to ask for the recipe. After consulting her collection of cookbooks for ideas, a #2 WOMAN improvises, measuring casually and tasting as she goes.

Hers is the home of a consummate collector. Be it potholders or paintings, her drawers and shelves will be filled with a lifetime accumulation of beloved objects.

FRIEND

Your deepest secret is safe with a #2 FRIEND. No one listens better than she does—not even your therapist. She's the kind of friend who may know you better than you know yourself, and will inspire you to pursue the best that is in you.

She always has a solution to your problem and her resources are endless. Who else can find an antique fire engine for your five-year-old's birthday party, or a vintage limo for your seventeen-year-old's prom?

To maintain your friendship with a #2 WOMAN, respect her sensitivity and don't make a joke that she could take personally.

LOVER

Polish up your suit of armor; the #2 WOMAN swoons over gallant heros. Wine her and dine her, and don't forget to hold her seat. If you mind your manners, she just might be your dessert. She may be shy at first, but don't be fooled; just wait until the bedroom door is closed! Always the serious student, she's more than willing to learn a few new tricks—even in bed. Fortunately for you, she likes to oblige and rarely says no.

Partnership and togetherness are important to her. She originated the expression "It takes two to tango."

Cradle your sexy and sensitive #2 WOMAN gently, since she's finely tuned. Leave her a note on the pillow, or call her just to say "I love you," and she'll be yours forever.

Don't ever lie to the #2 WOMAN. She can forgive, but she won't forget deceit.

MOTHER

A natural people pleaser, the #2 MOTHER is dedicated, often referred to as a "smother mother." Her children know her as a good listener and confidante who considers both sides of the story before rendering a decision.

Her home is a favorite gathering place for the neighborhood children; she succeeds in providing creative entertainment that is also educational. Patient and resourceful, she's able to help children with special needs.

Although she hates to say no, her children will tell you she does have her limits: too much noise, rude language, and not enough appreciation provoke her anger.

BUSINESS

The #2 WOMAN is a natural partner who can intuitively bring out the best in her associate. Her attention to detail and ability to develop organizational systems are enormous assets to any business. Under pressure, the #2 WOMAN remains calm. You can rely on her to be an arbitrator and peacemaker. Her tactful and sensitive approach will ensure the success of the most critical negotiations.

Clients and customers gravitate to her. She remembers their names and special requirements. Her office is a comfortable, nonthreatening place to do business. If you have a potential client who needs to be persuaded, a #2 WOMAN can close the deal with apparent ease.

Although she seems to make business decisions effortlessly, be assured that she carefully considers all the alternatives.

BOSS

She will amaze you with her resourcefulness and her limitless supply of ideas. You will continue to learn while you work for her because she enjoys sharing her knowledge. She answers all questions authoritatively, but if she doesn't know the answer, she is not afraid to admit it.

Although she hates to say no, when she puts her foot down, she always has her employee's interest at heart.

Appreciate and acknowledge the extra time she gives you. Never mistake her sensitive approach to business for weakness. She expects you to work as hard as she does. Although she may not have an iron hand, there is real strength inside her kid glove.

EMPLOYEE

Fill a job that requires diplomacy and an eye for detail with a #2 WOMAN. She's resourceful, reliable, and very organized.

Send her to cover a meeting, and she'll return with a detailed account of everything that happened. If you suspect a problem is brewing in the office, trust her sense of the emotional climate and her instincts about how to resolve it.

Sensitive and intelligent, #2 EMPLOYEE knows how to entertain an important client to make him feel special. After the initial meeting, she will have ideas for doing business with him (or her) more effectively in the future.

Assign a new employee to a #2, whose teaching instincts will help the trainee adjust quickly. Don't forget to thank her for all she does to make your business life run smoothly. If you treat her well, her loyalty and cooperation will help make your business a huge success.

HEALTH, DIET, EXERCISE

Consult the #2 WOMAN if you need the latest word on health, diet, or exercise. Once motivated to improve her physical condition, she leaves no page unturned in researching the best systems and products available.

With her collection of diet books and unused exercise equipment, she is a veritable fountain of information. And the professional quality of her wardrobe belies her amateur status.

If you are watching your weight, this sympathetic, seasoned dieter will serve you a 100-calorie salad that looks and tastes like a million. And your imported mineral water, garnished with fresh lime, will be served in stemmed crystal.

If you are sick, a #2 WOMAN will come to the rescue armed with the latest pain remedy, her copy of *Physicians' Desk Reference*, and a Thermos of homemade chicken soup.

TRAVEL

You'd be hard pressed to find a better traveling companion than an agreeable, thoughtful #2 WOMAN. Count on her to make reservations well in advance and to call ahead early on the day of departure for the weather report.

Overbooked flight? The #2 WOMAN will convince the airline to find space. At the hotel, she'll diplomatically change rooms three times until it feels "just right," and leave the desk clerk smiling in spite of her requests.

Within minutes of landing, she'll ask around to find the memorable sights, the "in" restaurants, and the best shops. When it's time to leave, she'll produce a collapsible suitcase to pack the souvenirs for friends at home.

GIFTS

She appreciates the wrapping as much as the gift, so take extra care with the way you present your present. She responds more to the thought behind the gift than its cost.

Remember the Depression glass in her breakfast room, or the display of crystal paperweights in her office? Add another piece to her collection or select a book that will provide her with more knowledge about her favorite things.

She is always pleased to receive a new toy for her kitchen. Since she cooks by the dump method, skip the measuring spoons; she doesn't use them. Instead, choose clever tools such as mushroom fluters, radish rose makers, and melon ballers in graduated sizes; she loves the finishing touches.

The least costly and most appreciated gift for a #2 WOMAN is a personal note saying thank you.

THE NAME #2 CHILD

So adaptable and adorable is he (or she) that the delivery-room nurse will swear that he was born with a halo. A #2 BABY instinctively knows that smiles and coos bring him lots of attention. (He or she will learn to apple polish before he can walk.) His built-in radar enables him to sense the tension in a household, or the messages from a nervous mother.

The #2 CHILD is a social creature. He (or she) makes friends of everyone he encounters, and never leaves the butcher shop without a piece of bologna in his little hand.

He is the teacher's pet and works hard to please. At recess, he is usually among the first chosen for a team because he is so cooperative. Although he is not especially competitive, he will try hard to win for his team.

His curiosity makes him an enthusiastic student, with a great capacity to learn. But it's not just facts he picks up: be sure to check his pockets before you toss the jeans in the wash. Hire a bulldozer to shovel out his room periodically, but be sure he has a chance to sort out his special treasures first.

Encourage his hobbies and artistic or musical interests. Don't be too concerned if he embroiders the truth; he is a born lily gilder.

Generous to a fault, he'll run out and spend his first paycheck on presents for you, and he'll be there to grace your old age with his quiet reassurance.

THE NAME #3 MAN

The #3 MAN uses his tremendous personal charm to get what he wants. An eternal optimist, he has the versatility to excel in many areas, but he claims his fame as a great communicator. His facility with words extends from writing and speaking to singing, if only in the shower.

With his dramatic flair and lighthearted attitude, the #3 MAN brings fun and humor to all aspects of his life. A kid at heart, his motto reads, "Whoever ends up with the most toys wins."

The more self-confident he feels, the more gregarious he is. Seeking a good time wherever he goes, he's welcomed by people of all ages. A natural entertainer, he thrives on the response of an appreciative audience. He claims center stage with his "look-at-me" tricks.

Although he may appear scattered and dependent on people, #3 occasionally becomes single-minded as he focuses on one project.

His glossy exterior may hide a lack of self-assurance, which makes some #3s very shy. But like a good wine that improves with age, a #3 MAN becomes more confident the older he gets.

HOME

Full of friends and family, the house of a #3 MAN is apt to be more like a busy train station than a private residence. The door is always open to his party palace, which contains every audio/video gadget available, plus a garage full of grown-up "wheel toys." There is at least one room where #3 can retreat to do exactly as he pleases.

Happiest when surrounded by people, this genial host really means it when he says, "The more the merrier." He's ready to drop everything for an impromptu party, and they know him by name at the twenty-four-hour gourmet takeout restaurant. All gatherings are lively because of #3's childlike spontaneity, and his planned parties usually have outlandish themes and exotic entertainment.

His phones never stop ringing; they are his lifeline, especially on the rare occasion when he's obsessed with a special project.

FRIEND

The gregarious #3 MAN is the center of his large circle of friends. The eternal optimist, he sees the best in others and loves everyone. His contagious enthusiasm is guaranteed to chase away your blues.

Pleasure-seeking #3 loves spur-of-the-moment diversions; he's a walking party looking for a place to happen. In his enthusiasm, he tends to overextend himself and accept too many invitations, so be patient if he's late or calls with an excuse to cancel.

To maintain his exuberance, bolster his ego and reassure him whenever you can. If a frown threatens to line his youthful brow, give in; he sulks when he doesn't get his way.

LOVER

Virile #3 is full of fun and games in bed. The flirtatious twinkle in his eye makes him irresistible; he's so popular you may have to take a number and stand in line!

A talented sweet-talker, the #3 LOVER is so clever with words he can write you a sonnet, or at least some sizzling love letters.

Sometimes shy, but always imaginative, he'll surprise you with his last-minute plans for a weekend getaway. Nothing keeps this energetic lover down for long; he's always ready for another round.

He loves to be admired and to get his way, so pamper him and stroke his ego, among other things. In return, he'll work hard to please you. With a #3 MAN, the honeymoon is never over.

FATHER

A #3 DAD understands what it's like to be a kid, because part of him will never grow up. He loves all children and has been known to drop everything to take a carload of kids to the beach or the amusement park.

When teachers assign essays or school elections call for slogans and speeches, the word-whiz #3 FATHER is eager to help. And he's the first one to offer his home for the swim team or drama-club party.

He will admit to spoiling his children, but they had better not act like it! Not only does he shower them with affection, he showers them with toys, especially the ones *he* wants to play with.

A #3 FATHER has great sympathy for shy children because he probably lacked self-confidence as a boy. And his own creativity explains why he encourages his children's artistic and musical talents.

BUSINESS

#3's versatile, creative mind earns him the title of jack-of-all-trades. At his best when he has an audience, #3 has a way with words. He can make himself known to everyone at a convention, or preside as master of ceremonies. Shy #3s, who are more comfortable moving among the public than in front of it, write the speeches that more outgoing #3s deliver.

Charm and magnetism are the keys he uses to open professional doors. With a tendency to exaggerate, he can talk his way into or out of anything.

Upbeat and optimistic, he motivates others; in the midst of serious business, he adds a touch of levity. Co-workers and clients appreciate his enthusiasm, even when he scatters his energies and overcommits his time in an effort to please.

On occasion, #3 will choose to concentrate on a single goal. This seemingly uncharacteristic behavior may perplex his associates, but when it's combined with his otherwise gregarious personality, the results spell success in the business world.

BOSS

The #3 BOSS wants to be liked by his employees. He may joke about a problem, but take him seriously because he actually means business. As long as the work gets done and you cover your bases, he'll understand if you want to set your own hours so you can leave early.

He's a master of verbal expression; no dull memos come out of his office!

Optimistic and good-natured, he's skilled at motivating employees. He makes an effort to vary otherwise boring routines and to inject humor into the business day. You'll receive positive reinforcement from a #3 BOSS and he'll help you see the bright side of your predicaments.

Even though he's flexible, remember he likes to get his own way and needs attention. He's human, after all!

EMPLOYEE

Assign paperwork and dull, routine tasks to someone else; #3 has a creative flair that must not be ignored. His unorthodox suggestions can expand many projects, and his verbal proficiency enables him to write excellent promotional material and speeches.

A #3 EMPLOYEE's positive attitude and personal charm enhance any office. Co-workers are uplifted by this friendly, entertaining man.

Even though he's socially adept, remind him not to do all the talking when he entertains clients. Be sure he stays within the budget, especially when he plans the office party.

Within a reasonable framework, allow him to vary standard routines and procedures to fit his own needs. Help him to set priorities so he doesn't overextend himself and promise projects he can't deliver on time. Harness his enthusiasm and energy and you've got a winner.

HEALTH, DIET, EXERCISE

A believer in preventive medicine, #3 takes good care of himself so he can burn the candle at both ends. Although nothing keeps this optimist down for long, he wants to be pampered whenever he's sick. If you're the patient, call on #3 to revitalize you with his cheerful manner; but when you need rest, gently tell him to stop talking.

Even though the #3 MAN values a trim body, his busy social life makes it difficult for him to count calories. Conscious of his youthful appearance, he enjoys flattery, so while he's dieting encourage him with compliments about his physique.

Loquacious #3 talks a good game. In fact, his jaw muscles are the most exercised part of his body! A group activity or a sport that reminds him of his youth will satisfy this social animal. Roller-skating, anyone?

TRAVEL

A #3 MAN lives by the pleasure principle. When he travels, he wants to go where the action is. He likes to meet new people and mingle with the multitudes.

Hour-by-hour itineraries restrict his love of the impromptu; he needs flexible plans so he can take the next flight if the spirit moves him.

His talent with words saves him in any strange land; expect him to pick up a new language as well as new friends.

When the mail comes, get out your magnifying glass. Wordy #3 can write more on a postcard than most people put in a letter! And when he offers to show you his pictures, be prepared to see more people than scenic vistas and hear more life stories than historic facts.

GIFTS

A #3 MAN loves the attention a gift implies. Give him a joke book, since he's usually the life of the party and always needs new material. To remind him of his childhood, present him with a bag of peanuts containing two tickets to a ballgame. Best of all, give your #3 Captain Communication a car phone or cordless extension to facilitate his favorite habit.

At his best with an audience, #3 is a perfect candidate for a "This Is Your Life" party. Videotape the whole affair so you can preserve his colorful ad libs.

THE NAME #3 WOMAN

In her desire to be popular, the #3 WOMAN attempts to be the E-type Woman—everything to everybody. Outgoing or shy, she knows how to attract attention by telling entertaining stories and skillfully performing "watch-me" tricks.

Although talented in many areas of creative expression, she may lack self-assurance. Most #3 women overcome their timidity and grow more confident with age.

Playful, animated #3 is attracted to the less serious side of life. Not one to keep her nose to the grindstone indefinitely, she believes that all work and no play makes life dull. She rewards herself with fun at every turn. She has an optimistic view and is not easily discouraged. Versatile #3 thinks on her feet and talks her way around any problem. Even though she enjoys keeping many irons in the fire, she can be very single-minded at times.

Conscious of her youthful appearance, she goes to great lengths to preserve and enhance it. A lover of beautiful things and luxurious surroundings, she also craves the latest gadgets. The telephone is her favorite modern convenience; she has as many extensions and extra services as she can afford to help her keep track of a busy social life.

HOME

The welcome mat of this fun-loving lady is well used by a constant stream of guests eager to enjoy her hospitality.

She runs her home like a three-ring circus, and there is always room for one more at her table. The cupboard is never bare, but don't expect to eat on time. If she is running late, the party moves to the kitchen while she adds the finishing touches. Variety is the spice in her recipes; she never serves the same menu twice. Expect at least one concoction made with her new pasta machine or served flambé.

Even if she's shy, the #3 WOMAN is in her element at home. A charming hostess, she uses her artistic flair to create a pleasant atmosphere conducive to entertaining.

FRIEND

If you're feeling blue, count on a cheerful #3 FRIEND to improve your outlook. She invests a lot of time pleasing her friends; when you really need her, she'll drop everything.

Catch this social butterfly on the run by leaving a message on her answering machine. She's perpetually overbooked, so don't be offended when she cancels your date with an artful excuse.

Count on her to be the first to send you a clipping when you make the news. And when you want to take in an avant garde play or concert, she's always a willing companion.

In return, she needs your reassurance to build her self-confidence. Laugh at her stories, admire her new dress, and give in when she wants her way. It's a small price to pay for such a friend.

LOVER

When she spots someone attractive, the #3 LOVER goes to great lengths to capture his attention with her youthful good looks and a variety of entertaining opening gambits.

Frisky and brazen in her baby dolls or childlike and shy in her Dr. Dentons, the flirtatious #3 knows how to charm her sugar daddy. Don't let the baby talk fool you; by pen or by tongue, she's an expert in intimate linguistics, her favorite romance language. She'll talk you into and out of the most compromising positions.

Love-making is an excellent outlet for a creative #3; with her imagination, the sky's the limit. This playmate loves fun and games in the bedroom, so count on her to provide the toys and gadgets.

Even though #3's little-girl ways are enticing, she needs reassurance that she's attractive and desirable. Send her a telegram the next day saying "Nobody does it better."

MOTHER

The imaginative #3 MOM tells the best bedtime stories on the block. A kid at heart, she loves birthday parties, holiday stockings, and baskets of jelly beans as much as her children do.

A #3 MOTHER knows that chores can be boring, so she'll vary the routine or throw it out the window when she wants to have fun. As long as they play the game her way, the neighborhood children have an open invitation to her house. She's lavish in expressing her love and lenient in her discipline. Her philosophy is spare the rod and spoil the child. A clotheshorse herself, #3's a pushover when it comes to buying her children the latest fads in fashion.

Don't be surprised when a #3 MOM jumps at the chance to drive the getaway car the night the slumber party guests festoon the quarterback's home with toilet paper. She'll even sweet-talk the neighborhood cop out of a curfew warning and giggle when he tells her she looks like one of the girls!

BUSINESS

Skilled in communications, the #3 WOMAN is a valuable asset to any business team. A shy #3 expresses herself well in elaborate reports or in one-on-one client contact; more outgoing #3 interacts well at conventions or board meetings. Positive and fun loving, she uses humor to get results and boost morale. She can persuade people to hop on her bandwagon, and when she believes in it, she can sell any product.

A new travel assignment or an extra account will not bother a flexible #3; in fact, she thrives on a varied routine. Just as her colleagues get used to her perpetual motion, she may surprise them and focus on one important project. And even when she overextends herself in her desire to please, they come to her rescue.

BOSS

To enjoy work and to be popular with employees are top priorities for a #3 BOSS. She applies humor and variety in liberal doses to liven up office procedures. In her book, rules are made to be broken. Once you understand that she likes to get her way, you'll know how to approach her when you want an afternoon off.

A wizard with words who delights in an audience, the #3 BOSS seeks the limelight. Nobody tells a better story; the entire company looks forward to her impromptu performance at the annual office party.

She's an optimist who can handle all kinds of people and help others view their problems in a positive light. A #3 BOSS can show you how to roll with the punches and stretch your creative limits.

EMPLOYEE

A solitary job demanding little imagination does not satisfy a #3 EMPLOYEE. Assign her to a variety of projects and trust her to represent you in the field. She likes people and wants them to like her.

Beneath her pleasant manner lie valuable communication skills; she can write as well as deliver a speech. Effective on the telephone, she can charm a disgruntled client. She invented Customer Service!

Since she tends to be scattered, help her to set priorities and keep a checklist. She has her own style of organization, even though her desk looks as if a cyclone hit it!

HEALTH, DIET, EXERCISE

Until she locates the fountain of youth, the #3 WOMAN will expend time and money to preserve and enhance her appearance. She lives by the pleasure principle and has a difficult time denying herself; consequently, her expansive nature extends to her waistline in a continuing battle with her high-calorie social life.

Exercise to the rescue! She'll try anything as long as it involves people, a few laughs, and a cute outfit! Catching sight of her shrinking image in the mirror and receiving a few compliments will spur her on.

When she is sick, surround her with pillows and constant attention; she loves to be babied. Don't worry, it won't last; she'll be out of bed in time for the next party.

In return, be prepared to survive her "intensive care" when you are sick. Don't let her doctor you to death. You'll recover quickly just to get some relief from well-meaning #3's continual chatter!

TRAVEL

The #3 WOMAN finds new faces as fascinating as new places. She loves to travel with a group but hates routines; even though she's the most entertaining person on the bus, she's the last one to board every morning.

Her idea of planning is to pack an outfit for every occasion and leave the itinerary to chance. Ask her to choose the accommodations and she'll go for charm every time; never mind details such as hot water and central heat. Fortunately she loves to laugh, and her sense of humor sees her through when her plans don't.

When you meet her at the plane, consider her habits before driving the two-seater. If you think she needs the big car just for her wardrobe trunks, look again; she brings home two-legged souvenirs who need rides!

GIFTS

The #3 WOMAN enjoys receiving a number of imaginative presents as much as one important gift. Cleverness appeals to her, so skip the gift certificate, unless it's for a day of self-indulgence at her favorite salon.

Since she believes in positive thinking, give her an inspirational book to add to her library.

Present two tickets hidden in a box of animal crackers for the center ring at the circus if you want to delight the little girl in your #3 WOMAN.

THE NAME #3 CHILD

From the moment of birth, the irresistible #3 CHILD not only expects attention, he gets it. Shy or outgoing, he (or she) flirts coyly from behind his mother's skirts or chatters incessantly to the first person who smiles at him.

Eager to learn, even if by unconventional methods, the #3 CHILD acquires knowledge through experience. A flexible teacher who appreciates his ability to "show and exaggerate" should help versatile #3 to concentrate on one thing at a time and to be prompt. A restless student, he dislikes routine; but when something catches his interest, he excels.

With a million tricks up his sleeve, he can dish out a prank, though he can't take it. If patience fails to corral the mischievous #3 CHILD, deprive him of the audience he loves; isolation is the ultimate punishment.

Charming #3 can talk his way around any problem and has an excuse for every occasion, especially when he forgets his homework or loses his jacket. Discourage his whining and realize that little things won't get him down for long; he's got a stiff upper lip, but his lower one tends to pout.

Don't be surprised if he and his kids ring the doorbell and run when they arrive to celebrate your eightieth birthday with balloons and toys!

THE NAME #4 MAN

Happiest when busy, #4 was born to work hard. The ultimate planner, he makes lists of his lists. And once he has organized his home or office system, he won't change it.

Rely on the #4 MAN to keep his promises; he's careful not to overextend himself because he hates to be caught short when a deadline approaches. With a reputation for being honest and trustworthy, #4 is not a likely candidate to misappropriate funds or abuse equipment. He returns items promptly and in better condition than he borrowed them. No gambler when it comes to money or safety, #4 always takes the prudent approach.

Despite his serious, structured approach to life, sentimental #4 treasures traditions involving family and friends. A lover of ritual, creature of habit, he carefully nurtures long-lasting commitments.

Attached to things as well as people, he would rather retread his ten-year-old running shoes than replace them. Once #4 sets his course on the straight and narrow, he will follow it to achieve his goal. Like the tortoise, #4 wins the race carrying his fortress on his back.

HOME

The #4 MAN's house is the one with the fresh paint, flag flying, and manicured lawn. Armed with a green thumb and a maintenance schedule, this Mr. Fix-It perpetually putters to make his home functional; though it's comfortable, it's not pretentious.

Be sure to find out when he's hanging wallpaper or changing his oil; you can learn a lot from #4. Not only does he have the material and the tools, he has the time set aside and the manual dexterity to achieve the result he desires—perfection. Watch him and weep while you clutch your ten thumbs behind your back.

He's insured to the hilt and heads up the neighborhood watch program. Smoke alarms are checked quarterly and scheduled fire drills are routine for his family. His car has a fire extinguisher, first-aid kit, and flares.

Parties are a pleasure on his newly built deck or in his cabana. This chef knows the difference between rare and medium, and he can grow his own salads.

FRIEND

The #4 MAN is a down-to-earth friend; call on him if you want practical advice. After outlining the pros and cons of your quandary, he will leave the final decision to you; it's hard for self-reliant #4 to walk in another man's shoes. No matter, his feet are firmly planted, sometimes in cement.

He budgets his time, so don't expect him to drop everything when you arrive unannounced. You won't mind visiting in the garage; it's so clean you could eat off the floor. When you need to borrow from his extensive tool collection, you'll notice that his check-out procedure rivals the public library system. Generous with the how-to instructions, he's not so liberal when his favorite tool is overdue. The postcard reminder will say "Return my hacksaw and I'll bury the hatchet." Serious #4 has a pointed sense of humor.

When you do go out on the town, expect him to choose the same place every time and arrive early. He's easy to spot at his favorite table. The #4 FRIEND loves to reminisce and recalls the most amazing trivia; he even remembers your family members' birthdays.

LOVER

If you're looking for a faithful, patient partner, choose a #4 LOVER. Not a love-'em-and-leave-'em type, he'll be here today and tomorrow.

More a doer than a dreamer, #4 would rather act on something than talk about it. Even though he may not express his emotions verbally, he is very affectionate and sentimental; #4 shows how much he cares by never failing to remember a special moment or anniversary. He loves rituals, so count on him for a repeat performance of a romantic occasion.

Not experimental by nature, #4 is a perfectionist who works hard to please. He is self-disciplined and has stick-to-itiveness; he keeps it up until he gets it right.

If #4 says he will pick you up at 7:00, be ready at 6:58. You'll love punctual, reliable #4; he comes when he says he will.

FATHER

The conscientious #4 FATHER runs a tight ship; his kids learn early not to rock the boat. He loves his family and wants a secure future for them.

A #4 FATHER teaches fiscal responsibility with the first quarter he gives for Saturday chores. But before his children dash out the door they had better do their jobs to his satisfaction.

Summer camping is a family favorite. Though nature-loving #4 DAD may choose an outdoor vacation to save on motel bills, his family won't miss the comforts of home. He brings everything they need: extra rain tarps and a portable shower to rig, plus enough games up his sleeve to make the long drive entertaining. At the campsite he'll keep his children busy hunting for wood to whittle into marshmallow roasting sticks—just as his father did.

During the school year, he oversees the homework, especially in math. And he doesn't mind rolling up his patriotic sleeves to organize the boy scout fund-raiser. A #4 DAD lives by the rules and takes his job as a parent seriously.

BUSINESS

A #4 MAN is a superior long-range planner; he doesn't get caught without supplies to start or time to finish. Given a project, he likes to mull over the facts and come up with a better mousetrap. #4 has the patience and perseverance to keep plugging until he succeeds.

Proficient in math, he is a shrewd financial manager who knows the value of a dollar and wants his money's worth. He doesn't order more than he needs and he doesn't waste what he has. He insists on a firm credit policy: "In God we trust; all others pay cash."

Beyond economy, #4 values security and sees the importance of controlling money and inventory. He doesn't speculate with funds or gamble with the future. A prudent investor who is conscious of good fringe benefits, #4 plans for a secure, comfortable retirement.

Ethical business practices are at the top of his value system; #4 won't tolerate dishonesty or cutthroat schemes. He always operates by the book.

BOSS

Be sure you like pick-and-shovel work before you hire on with a #4 BOSS; he digs until he finds the answers. A mastermind, he develops the most efficient method and expects his employees to implement it.

He's been known to repeat, "If it works, don't change it." Until he's convinced that a new system is more efficient and cost-effective, he's not likely to replace a perfectly good computer with the latest model.

Earn his respect by coming in early and staying late. Take your cue from him; be precise and take pride in your work. He can be patient if you have an off day, but skip the excuses and make up the work on your own time. Even though family is high on his list, a #4 BOSS expects you to call home during breaks and use the pay phone he's installed on each floor.

The quickest way to get your walking papers is to be petty or unethical. The loyal #4 BOSS is proud of his hard workers; the rest don't last long.

EMPLOYEE

Choose a reliable #4 EMPLOYEE to bring a complicated project in on time. When you tell him exactly what you need, he comes back with a detailed schedule, including manpower and equipment requirements. Expect his office to buzz like a beehive when you are ready to begin according to plan; warn him in advance if you need to make changes.

Accurate to the minute and penny, the #4 EMPLOYEE comes equipped with a green visor and an incredible memory; he can smell a mistake or an oversight. Don't expect him to create a new idea; let him critique an old one and make it better.

Conservative and set in his ways, he would feel uncomfortable stepping out of line. He won't embarrass you by talking out of turn or going over your head. As long as he can keep busy and moving forward on a project, he's satisfied. Fair compensation and a position with a future have more meaning to him than a pretentious title.

HEALTH, DIET, EXERCISE

The #4 MAN decided early in life that moderation would be his motto; consequently, he doesn't need a reducing diet. By eating well-balanced meals he maintains his weight according to the life insurance age, weight, and height tables. He can't understand why other people complain about dieting's yo-yo syndrome.

Exercise was invented by coordinated #4, who truly enjoys perfecting his technique. Adequate equipment and utilitarian sports attire are all he needs. Diligent #4 counts on regular exercise to relieve any stress brought on by unexpected changes in his daily routine.

If you are sick, send #4 to the pharmacy where he will insist on a less expensive, generic drug for your prescription. He'll make sure you take your medicine on time, even if he has to set the alarm clock and awaken you. If your insurance company fails to pay on a timely basis, put #4 on the job; he'll see that you get the benefits to which you are entitled. When #4 is sick, he's a doctor's dream; he follows directions to the letter.

TRAVEL

Patriotic #4 may want to see America first, but whatever his destination, you can be sure he plans ahead. Package tours with air fare included appeal to this cost-conscious traveler.

He's the first one on the bus every morning so he can get his regular seat. When others stay behind to rest, tireless #4 will show up for all the side trips to get his money's worth.

He has packing down to a science; his suitcase is as neatly arranged on the way home as it was when he left. Prepared for any eventuality, he brings a copy of his eyeglass prescription and carries the traveler's check serial numbers separately from the checks. Fellow passengers soon catch on that he has every important item they have forgotten, such as moleskin for blisters and digestive remedies.

Be on time to pick him up at the airport. Customs won't take long; he's made a list of receipts and packed purchases together for easy inspection. Don't expect #4 to bring home cute souvenirs; he'd rather take you out to dinner at his favorite restaurant on the way home from the airport with the money he's saved.

GIFTS

Choose practical over extravagant when you shop for #4; he's uncomfortable receiving anything he feels you can't afford. In fact, he would rather have something handmade or home grown than an expensive "doodad." The way to a #4 MAN's heart is definitely through his stomach. Homemade goodies appeal to his practical, yet sentimental tastes.

If #4 appears to have everything he needs, he probably does. Look for quality in whatever you buy and don't overlook organizers that he could use to further systematize his possessions. How-to books as well as useful materials such as film or blank tapes appeal to the do-it-yourself #4.

THE NAME #4 WOMAN

The #4 WOMAN has her act together and is capable of taking it on the road. A born systems expert, she successfully juggles responsibilities at home and at the office. Her secrets are planning, concentration, and hard work. She's a realist who knows her capabilities and does not overcommit.

Not easily distracted, she concentrates on a problem until she finds a logical solution. Once settled on the best course, she will not make changes unless someone can prove the merit of a new method. Ask her how long she's patronized her favorite store or beauty salon and she'll say "forever."

Like her possessions, her ideas are carefully chosen and put neatly into categories. She has an excellent memory and a great store of practical knowledge. While math and logical reasoning are her forte, she's also very good with her hands.

The #4 WOMAN is a perfectionist who types entries into her address book and balances her checkbook to the penny the same day she receives her statement. She buys greeting cards a year in advance and files them by the month. Traditional Monday wash day, Tuesday ironing day, etcetera was invented by a #4

WOMAN; and today's #4 WOMAN probably serves meat loaf every Thursday. Count on her to arrange her errands to save gas and to write her grocery list according to the layout of the store.

HOME

Calm, cool, and collected describes the atmosphere in the home of a #4 WOMAN. It's a great place to relax, but don't put your feet up. #4 is an excellent housekeeper who doesn't like clutter, much less dirty shoes on her freshly polished coffee table.

She is prepared for any eventuality. Pipe wrench at her fingertips, she can fish a contact lens unscratched from a sink trap as efficiently as any plumber.

#4 is an avid list maker; her loved ones have been known to receive a "Honey Do" list, as in "Honey, do this. Honey, do that." She's organized her closets so they're the safest in town; open the door and nothing falls out. She even has a security closet for all her valuables and an itemized list with photographs and insurance appraisals stashed in the bank safety deposit box.

Expect a patriotic #4 to organize a bang-up Fourth of July block party, right down to the city permit required to close off the street. There will be plenty of salads and desserts and games to keep the kids busy. Thrifty #4 purchases her steaks ahead on special. No last-minute rush for her; she'll be ready and waiting for the party to begin.

FRIEND

A #4 uses ink, not pencil, when she writes your name on her calendar; she keeps her promises and arrives on time.

When you volunteer to arrange a fund-raising dinner on a limited budget, call on your #4 FRIEND. She'll tell you to cancel the caterer and will organize the menu herself, preparing a delicious meal at a modest cost.

When you return the favor by offering to do her errands, #4 gives you a list complete with instructions, the correct amount of change, and an envelope for the receipts.

It's smart to shop with a #4; she knows value and design when she sees it, gives honest opinions, and can help friends zero in on what they want.

Capable #4 makes a sentimental friend; she remembers what you like and goes out of her way to please. If she knows you are going to a luau, she'll use the hibiscus from her garden and dental floss to string a lei to match your pink dress.

LOVER

The #4 WOMAN is an earthy, sensual lover whose life is so organized she's always able to fit you in. This sentimental lady savors all your love letters and perfumes her lingerie with the petals of every rose you send.

If you like to relive past moments of ecstasy, she can remember each passionate detail and give you a blow-by-blow account during the repeat performance. Though she's a creature of habit and somewhat rigid herself, she won't mind it in you; nor will she object to your being stuck in a rut, as long as it's hers.

Intimate moments with #4 include extra benefits such as rubdowns and massages. Patient and thorough, she's great with her hands and will work hard to get it just the way you want it.

MOTHER

A #4 MOM keeps her kids busy and uses charts and gold stars to reward jobs well done. Children learn good habits and gain practical knowledge from a sensible #4 MOTHER who doesn't believe in wasting a minute or a morsel.

She budgets the basics and hands out the extras sparingly. She has the skills to copy a designer dress for the prom, but don't expect her to let you spend the money she's saved on rhinestone-studded spike heels to go with it.

Because #4 has the family and house running like clockwork, she can manage an outside job or community activities. Service clubs love her; whoever said, "Give the job to a busy person if you want it done," had a #4 in mind!

Family life is her foundation. She takes her parenting responsibilities seriously, right down to recordkeeping; she writes names and dates on every snapshot, fills in baby books, and saves newspaper clippings. When her children are grown, she will still be able to recall the exact date they had chicken pox and will still be reminding them to lock the car doors and wear their seat belts!

BUSINESS

The professional woman personified, #4 has the logical, disciplined mind necessary not only to survive but to prosper in a high-pressure career. Systems-oriented, she naturally makes good use of her time and organizes her workplace with an eye toward efficiency.

A talented money manager, she has never heard of math anxiety. Whether clipping coupons at the bank or from the food section of the paper, #4 values thrift and security. She makes purchases with an eye for utility and knows exactly what she needs to get the job done. Waste and extravagance are not in her vocabulary.

Goal-oriented, the #4 businesswoman makes precise plans to achieve tangible results. From past experience she knows that patience and hard work pay off. This woman of integrity has a reputation for playing by the rules.

BOSS

Even though she expects you to work hard within her system, she never asks you to do anything she wouldn't do herself. After careful consideration she decides what it takes to get a job done and gives precise instructions. She dislikes changes; approach her well in advance with all the facts, so she can deal with the situation in her usual calm and logical manner.

Her serious, no-nonsense approach gives way to a dry sense of humor and real sentiment when the job is done. Think about your thrifty, time-conscious boss when a client rambles on the phone. Straighten out your "in" basket instead of the paper clips, and for heaven's sake, don't doodle wastefully on company stationery.

Take your lead from her businesslike wardrobe; keep your tie on and your jacket handy—and no jangling bracelets or flowing sleeves near the paper shredder. She balances her home and office obligations and expects the same of you. Get her permission ahead of time to attend your child's school program; plan teacher conferences after work, and have a back-up baby-sitter.

EMPLOYEE

Hire a precise #4 EMPLOYEE to follow your directions to the letter. As long as you provide tangible guidelines, she is capable of devising her own method to do the job. Although she doesn't require your close supervision, be accessible to approve any changes.

With her eye for detail and ability to develop systems, she's the perfect candidate for office manager. She lives by the company policy manual; she knows who is taking long lunch hours or abusing the WATS line. Gossip is not her style, so expect her to handle problems with her subordinates by going through channels.

She's punctual and rather enjoys punching the time clock; in fact, she'll be the first one to point out if it's off. A good shopper with an eye for value, the #4 makes an ideal purchasing agent, buying supplies wisely and keeping track of their use.

She treasures your approval and respect, and values a secure job with good benefits more than a title.

HEALTH, DIET, EXERCISE

A #4 WOMAN has the willpower to diet, even in the face of temptation. With the memory of an elephant, this math whiz keeps a mental list of what, when, and where she ate, down to the last calorie and ounce.

On a given day, she chooses her exercise by calculating the number of calories burned per hour to compensate for a dinner out or an unexpected slice of birthday cake at the office. The #4 WOMAN likes routine, so she joins the new health spa a month before it opens to get a deal. Three years later, with her eleventh instructor, she'll still be attending the same class. If her spa gives out awards, she'll have the trophy for being the most faithful member.

If you are sick, count on #4 to follow the doctor's instructions to the letter, and to ask plenty of questions to clarify any details. Efficient #4 will be at your beck and call to attend to your every need.

If she is sick, her household will run smoothly without her. At any given time, she is prepared for emergencies with a freezer and refrigerator full of food, menus posted, and laundry up to date.

TRAVEL

When she chooses a tour, the #4 WOMAN takes one that visits the most cities for the best price. She packs a complete change of clothes and all the necessities in her carry-on bag, in case her baggage is lost.

She doesn't miss a meal, but eats sparingly with attention to calories and a well-balanced diet. You wonder when she sleeps, because she attends every function on the itinerary and still has time to write in her daily journal.

An astute shopper, she goes straight to the best deal and comes away with useful gifts of real quality instead of "native Indian" carved beetles made in Taiwan. When you get stuck without an aspirin or there are no tissues in the ladies' room, be glad there's a #4 WOMAN around; she even has an extra bottle of Pepto-Bismol to swig when yesterday's salad takes its revenge.

GIFTS

She is a keen, discriminating buyer, so look for quality in any gift you choose for a #4 WOMAN. Don't go overboard in the number of gifts or the cost; she's not impressed by extravagance.

Sentimental #4 appreciates a useful handmade gift such as an afghan to ward off the evening's chill, an apron, or a needlepoint pillow. A container of your famous soup or applesauce, timed to arrive on a regular basis, makes a perfect gift. She has a green thumb, so visit a nursery for plants or a basket of garden accessories. Bounty from your own garden would be doubly welcome, especially if it has been turned into jam or preserves.

An inveterate list maker, the #4 WOMAN would enjoy personalized note pads or desk organizers. Keep it simple, sentimental, and useful to please a #4.

THE NAME #4 CHILD

The #4 BABY is born with a built-in clock, and you can set yours by the precision of his (or her) hunger cries; be punctual with his pabulum or you'll hear about it. From the start, this child wants to be clean and dry, not to mention on schedule!

When he takes the spoon out of your hand at an early age to feed himself, and begins to tinker with his toys, you'll recognize his exceptional manual dexterity. Self-reliant #4 amuses himself for hours with blocks and puzzles. Not one to force a square peg into a round hole, he shows early that he has a practical approach to problems. The #4 CHILD keeps his (or her) toy soldiers all in a row, and woe to the mother who moves one stuffed animal on the bed.

His favorite color is green—as in money and growing things.

He stashes his cash, so family members frequently hit him up for a quick loan, in spite of the interest he charges. From the moment he picks flowers in the backyard and peddles the posies from his little red wagon, to his lawn business courtesy of Dad's mower and gasoline, he knows how to turn a profit.

At school, #4 is a diligent student who forgoes television in order to finish his homework. After school he's early for team practice to perfect his skills, and she's on time to her tap class. Heaven help the teacher who changes one step in the routine. Rhythmic #4 is bound to respond, "That's not the way we did it last week."

Covet the phone number of a #4 baby-sitter. She's in charge, has the kids under control, and if the schedule says 7:30, #4 has the wee ones in bed, complete with brushed teeth, at 7:28.

Comfort yourself with the thought that your trustworthy #4 child will preserve the family fortune and carry on your good name, long after you have departed.

THE NAME #5 MAN

The #5 MAN is intensely aware of the world around him. Up on the latest news and positioned in the center of the action, he is eager to know what others are thinking. He approaches people in a cheerful, friendly manner and usually gets the answers he's after.

Restless #5 needs freedom to follow the most intriguing path; he refuses to be restricted by a possessive relationship or routine job. Often acting impulsively, he succeeds in making his life a true adventure.

Ruled by his five senses, he is easily enticed by a new sight or sound. An innovative thinker, #5 sees fresh possibilities in everyday situations and adapts easily to many settings because he is so versatile. Where a more sedate man would flounder, daring #5 is quick to size up a situation and leaps in with both feet.

HOME

"The true value of a property is its location." That's the real estate adage the #5 MAN lives by. His spacious house has convenient access to the freeway, the airport, and the action. He'd like to install a revolving door to facilitate his frequent comings and goings, but the family won't go along with any more of his unconventional ideas.

When he's in residence—and he may have several, including one on wheels—#5 has his fingers in many pies. He buys any gadget that plugs in—TV, VCR, radio, and portable tools—and leaves projects in various stages of development around the house. To save time, he works or eats standing up.

The #5 MAN prefers impromptu progressive parties that move from house to house or room to room, featuring cook-your-own steaks or hand-cranked ice cream to involve the guests. He is an active host who likes to man the barbecue and tend bar while he table hops to make sure everyone is having as much fun as he is.

FRIEND

When your #5 FRIEND calls on an impulse to ask you out for a quiet drink or a simple movie, don't you believe him! Sociable #5 attracts attention wherever he goes and stirs up fun, turning the most ordinary occasion into an event. The quiet drink will be a bizarre brew at a lively dive and the movie will be exotic, to say the least.

His mind works so quickly he often interrupts before he loses his thought. #5 talks in shorthand, leaving unfinished sentences he expects you to complete; after all, he finishes yours.

Fascinated by people, the #5 MAN is full of information about his recently acquired friends and digs for news about your mutual acquaintances.

LOVER

A #5 LOVER wants action and plenty of it. With an insatiable appetite for sensual pleasures, he wants to taste all the erotic experiences life has to offer.

He enjoys the challenge of a quick encounter on the run; so change your hair color and wear a new outfit when you surprise him with a "nooner." Always on the go, #5 is hard to pin down; don't try. The only way to keep him is to supply him with variety and to leave the door open.

Adventure calls curious #5, and he loves to experiment with novel ways and places to make love. He has a probing mind and monotony bores him stiff. He is always in motion, and his actions speak louder than his words even though his tongue can move as fast as his feet.

In bed and out, the #5 MAN is versatile and can do many things at once; for your own sake, make sure he finishes what he starts.

FATHER

A spontaneous, fun-loving #5 makes an enthusiastic father who can keep up with the most energetic kids.

He won't allow his children to sit around all weekend watching TV. If it's audiovisual entertainment they want, he'll take them to a marathon day at the movies: two action-packed double features at two different theaters.

Dad gets impatient when his kids drag their feet about chores or studying. He's willing to help out with homework, but only if the teacher accepts short division in place of long division; #5 always shows you the shortcuts.

A #5 DAD is a clever type who can assemble battery-powered robot cars without reading the directions. He has eyes in the back of his head when it comes to sneaky kids; he can spot a contraband candy bar in seconds and demand a bite as "hush money."

A man who likes to live on the edge, the #5 FATHER gives his children the same freedom to take chances and grow. They learn to take his short fuse in stride as they anticipate the next adventure with their energetic parent.

BUSINESS

Multitalented #5 accomplishes more in one day than an entire team, and he still has the energy to socialize in the evening.

Colleagues refer to him as a "quick study" because he sizes up situations immediately. Curious to a fault, he pursues answers relentlessly and can charm information out of the toughest receptionist before she realizes what has happened. In the brief moments when he isn't talking, you can actually hear the wheels spinning in his head.

Unconventional in his approach, the #5 BUSINESSMAN works best on the move, unfettered by a schedule. He plays things by ear and likes to float free of the office, attached only by a telephone or beeper.

A risk taker, #5 pursues new contacts, leaving his less-adventurous associates choking in his cloud of dust.

BOSS

Like a pony-express rider who keeps going with a fresh horse, the #5 BOSS may go through a whole stable of secretaries. He talks faster than the speed of sound, giving last-minute directions over his shoulder as he goes out the door.

He likes to be the boss because he hates routine imposed by others; as captain of the ship, he can change course whenever he wants to. His memos are to the point; he assumes others have as little time to read wordy messages as he has to write them.

Be prepared to work behind the scenes for a creative #5 BOSS. His inquiring mind sets lots of wheels in motion; he pays attention to the squeaky ones and counts on you to take care of the others.

No matter how hard you work, you'll have fun with a #5 BOSS. Hating to be tied down himself, he will vary your routine and see that you aren't a constant slave to detail.

EMPLOYEE

The #5 EMPLOYEE is an outgoing man who can read the sales potential of an area and assess the needs of a client quickly. He thinks on his feet and asks the right questions.

Naturally inquisitive, #5 enjoys meeting different people; fresh contacts provide the variety he craves. He needs a challenge; let him stir things up and investigate the possibilities of a new approach.

Vary #5's assignments so he won't become bored, and pair him with a nine-to-five detail person to follow up on his leads. After listening to his barrage of timesaving ideas and answering his intelligent questions, you will realize what a valuable asset the #5 EMPLOYEE can be.

HEALTH, DIET, EXERCISE

Active, energetic #5 naturally keeps himself fit. Constantly in search of new experiences, he likes to ski fast, shoot the rougher rapids, and climb the more challenging rocks; mostly he's curious to see what's around the next bend or over the next hill.

Not one to waste time, he often eats on the run or while standing at the kitchen counter and reading. If he needs to lose weight, he chooses a diet with a variety of foods that are quick to prepare.

Two speeds—stop and go at full throttle—keep #5 so busy he doesn't have time to be sick. When he is housebound, boredom from lack of activity will do him in faster than any illness. When you are sick, expect lots of encouragement to get well soon. He misses your company.

TRAVEL

At a moment's notice, #5 tosses his prepacked shaving kit into his ever-ready carry-on luggage and heads for the airport. He books a direct flight and requests an aisle seat in case he gets restless.

The #5 TRAVELER feels right at home in the hustle and bustle of a strange city; he'll pack his business trip with as much sightseeing as his schedule will allow. Authentic inns serving local specialties are his choice over chain hotels that dish up the same roast beef and frozen peas worldwide.

Genial #5 makes a great traveling companion if you want to meet people easily. But take your roller skates if you expect to keep up with him, and be prepared for a few out-of-the-way escapades. He takes a wrong turn in stride; it spells adventure in his book. After all, he's never been to Zanzibar!

GIFTS

Energetic, on-the-go #5 loves the excitement of a surprise party. Wrap up a can of red paint and a brush with an invitation to paint the town red. The evening doesn't have to be expensive, just unconventional: a lively mix of guests, a new night spot, exotic cuisine.

Buy him an answering machine to handle all the calls he misses because he's rarely home. A tiny alarm clock that tells international time or any other travel gift appeals to this wayfaring man. If he isn't actually gadding about, he's at least perpetually in motion, so give him a mini-trampoline to use while he watches the news. For his restorative catnaps, give the sensual #5 MAN the softest afghan or coziest slippers to rest his weary feet.

THE NAME #5 WOMAN

Multifaceted #5 sparkles in any arena where her quick wit and inquiring mind can operate freely. Always on the move, she gathers ideas and makes friends wherever she goes.

The #5 WOMAN is a doer with an impressive list of experiences to her credit. Easily bored, she has a genuine need to keep busy, and moves from one activity to another at full speed ahead until she drops.

The sensual #5 WOMAN operates on messages she receives through her five senses; reactions to aromas, tastes, sounds, and sights crop up frequently in her conversation. She often fondles and exclaims over objects she finds touchable.

While routines imposed by others restrict her freedom, she is not without a sense of organization; to move quickly and easily, she streamlines her life. No matter what she does or where she goes, she maintains a sense of humor and excitement that attracts everyone she meets.

HOME

Unrestricted spaces and adequate storage for luggage are top priorities when #5 selects a home.

In a typical day, the #5 WOMAN's home hums with activity. The TV, radio, phones, and electrical gadgets generate an astronomical monthly bill—much to the delight of the local utility company.

Her approach to housecleaning is sheer speed; stay out of her way when she's on the other end of the vacuum cleaner. You can tell when she has cleaned; to make the effort worthwhile and to satisfy her need for variety, she rearranges the furniture as often as other people dust.

If you ever offer to help her paint, wear a hat and a drop cloth—#5 buys a gallon of paint for the walls and an extra one for herself.

Capable of doing many things simultaneously, she's happy to toss routine out the window to whip up an impromptu party. She prepares multicourse feasts featuring an interesting mix of flavors and guests. To keep the evening moving, she favors menus with diner participation, such as curry with myriad bowls of exotic condiments to pass around the table.

FRIEND

Be sure your shoes are handy if you have an adventurous #5 FRIEND. She loves to dream up exciting escapades and give you five minutes' notice.

Mentally agile #5 can read people's minds, and she has been known to finish their sentences or tap her toes if they are slow to make a point. Her mind, of course, works faster than her high-velocity mouth. When she tells a joke, #5 laughs in the middle; she's already enjoying the punchline.

The #5 WOMAN has a nose for news; when she asks pointed questions, tell her that you will forgive her for asking if she will forgive you for not answering.

LOVER

Quick to respond, #5 is a provocative, sensual lover who is intoxicated by your aftershave. She laps up your tasty kisses, quivers visibly at your touch, and simmers passionately when you say the magic word.

Adventurous to the core, a #5 LOVER likes to sink her teeth into new and unusual experiences. Constantly on the move, sometimes she just has time to eat and run. You may have to remind her to take off her track shoes and sweat socks unless, of course, you're fit for strenuous athletics. Remember, she's curious but loves to be kept in the dark; try not to let her know up front what you have in mind. To keep her, accept the fact that she needs her freedom; give her a long leash.

MOTHER

A lively #5 MOM is as active and inquisitive as her kids. On a field trip, everybody clamors to ride in her car because she's so much fun. When she drops off the kids at the ice palace, she's likely to take a twirl around the rink herself.

Knowing how quickly she can detect a shaky alibi, her kids always conform to house curfew. She may be impatient when they take their time with the chores, but she isn't fazed by last-minute changes in plans or extra guests. Casual about ordinary scrapes and other minor injuries, a #5 MOTHER understands, because she's apt to be accident-prone herself.

When her kids go out on a limb, don't expect her to rush a ladder to the rescue. She feels that children who take chances need to live with the consequences. She waits up to hear all about the evening's adventure; not one to sit around, she probably wants to share hers, too.

BUSINESS

Energetic, multitalented #5 brings a fresh approach to business. Because she can juggle so many projects at once, she runs circles around her colleagues. With her inquiring mind and need to keep moving, she's at her best traveling and meeting new people. A natural in sales, the #5 WOMAN is quick to assess the needs of the customer and can give him (or her) many good reasons to buy her product.

Her sense of adventure makes her open to novel concepts and willing to make new contacts. Curious #5 thinks on her feet and loves to investigate. She is quick to ask the kinds of questions that will give her the answers she needs to make good business decisions.

BOSS

Clear the decks and line up the support team, here comes the whirlwind! The fast-moving #5 BOSS enters the office asking pertinent questions and expects high-speed replies.

Pity the secretary who takes #5's dictation; this boss not only talks nonstop off the top of her head but also in capital letters and exclamation points.

Performing many tasks simultaneously, the #5 BOSS speaks on the phone, thumbs through papers, signs letters, and overhears conversations. Just because she looks busy doesn't mean she's not listening. If you are her right hand, don't be surprised if neither of you knows what her left hand is doing.

Boredom never becomes a problem if you work for #5; she varies your duties and your hours, and is always thinking of exciting new projects.

EMPLOYEE

The versatile #5 EMPLOYEE wears many hats in an organization and thrives on frequent changes of assignment and location. She dislikes routine and becomes restless if she is tied to a desk.

Take advantage of her flexibility and let her be the "gofer" who runs errands outside the office.

Easily sidetracked, #5 may return late, but she gathers important information and spreads goodwill while calling on suppliers and customers. She loves to ask questions, and her creative mind ranges into many fields. Keep her on the right track, and she may come up with improvements and new uses for your products. Once she's tuned in to your wavelength, quick-witted #5 can finish your sentences and guess the content of her next assignment.

HEALTH, DIET, EXERCISE

Monotonous exercise does not appeal to a #5 WOMAN; always thinking, always moving, she looks for vigorous action and a bit of risk or excitement in her sports. Born with natural pep in her step, she'd rather run than walk, and she'd rather dive for a ball or reach for an impossible shot than stand around.

Constantly on the go, #5 sometimes eats too fast or isn't hungry when it's time to eat. Impulsive by nature, she may indulge on a whim and find herself needing to diet. Strict regimen does not appeal to her, so she chooses a variety of exercises and a diet with a wide assortment of foods.

The #5 WOMAN burns the candle at both ends; she may drop from exhaustion more often than she is actually sick, but won't stay down long. If you become ill, #5 predicts rapid recovery assuming you are just as bored as she is with the idea of staying home; besides, she misses your company in the fast lane.

TRAVEL

The #5 TRAVELER lives with her hat on and her trunks packed. She's always ready for adventure and copes easily with the problems travel presents. Instead of sitting and twiddling her thumbs in the airport when a flight is canceled, she hops the first bus for a day in the hustle and bustle of the central city, taking in as many new sights as she can.

The #5 WOMAN travels light and packs her luggage to save time at her destination; cosmetics go in clear plastic cases and lingerie is divided into hanging pockets that go directly into the closet.

She has a mix-and-match travel wardrobe and doesn't waste

time going back to the hotel to change; with the dressy accessories in her purse, she takes only a minute to transform herself for the evening.

GIFTS

Surprise a #5 WOMAN with a mystery day; keep the party active and on the move. Provide rest stops for the guests or have a fresh group join you for the evening; #5 won't fade, provided you feed her.

An old-fashioned scavenger hunt appeals to #5, who is whimsical enough to enjoy an adventurous hour knocking on strange doors asking for a list of odd objects.

Buy her the newest gadget, something currently in vogue, or a sensual gift she can taste, touch, hear, see, or smell with pleasure.

Always on the go, the #5 WOMAN runs her feet into the ground; present her with a gift certificate for a pedicure or a foot reflexology treatment.

THE NAME #5 CHILD

If you have a #5 CHILD, take your vitamins as you pursue this guided missile. From his (or her) first days on earth the #5 BABY follows every movement with his eyes, eagerly awaiting his first launch.

Childproof the house for curious #5, removing cleaning supplies and sharp objects that would intrigue his well-developed imagination. Post the poison control number next to the phone and carry Band-Aids at all times.

Don't leave an active #5 BABY napping in the middle of Grandma's big bed or unattended on the changing table—unless you want to witness his first solo flight. To corral experimental #5, keep a well-stocked playpen. With his motor perpetually in high gear, he will drop one toy after another to the floor, but at least you know he's safe for a few minutes until he wails his loud version of the old cowboy song, "Don't fence me in."

The restless, inquisitive #5 CHILD needs a teacher who keeps him (or her) interested and knows when his frequent questions lead her off the subject. His favorite word is *why*.

Sports provide a good outlet for physically agile #5. Judging from the way he manages to watch TV, listen to the radio, do his homework, chat on the phone, and play with the dog simultaneously, you might think juggling is his favorite activity.

A fearless speed demon on his first scooter, the #5 CHILD leads the world on a merry chase. He's impossible to surprise because he is driven to search out hidden presents and do more than rattle the boxes.

Count on your #5 CHILD to bring his sense of adventure into your life; he won't let you get in a rut.

THE NAME #6 MAN

The responsible #6 MAN dedicates himself to the happiness and well-being of his family and friends. Always ready to lend a helping hand, he tries to ease the way for those he loves and goes to the defense of anyone needing his protection. Ordinarily a peace-loving man, #6 will fight for principles; faced with injustice, he comes out swinging.

#6 is careful to weigh the facts before passing judgment. Reluctant to point the accusing finger at others, he is cut to the quick when he feels rejected or becomes the target for unfounded criticism; a disagreement ruins his whole day. Not one to burn bridges, he always phrases his comments in positive terms.

Aware of beauty and quality, the #6 MAN wants the best that money can buy. Before he accepts an inferior substitute, he'll do without the flawlessly tailored cashmere jacket or the Italian shoes until he can afford them. The #6 MAN tries to look and do his best and appreciates sincere flattery, but only when he feels he is deserving.

HOME

"There's no place like home," according to the #6 MAN. Proud of every nook and cranny, he is especially pleased with its sound construction and quality materials. A haven for family and friends, his home is the perfect place to curl up in a comfortable chair or wade barefoot through lush carpet. Guests feel especially welcome because he sees to their needs so hospitably.

#6 loves good food; nothing pleases him more than to play the role of the genial host. He plies his guests with premium meats, the freshest vegetables, and homemade desserts piled high with real whipped cream. Beaming from the head of his table, he feasts with his eyes, taking in the beautiful food and the good company.

With a deep sense of tradition, the #6 MAN proudly displays his family's keepsakes and makes an effort to acquire beautiful treasures for future generations.

FRIEND

Congenial #6 knows how to win friends and influence people. Because he's a solid citizen and a good listener, his friends regard him as a port in a storm. He gives carefully considered counsel, and when the chips are down, you can rely on him to keep his word and come to your rescue.

When a #6 FRIEND arranges your birthday dinner, you won't dine on substandard fare; nor will he allow the cocktail waitress to bring you anything but your favorite brand. His idea of a good time is the best his budget can handle. Don't be surprised when he includes your favorite sibling or long-lost cousin. Family ties are important to him, and no amount of effort is too great for a friend.

LOVER

A #6 MAN sends flowers and puts his lover on a pedestal. He loves it when you climb down once in a while or move over and invite him up.

When a peace- and home-loving #6 asks, "Your place or mine?" opt for his. He'll not only keep the home fires burning, but he'll stoke your fire as well. Surrounded by comfort and beauty, you'll be so drawn to this magnetic man that you won't want to come unstuck.

Affectionate #6 makes a devoted lover who attunes himself skillfully in duets; count on him to ring your chimes. Whether in business or pleasure, his sense of fealty keeps him up all night to fulfill his promises.

Sex and your #6 LOVER are synonymous. He's a generous, sweet-talking sugar daddy who is so delicious you'll want to gobble him up.

FATHER

A #6 FATHER knows best and has the greatest kids in the world. Just ask him; he has pictures and newspaper clippings to prove it. Nothing is too good for his children; his greatest pleasure is providing a quality life for them. He buys his son the best bat and glove he can without choking his budget and tells him home-run stories every night. He caters to his daughter's every whim, providing the frilliest dolls and party dresses money can buy. The #6 DAD treats his kids' birthdays like national holidays. Everyone has a good time because #6 doesn't allow tiffs and disruptions.

Even though a #6 DAD is a stickler for "thank you" and "please," he rarely reprimands his children in a harsh way. He establishes a feeling of mutual respect and keeps conflicts to a minimum. A wonderful father, he attracts all kids with his warmth, patience, and generosity.

BUSINESS

His warm handshake is as solid as his word. When colleagues refer to #6 as "the judge," you know he has a reputation for being fair and objective.

At community service meetings, the charismatic #6 MAN attracts throngs of people who trust him and respect the way he fights for his favorite causes around town. Both in business and in the community, he takes his responsibilities seriously.

#6 understands people and is quick to assess their needs, making him very successful in a service-oriented business. He has an uncanny ability for putting people at ease.

The #6 MAN is never satisfied with second best; quality is his watchword. In a competitive market, he believes excellence is its own reward.

BOSS

The #6 BOSS runs his department like a team and expects his players to cooperate and work toward a common goal. A smart coach, he picks people who play fair; those who don't get dropped.

Respected for his honesty, he is often asked to write letters of recommendation. Although #6 ordinarily overlooks others' faults, he has a knack for making impartial statements. He includes fair mention of weakness, but emphasizes strengths, putting his subject in the best light possible.

A #6 BOSS creates a comfortable environment in his office, even if it's just to display his family's pictures on his desk. Don't be surprised when he gives his staff Thanksgiving turkeys and the Friday after the holiday off.

When his secretary tells him that she's been offered a job with a better future, #6 is likely to insist that she move on with his blessings.

EMPLOYEE

Pat yourself on the back if you had the foresight to hire a #6 EMPLOYEE. His agreeable nature enables him to foster good relationships with clients.

He holds himself accountable for his own work, but will also step in to help others when he senses the need. He's such a responsible member of the squad, you expect to see him wearing a team shirt under his jacket.

When he sees that you're down to the last box of computer paper, he'll call the supplier without being asked, charm the clerk at the order desk, and get a rush delivery free of charge.

He prefers peaceful working conditions and, like a one-man cavalry unit, heads off potential disputes at the pass.

HEALTH, DIET, EXERCISE

Perfectly pleated, pressed, and starched, the #6 MAN looks as if he has a valet or just stepped off the ironing board. Under it all is the frame he likes to keep fit, using the Cadillac of rowing machines or exercise bikes parked in his den.

When his love of gourmet food takes its toll, #6 continues to order lobster, substituting lemon for butter. Vintage sherry becomes dry white wine, and pâté becomes mushrooms or dilled cucumber slices.

When he gets sick, responsible #6 doesn't like to miss work; but when others are ill, he exerts his restorative powers. A pillow fluffer extraordinaire, he arrives bearing flowers and is apt to kill you with kindness.

TRAVEL

The #6 TRAVELER has champagne tastes and wants to go straight to the source for a guided tour of the Mumm winery in France. If he can't swing it financially until next year, he's satisfied for the time being with an afternoon in the beer garden of the local brewery.

After much consideration, #6 chooses quaint, first-class hotels with just the right ambiance, a full room-service menu, and fresh fruit baskets and flowers replenished daily.

Wherever he goes, #6 buys the best each country has to offer: Waterford crystal from the factory in Ireland, perfect pearls from Mikimoto Island in Japan, or emeralds from Colombia.

While he's away, he takes time to send gorgeous postcards picturing the highlights of his trip. Don't be surprised when he calls person-to-person to say "Wish you were here."

GIFTS

Any gift that contributes to his personal comfort pleases #6. Give him a soft bathrobe, a recliner, or a gift certificate for a massage. A lover of elegance, he'd like a solid gold pen or a 14-karat key for his car.

If his ship hasn't come in yet, give him a captain's hat and a day on a yacht with six friends. Capture the best moments for posterity with an instant-photo camera. As he steps onto the dock at sunset, present him with a picture-filled album commemorating the voyage.

Quality counts with a #6 MAN; one superior bottle of wine will please him more than a case of average stock.

THE NAME #6 WOMAN

The hand of a warmhearted #6 WOMAN is perpetually extended to help her family and friends. Fair and impartial, she's not one to jump to conclusions until she listens or sees for herself. Once she judges a cause worthwhile, she has the dedication to right any wrong.

Nothing is too good for her loved ones; she delights in taking responsibility for their comfort and pleasure. Unlike the nature lover who leaves her campsite the way she found it, the #6 WOMAN improves the places she visits and the lives she touches.

Quality conscious, #6 wants the finest that money can buy; she'll search relentlessly until she finds exactly what she wants. Beauty and harmony are her basic requirements. She looks good and smells good, and she adores flowers and colorful, comfortable surroundings.

To maintain her composure, #6 creates a peaceful atmosphere by her example, taking great care to establish positive lines of communication.

She appreciates honest flattery as long as she thinks she deserves it.

HOME

Home is where her heart is; surrounded by family and friends, #6 creates a loving atmosphere and keeps the home fires burning. Beside her door a plaque reads: OUR HOME IS OPEN TO SUNSHINE, LAUGHTER, FRIENDS, AND GUESTS.

#6 often sends dinner invitations to close friends, asking each of them to bring a special someone she hasn't met. Watching her cook, you'll notice #6 loves to fuss in the kitchen, producing tender, succulent morsels from steaming pots and heavenly smelling confections warm from the oven. No matter when you arrive, she can supply a bountiful snack, thanks to her well-stocked pantry.

The #6 WOMAN feathers her cozy nest with beautiful things carefully chosen or handed down in her family. The china and silver make their appearance often on her artistically arranged table; she likes to dine elegantly, not merely eat. Instead of furnishing her home with early Goodwill, #6 buys one piece of French Provincial at a time, until she has exactly what she wants.

FRIEND

Her standard greeting is an enthusiastic hug. She's a one-woman fan club who never fails to point out your sterling qualities. She overlooks your faults, even after she's listened sympathetically while you complain for an hour.

If you give a #6 FRIEND the key to your home when you go on vacation, you'll come home to greener plants and a dog who expects to be walked, not just fed and watered.

When she takes you to dinner at one of her favorite spots, don't be suprised if the waiter knows her by name and the chef is willing to whip up something special.

A #6 is the friend to call when you need sound advice; say "uncle" when you've heard enough.

LOVER

The epitome of womanhood and the essence of seduction, the alluring #6 WOMAN sets a tender trap for the man she loves. When she wants to play house, you're in for a gratifying experience; #6 will cater to your every wish, and spoil you outrageously.

Don't let her sweet looks fool you; she has a lusty laugh which gives her away. #6 needs no encouragement to slip into something more comfortable. After dinner by candlelight, she likes to serve dessert by the fire. When she suggests banana splits and brings out the bowl of whipped cream you'll know what your sexy #6 LOVER has in mind.

MOTHER

You can spot a #6 mother hen proudly parading her well-dressed chicks. Camera in hand, she documents the most minor occasions. Fat little scrapbooks all in a row attest to the first-rate accomplishments of her children, who can do no wrong in her eyes. Beware of the brag book she carries, and don't ask about her kids unless you have an hour to spare.

She's a room mother, den mother, and godmother to dozens. Popular with stray kids and cats who congregate on her doorstep, she's always good for a treat from her cookie jar, which enjoys national monument status. Between carpools to scout meetings and orthodontist appointments, she still has time to listen.

No pushover, the #6 MOTHER puts her foot down sweetly and keeps peace in a firm, but loving way.

BUSINESS

The #6 WOMAN enjoys a reputation for being honest and responsible. Her word is as solid as her handshake. When a report comes through with her name on it, you know you can rely on the information.

She believes that there is enough business out there for everyone; unscrupulous business practices do not meet with her approval. Concerned with the welfare of others, the #6 WOMAN is well suited to a helping profession or service-oriented business.

Noted for her loyalty, she has been observed in the lobby nodding her allegiance to the portrait of the company founder as she goes to work. A sure candidate for the twenty-five-year diamond pin, #6 is at her best working in cooperation with others to produce a quality product.

BOSS

The highly principled #6 BOSS is a staunch company supporter who will not tolerate padding the expense account or altering the time reports. She wants her department to run smoothly and goes out of her way to create a peaceful atmosphere in which her employees cooperate.

She takes her professional role seriously, but a touch of home is evident in her office. She approves the display of family photographs and small personal items, but raises an eyebrow if she spots a loud shirt or an inappropriate dress.

Considerate but firm, a #6 BOSS expects from her employees the same high degree of loyalty and performance she gives. When it comes to family obligations, she's understanding, but be sure to make up the time you took off for your child's spring music program.

EMPLOYEE

The popular #6 EMPLOYEE treats her office mates as an extension of her family. She singlehandedly supports the greeting card business, marking every occasion with a thoughtful message. She adds homey touches to her work space and contributes regularly to coffee breaks with freshly baked goodies.

Cooperative by nature, #6 goes out of her way to keep peace. A good listener, she can correct a problem before it becomes a confrontation. Great at "putting out fires," she has a sixth sense when it comes to knowing if someone needs extra help. When she sees that you are inundated with work on the eve of a business trip, she'll stay late to help without being asked. When a report is due in a half hour, it's #6 to the rescue as she offers to collate and staple the pages.

She is completely trustworthy, and her word is as good as the top-quality work she consistently performs on a timely basis.

HEALTH, DIET, EXERCISE

A love of beauty and comfort sends #6 to the health spa regularly. She exercises to keep a trim figure for her closetful of beautiful clothes, but she likes to be steamed, massaged, and manicured afterward.

Dieting is sometimes a necessity for the self-indulgent #6 WOMAN. Not one to feel deprived, she cuts down on calories but maintains the quality and eye appeal of her food. The jumbo shrimp salad garnished with celery fans and radish roses remains; only the creamy dressing disappears temporarily.

If you are sick, expect a visit from this modern-day Little Red Riding Hood. In addition to the crock of butter and blueberry muffins, she'll produce a tureen of her famous barley soup from the basket. She'll mother you until you recover or die of sheer joy. If she's sick, make her cozy and comfortable. Remember, flowers are her best medicine.

TRAVEL

When the #6 TRAVELER plans the grand tour, she arranges for a house-sitter who knows the pets and leaves a number where she can be reached at every stop.

The biggest suitcase, also the lightest, is the most important because it contains her down pillows and her travel steam iron. Immediately upon checking in, #6 phones the concierge to arrange for a hair appointment and a massage to get out the travel kinks.

In the room, #6 starts the coffee maker, fills the refrigerator, and dials housekeeping for the ironing board.

When she checks out, the computer printout of her hotel bill, including long-distance calls home, is as long as she is tall.

When you meet her plane, bring her loved ones along and a WELCOME HOME banner.

GIFTS

Plan a "beauty day" for #6 at her favorite salon; she loves to be pampered head to toe. Lavish her with beautiful lingerie, a bottle of her favorite perfume, or a silk crepe de chine blouse. Remember, she searches hard and long for the best for herself, so present her with one quality item rather than several gifts of lesser value.

When you plan a birthday celebration, include her loved ones and have the party at home or at a restaurant that specializes in impeccable service. If Chateaubriand or lobster is not within your budget, select breast of chicken en croute and a salad so gorgeous you might mistake it for the centerpiece.

THE NAME #6 CHILD

The #6 BABY was born with charm; he (or she) loves to be held and endears himself to everyone who falls within range of his smile. As long as his surroundings are serene, this cuddly bundle of joy remains calm, but add tension and he starts to fuss.

The #6 CHILD genuinely enjoys being part of a family; he (or she) actually likes his siblings and is happy to share a room and even his toys upon occasion. Relatives are important to him from the time he toddles around at family gatherings; he makes lasting friendships with his cousins and paints pictures to send to his far-away grandparents.

Popular with friends, he tries hard to get along with others. Happiest at home, he is a precocious host; provide an extra bed or a sleeping bag for frequent overnight guests.

#6 will do anything to avoid rejection or criticism; consequently he attempts to perform at perfection levels. At home, #6 is Mother's little helper, taking his responsibilities seriously. Pets and plants flourish under his care, and he sets the table carefully, seeing that the napkins are folded "just right."

Your #6 scholar strives for high marks in every subject. He often displays artistic or musical talent, and enjoys the praise and recognition he receives. A reliable team player, he goes all out to win for the squad.

A responsible sitter who adores babies and young children, #6 shows strong parental instincts at an early age. You can be sure that he'll keep the peace and settle disputes fairly and quickly.

If he has a newspaper route, he is careful to put the paper on the porch so the older gentleman on the next street doesn't need to go up and down stairs.

It's hard for #6 to cut family ties; he will call often and come home for family celebrations at holiday time. Count on him to be there when you need him.

THE NAME #7 MAN

The #7 MAN is a class act. The picture of a gentleman, he is impeccably groomed and well-dressed—thanks to an excellent tailor and quality dry cleaner.

Behind the polished exterior is a man who may seem quiet because he's so busy observing the world around him. Not one to make casual, offhand remarks, he speaks only when he's sure of his facts. Believing only what he can prove, #7 can't be bothered with rumors and hearsay.

A mystery man at first meeting, the #7 MAN is well worth the time it takes to know him. Full of surprises, this ordinarily tranquil, nature-loving man will fight for his principles; #7 doesn't make threats, he makes promises.

From the sympathy evident in his eyes, it is obvious that he cares deeply for all creatures great and small. The resident spider and his pet spaniel receive equal respect, as do the man with a tin cup and the tycoon with millions.

HOME

The #7 MAN'S home is nestled in a lush garden. Beside the front door a small, tasteful sign reads NO SOLICITORS. Surrounded by exotic plants, books, and perhaps a pet or two, #7 regards his home as a place where he can be alone without being lonely.

If you have his unlisted phone number, be sure to use it before you pay him a visit; never arrive unannounced. But when you're called upon, give a resounding "yes" to his invitation for dinner. You'll be treated to stimulating conversation without the usual small or shop talk. His sense of humor is as dry as the fine wines he serves, and he's famous for his wickedly accurate imitations.

FRIEND

Your deepest secrets are safe with a #7 FRIEND; not even Chinese water torture or sticks under his fingernails would convince him to betray your trust. When you bend his ear, count on him to dissolve your self-pity with a candid response to your dilemma.

#7's idea of a good time is to invite you to a concert or an afternoon nature walk. He is content to share periods of companionable silence, and if he accepts your offer of a "penny for his thoughts," you are getting a great bargain.

The #7 FRIEND will clam up when quizzed about personal matters. He doesn't gossip about others, and his humor is rarely at anyone else's expense.

LOVER

Don't let #7's conservative appearance fool you. Cool on the outside, he simmers passionately on the inside. Even though he's got it, don't expect him to flaunt it.

The inquisitive #7 MAN isn't satisfied until he's penetrated the depths of your soul. He loves to experiment and explores all the ins and outs of love until he finds the source of his partner's pleasure.

This amorous nature boy's idea of the perfect indoor/outdoor sport is spelunking; he may also suggest a tryst in the woods or a long, languorous encounter on a secluded beach.

No Don Juan or roving Romeo, #7 is a devoted lover; once he makes your bed, he's content to lie in it.

FATHER

A lover of fine music, the #7 FATHER encourages his children's budding talent. He buys Junior a slide trombone and Little Sis the violin of her dreams. At the same time, considerate #7 buys the rest of the family earplugs and gives strict instructions to remove them for the recital and not to laugh during the duet.

The term "quality time" was inspired by a #7 DAD. He's a patient teacher who knows that the secret to learning how to skip is step, hop, step, hop. Although he doesn't force his kids to join youth organizations, #7 supports them if they do. He's willing to help small groups of budding nature lovers earn merit badges.

Not one to overindulge his children, a #7 FATHER teaches them to care for their possessions; a carelessly broken truck is mended with his child's help, not replaced. A lover of animals, he utilizes family pets to teach compassion and responsibility.

#7 trusts his children; if they breach that trust, he expects them to analyze their actions. Once the penalty for misbehavior is set, a #7 DAD gives no reprieves.

BUSINESS

Dignified and well-groomed, #7 makes a good impression. By asking intelligent questions, he acquires information from others who afterward mistake their own monologue for a seemingly two-way conversation.

Not a gambler, the #7 BUSINESSMAN analyzes his position and makes a move only when the odds are in his favor. Blessed with a poker face, he plays his cards close to his chest and speaks up only when he has a winning hand. Hunches occur to him but he investigates them so thoroughly that he occasionally misses opportunities that require immediate action.

He refuses to be party to poor decisions and turns away business if he doesn't feel he can serve his client's best interest.

Time is his most precious commodity, and he manages it well. Never missing a chance to add to his considerable store of knowledge, #7 regards education as a lifelong pursuit.

BOSS

The #7 BOSS is a technical wizard whose command of language and desire for perfection are formidable. Beneath his reserved manners and keep-your-distance pinstripe suits is a warm human being.

Under pressure the #7 BOSS keeps his cool; he withholds comments until he's had time to examine the facts. Nothing escapes his scrutiny, so don't even consider taking advantage of him. Since his intellect rules his emotions, you'll be out on your ear if you lie—no matter how tragic your tale.

To a #7 BOSS, time is money. Respect his schedule and avoid unnecessary interruptions. Make every minute of your workday count; keep personal calls to a minimum and be sure to use your own quarters.

EMPLOYEE

Not the type to get hot under the collar during a heated discussion, #7 makes a dignified representative at any meeting, whether in-house or with a client. Count on him to return with an accurate report of the proceedings.

The #7 EMPLOYEE asks pertinent questions and interprets information well. His reports are comprehensive and carefully written. He is a master of semantics, so keep a dictionary on hand to decipher his extensive vocabulary.

Content to work alone, #7 doesn't require close supervision. He quickly assesses his role in office politics and avoids involvement in personal or departmental intrigues.

HEALTH, DIET, EXERCISE

Skeptical of fad and crash diets, the #7 man prefers fresh fruit and vegetables to the hidden calories and additives in processed foods. Just in case his chosen diet doesn't work, #7 keeps it to himself until someone else notices the results.

You won't find #7 in a windowless gym waiting in line for a rowing machine when he can be doing the same exercise on a lake. Aware of the mental as well as physical benefits of vigorous activity, he chooses a tranquil setting whenever possible.

A believer in preventive medicine, #7 eliminates the causes of disease so he won't need the cures. When he is sick, the #7 man suffers in silence and wants to be left alone. If you are ill, he'll help you examine your lifestyle and eating habits to prevent future bouts of poor health.

TRAVEL

Content to travel alone or in the company of a few select friends, #7 chooses a private guide instead of a tour. He makes arrangements himself rather than trust an untried travel agent.

Destinations of great natural beauty or architectural achievement inspire him. He prefers accommodations with charm and character, fireplaces and wood paneling to glass and brass.

When in Rome, the #7 TRAVELER does as the Romans do. Immersing himself in their language and culture, he successfully avoids the crowds and tourist traps.

On the flight home, #7 would rather relive the best moments of his foreign adventure to the music of his earphones than listen to the trials and tribulations of his loquacious seat mate.

GIFTS

For this master of words, the ultimate gift is a deluxe edition of the *Oxford English Dictionary* or personalized bookplates for his library.

An Audubon book and binoculars for bird watching would also appeal to nature-loving #7. Or buy a telescope so this mystical man can contemplate the secrets of the stars, while the voyeur in him checks out the curvaceous brunette across the street.

To celebrate his birthday, avoid establishments where the cake is ablaze with sparklers and served by waiters who sing "Happy Birthday" off-key. Instead, invite a select group of friends for an evening of wine tasting, elegantly conducted by a tuxedo-clad winery representative. Present the #7 MAN with a leatherbound wine diary in which to preserve labels and record his favorites.

THE NAME #7 WOMAN

With an air of mystery about her, the polished #7 WOMAN fascinates people because she holds a part of herself in reserve. Her Mona Lisa smile leaves people wondering what this introspective woman has in mind.

A lover of fine things, she has the carriage to wear classic styles well. Her manners are impeccable, and she treats others with respect. She reveres nature and loves animals, from her pet cat to the lowest earthworm in her garden.

The #7 WOMAN'S great strength lies in her ability to analyze problems and see projects through to completion. Her keen powers of observation also account for her talent to delight others with her imitations.

She chooses her path in life carefully, seeing the forest in spite of the trees.

HOME

The #7 WOMAN'S home is her private domain, a refuge from the stress of everyday living. Think twice before you invade her sanctuary; wait for an invitation or call first.

In the tranquil surroundings of her home, #7 can work magic on anything that grows; she's forever reviving a friend's grape ivy or adopting the runt of the litter.

Even though she's content with her own company, #7 is a considerate hostess who enjoys inviting special friends for an evening of surprises. Dinner is well-planned, cooked to perfection, and garnished with parsley she's grown in her garden. #7 frequently provides her guests with entertainment—a harpist to set the mood or perhaps a gypsy card reader to predict the future.

FRIEND

The three monkeys—Hear No Evil, See No Evil, and Speak No Evil—influence the #7 FRIEND, who avoids gossip and hearsay. Not one to gab indiscriminately on the phone, she communicates intuitively with friends. Skipping the small talk, she likes to share a meaningful conversation over lunch at a fine restaurant where she expects unobtrusive service and impeccable attention to detail. If your meal isn't right she'll send it back to the kitchen.

As a perceptive confidante, she has a knack for asking the right questions. Her friends often hear the solutions to their problems in the answers they give. No detail escapes the gaze of observant #7; she notices a new shade of hair color, the loss of those important first few pounds, or even signs that you might like to be alone.

LOVER

Salomé with her seven veils has nothing on the #7 LOVER, who understands the mysteries of love. Who would imagine that beneath her poised, cerebral exterior beats the heart of a belly dancer? Still waters run deep, and pleasure awaits the man who is willing to probe her depths.

The key to intriguing #7 is her mind, for it rules her heart. When she feels secure in your love, she'll reveal her talents. She's an accomplished prestidigitator with a magic box full of tricks and the skills to levitate you.

Although the #7 WOMAN may cherish your presence, she also needs time alone; be assured that she is so devoted and honest you can trust her with your heart and your family jewels.

MOTHER

An intuitive #7 MOTHER sympathizes if her children feel misunderstood or want to be alone. She analyzes their needs and schedules study and bedtimes accordingly.

A #7 MOM knows how to make learning fun. She teaches her children chemistry by making peanut brittle with a candy thermometer. She introduces new words and current events at dinner and instills good habits with rhymes such as "Mabel, Mabel, strong and able; get your elbows off the table."

Her children grow up with fond memories of quality time spent alone with their #7 MOM. She knows how to build a replica of the state capitol with sugar cubes, and she shares her love of books by reading aloud and introducing her kids to the library at an early age.

A #7 MOTHER is calm during a crisis. When the fire chief pulls up in front of the house to investigate the false alarm, she asks penetrating questions to get to the heart of the matter; her children better have the right answers, and the fire chief better have the right house!

BUSINESS

The analytical #7 WOMAN enjoys the mental discipline of a demanding job. Not one to leap without looking, she carefully sifts facts before combining her uncanny hunches with good judgment to reach sound business decisions.

Creating her own good fortune, #7 often manages to acquire the trump card. Guarding her advantage carefully, she always collects more information than she divulges.

Professional in her demeanor, #7 separates her business and private lives. Time is her most valuable asset, and she doesn't squander it on idle conversation. Always looking for ways to increase her knowledge, the #7 WOMAN is well-read in her field and pursues continuing education.

BOSS

Technically proficient in her area of expertise, the #7 BOSS is a perfectionist. She writes masterful memos and gives concise instructions. Woe to the subordinate who consistently turns in poor work accompanied by a lame excuse. Count on the #7 BOSS to document the substandard performance and invite the employee to a last supper with the personnel director.

It's her style to work alone without interruptions. To save time, she asks her employees to list questions as they occur and hold them for discussion at regularly scheduled meetings.

Dignified and in control of her emotions, #7 remains unflustered as a deadline approaches; she's confident in her staff's ability to maintain the schedule. Petty office politics do not interest her; she expects employees to substantiate their complaints with facts, and she handles the problems with dispatch.

EMPLOYEE

The #7 EMPLOYEE is the essence of decorum in her behavior and appearance. She's a perfectionist who spots typographical errors and can make minor repairs on the office equipment.

Intuitive when it comes to relationships, she tests the temperature of the office pool before getting in the swim of company politics. Gossip stops with #7. Good at keeping her feelings under wraps, she won't cry and fall apart under pressure.

Not one to waste her time or yours, #7 can quickly analyze a problem and generate a list of pertinent questions. An adept troubleshooter, she uses good judgment and needs little supervision.

Don't be surprised when she expresses an interest in pursuing her knowledge to develop a specialty.

HEALTH, DIET, EXERCISE

Skeptical of the current fad diet her friends are touting, the #7 WOMAN analyzes the best plan for her. A strong advocate of preventive medicine, she won't jeopardize her health by eliminating necessary nutrients. To avoid comments and sabotage by the office lunch bunch, #7 brown bags her low-cal midday meal and takes a walk in the park.

Outdoor sports such as hiking, tennis, and skiing appeal to #7; she'd rather jog with the dog or bend and stretch over her petunias than join a crowded exercise class.

When #7 is under the weather, she wants to be left alone to sleep it off. Assuming a sick friend feels the same way, she responds by sending a prayer plant and a brief, sympathetic note.

TRAVEL

Armed with her permanently crinkled cotton gauze wardrobe, cold water soap and toilet seat covers, she's off to see her own list of the Seven Wonders of the World. Personally selecting her itinerary, she avoids the crowds on the beaten path. The #7 WOMAN skips the fresh poi at the luau with casts of thousands and searches out the tiny restaurant for four, nestled in the branches of the huge banyan tree.

Stopping at every inspiration point along the way, the #7 TRAVELER is enriched by the beauty and power of nature and the great men who tamed it. Attracted by the quaint hotels and country inns, she selects a room with a past and the corner table on the veranda.

Don't be surprised if she doesn't publicize her return; travel-weary #7 is happy to find her own way home.

GIFTS

An embossed box of French milled soap and thick, fluffy towels are appropriate gifts for the squeaky-clean #7 WOMAN. A professional steam iron or a gift certificate from the Chinese hand laundry would satisfy her fastidious nature.

To mark the coming year, give her a calendar with a thought for each day or a leatherbound diary to record her own inspirations. A mystic of sorts, the #7 WOMAN would appreciate a book on palmistry or numerology.

To celebrate her birthday, invite her closest friends to take in a garden tour or plan an alfresco picnic at the arboretum. Arrange for some strolling strings and, if you must, allow the violinists to play their refined rendition of "Felicitations on Your Natal Day."

THE NAME #7 CHILD

From his (or her) first moments in the delivery room, the #7 BABY appears placid as he observes his new world. After he's been changed and fed in the morning, he's content to amuse himself with toys in his crib or to contemplate his navel until he falls back to sleep.

He shows early interest in words and books and may tinker on a typewriter or teach himself to read long before he enters school. His inquisitive, analytical mind makes subjects such as creative writing and science enjoyable for him.

A perfectionist, the #7 CHILD plans ahead and finishes what he (or she) starts. A disorganized coach or an unprepared teacher will not win his respect. An amateur sports psychologist, #7 motivates himself and plans strategies to improve his technique. Satisfy his desire to analyze his performance by videotaping his practice session or the big event.

#7 is his own best friend; aside from a few close chums, he's content with his own company and rarely falls prey to peer pressure. He needs to claim his territory and is fussy about his possessions; siblings who borrow games had better return them intact. A fastidious dresser, the #7 CHILD may reject your obvious attempts at mending and refuse to wear a garment that is wrinkled or missing a button.

He hates to be questioned or told what to do. When he feels misunderstood, the #7 CHILD heads for the hills with his dog or curls up with a good book.

By the time he is grown, the #7 CHILD will have told you in a hundred ways that he reveres you as a parent. Your immortality is assured in the stories he will tell his children about their wonderful grandparents.

THE NAME #8 MAN

The #8 MAN is a real go-getter who believes you never get a second chance to make a good first impression. He has the drive and the discipline to take control of an idea from conception to completion; one man's inspiration becomes #8's realization.

He delegates well and builds an effective team to follow his orders. Wielding power and influence, #8 seems to possess the Midas touch. He visualizes money, power, and success, and has the will to make dreams come true.

His physical stamina and organizational genius combine to make an unbeatable combination on any level; the #8 MAN is a giant in the business world and on the playing field. Winning a contract or a baseball game, he is a trophy hunter who frames his certificates and displays his medals.

HOME

The #8 MAN subscribes to the proven real estate strategy of buying the least expensive house in the best neighborhood. Renovating the outside first, he chooses a massive front door, selects an impressive light fixture, and plants a forest of full-grown trees in the front yard.

Acting as his own contractor to ensure a quality job at the most economical price, #8 hires experts to do the extensive restoration work calculated to transform his bargain abode into a showplace.

When he says "dinner at eight," he means it. Dress up and be on time or you'll miss the grand entrance of his first-course soufflé. Expect the linguine to be al dente and the company to be high powered.

When #8 conducts an afterdinner guided tour, be sure to admire all the time-and-energy-saving devices and his temperature-controlled wine cellar.

FRIEND

A #8 FRIEND is always level-headed in an emergency. When an avalanche buries the warming hut, he'll organize the skiers to dig a tunnel to meet the rescue party halfway.

When #8 issues an invitation, he's apt to kill two birds with one stone. He enjoys your company while he exercises at the gym and tops off the evening with a sumptuous dinner at his favorite restaurant. Encouraging his friends to be successful, he dares them to take chances. Share your brainstorm with #8 because he can recognize and implement your good ideas. If he's too busy, he'll persuade his influential friends to help you.

Based on his own winning record, the #8 FRIEND is a master at giving advice, but don't waste time offering him yours. When his counsel pays off, thank him publicly and arrange for a drum roll as you introduce him to your other friends.

LOVER

Not easily discouraged, the #8 LOVER won't take no for an answer. It's hard to keep this resilient romancer down for long. Up-and-coming #8 is a tower of strength with the potential to reach great heights. You'll nickname him "Marathon Man" and crawl breathlessly to the phone to tell your best friend that you've just discovered the Eighth Wonder of the World.

He's a take-charge guy who wants action, not talk. #8 won't use strong-arm tactics, but he's apt to forge his way in anywhere because he likes a little struggle in his snuggle to heighten his fun.

Generous #8 believes in sharing the wealth. When he offers to give you his family jewels—2 karats apiece for each earlobe—be sure to swoon at the size of his rocks.

FATHER

Inspired by his newborn's long, tapered fingers, the ambitious #8 FATHER rushes out to buy a baby grand piano.

A dynamic dad with high expectations, he encourages his children's money-making schemes. He's more than willing to float his budding entrepreneur a loan so that Jr. Cézanne and Co. can paint numbers on the neighborhood curbs.

The #8 FATHER handpicks sports for his children according to their talents. Up at the crack of dawn to help his daughter trace perfect figure 8s on ice, he makes time later on to coach his growing goalie. On the way home they stop at the trophy store window to visualize Junior's name on the biggest one.

When his kids get the winter sniffles, health-conscious #8 DAD whips up his family's recipe for horseradish. As an effective sinus treatment, it's guaranteed to put every ear, nose, and throat doctor within a hundred-mile radius out of practice.

BUSINESS

The #8 MAN doesn't wait for his ship to come in; he swims out to meet it, promoting himself to captain so he can chart his own course. With definite goals in mind and efficient systems in place, #8 meets challenges head on and commissions experts to perform each task.

Blessed with great physical stamina, #8 also knows the importance of mental balance. Emotions wreak havoc in the business arena, so #8 keeps his feelings under control with regular exercise. Instinctively sensing the pulse of the marketplace and consolidating his alliances, the #8 MAN surpasses his competition and climbs to the top.

BOSS

The #8 BOSS leaves no doubt in your mind that he is in charge. Choosing an ambitious route to the summit of the corporate mountain, he creates a productive system and delegates the work to hardy subordinates who can keep up with him. Once the wheels are in motion, he switches into high gear until he plants his flag on the penthouse.

From his prestigious corner office, the #8 BOSS wields power and builds empires. He sees every obstacle as a challenge; if you can match his stamina and adjust to the altitude, hang on for an exciting ascent and a key to the executive washroom.

EMPLOYEE

The bottom rung of the ladder is no resting place for ambitious #8. He likes a demanding assignment and, rain or shine, he'll be on the job as long as he feels there's a future. If you can't afford to give him a raise right away, buy time with an impressive title and a shiny new nameplate for his desk.

His budding managerial skills are evident in the way he takes charge of projects. You won't have to breathe down his neck because he quickly assesses the requirements, devises a plan, and organizes his co-workers.

When dealing with a #8 EMPLOYEE, remember that he hates to take orders; give your directions with a smile and use words such as "suggestion" and "we."

HEALTH, DIET, EXERCISE

According to #8, winning isn't everything—it's the only thing. He exercises to keep his body in tune and running on all eight cylinders. Pushing to increase his strength, he prides himself on the fact that the recreation he's chosen is on the leading edge of popularity. His definition of a contact sport depends on how many new clients it nets him.

A successful dieter, #8 burns off extra calories by taking the stairs instead of the elevator and beams breathlessly when his secretary exclaims over his feat.

With an ice pack in the freezer and a supply of Ace bandages handy, #8 guards against missing a game or admitting defeat in the form of illness or injury. When others are sidelined, he sends them bottles of vitamins and the telephone number of his sports medicine specialist.

TRAVEL

Self-appointed travel agent and tour director, the #8 MAN automatically assumes the leadership role—to the great relief and pleasure of his companions. He issues comprehensive lists with updates as the day of departure draws near, times his connections to avoid lengthy layovers, and books name hotels at "in" resorts.

No obstacles deter him; in the face of an impending airline strike, he makes alternate reservations. To facilitate baggage handling, he hands out identical luggage tags to each member of the group. At every border he handles immigration and locates the best rate of foreign exchange. Don't worry about ground transportation; chauffeurs will await you at the curb.

GIFTS

Buy the #8 MAN the best you can afford; a sterling silver key chain is better than an imitation alligator attaché case. And he would certainly treasure a gold coin minted in the year of his birth, but a monogrammed shirt would please him just as well.

Appeal to his athletic interests and present him with tickets to the playoff game. If you can't afford a sky writer to convey your greetings over the stadium, hang up a banner across his garage saying HAPPY BIRTHDAY, CHAMP.

When planning a party for #8, send engraved invitations to eight special friends for chilled Russian vodka and caviar. He won't mind adding another year to his age if the occasion is marked by a classy celebration.

THE NAME #8 WOMAN

According to the #8 WOMAN, "You can never be too rich or too thin." She is intent on building a positive image and she enjoys the material symbols of her success. From the cut of her clothes to the quality of their cloth, #8 gives the impression that she's a woman of status.

Respected for her competence, #8 has the organizational skills to manage a home and a full-time career. A pro at balancing the demands on her time, she loves a challenge: the more she has to do, the happier she is.

Able to take charge in any situation, the frank #8 WOMAN doesn't hesitate to give orders. People admire her executive ability and appreciate her efficiency at any task, from the simple to the most complex.

High voltage #8 is a vital addition to any gathering; her endless energy is contagious.

HOME

The #8 WOMAN is satisfied with a fixer-upper provided it has the right address in a prestigious location. She will refurbish it to be as impressive on the outside as it is organized on the inside.

The first on the block to invest in a microwave oven and a food processor, #8 has every other timesaving device known to humankind.

When she entertains, her countdown procedure rivals that of a space launch. A whiz with a wok, she slices and dices ahead in preparation for a quick stir-fry, leaving her more time to entertain her guests.

#8 believes in abundance, whether she's buying cases of staples on special or lugs of fruit to make jam. Her lavish buffets surpass any feast Henry VIII might have hosted. She'll present a table laden with delicious dishes and overflowing platters, banking the spaces in between with flaky croissants.

FRIEND

The #8 WOMAN is a true friend who gives practical advice and helps others choose their priorities by listing pros and cons. With a practiced eye for seeing the possibilities for success in all situations, she encourages you to reach for the brass ring.

Though she has the skill of a high-wire artist when it comes to balancing her emotions, #8 will send up a flare when she needs your help. She exchanges favors the way some people exchange money; while she may not keep score, the #8 FRIEND knows when the balance of trade needs adjusting.

Line up some cash when #8 asks you to go shopping; she knows where to find designer duds at discount prices. Before the day is over, energetic #8 will wear out your feet as well as your pocketbook. Don't let the white-gloved waiter serving high tea see you kick your shoes off under the table.

LOVER

Position is everything in the life of a #8 WOMAN; whether in the boardroom or the bedroom, she likes to be on top. Acrobatic and well-exercised, she knows which muscles to stretch and which to tighten. Deliberate in her moves, she makes every one count. Strong enough to wrestle, she's mastered some good holds and likes a man who can keep up with her.

Impressed by the finer things in life, #8 responds to tasteful gifts that attest to your affluence and influence. Don't be surprised if you catch her checking out your assets before she consolidates an alliance. When she sees a good thing, she hangs on to it.

MOTHER

A #8 MOM will do everything in her power to ensure the success of her children. Not only does she encourage little Olympians and Nobel prizewinners, she also prepares little financial geniuses to find their place in the world by giving them piggy banks and toy cash registers. She teaches the value of money; at her house the tooth fairy hasn't heard about inflation.

To encourage her son's first money-making efforts, #8 will get up at 4:00 A.M. to cook him a hearty breakfast before he delivers his papers. When her daughter shows culinary talent, she'll finance the flyers to promote Juliette the Child as a party helper-for-hire. #8 shows her children how to use their heads to get ahead.

A health-conscious #8 MOTHER sprinkles wheat germ on her kids' morning cereal and stirs protein powder in their bedtime Ovaltine. Count on her to give out boxes of raisins and shiny red apples on Halloween.

#8's happiest moments are frog hunting with her daughter (to find her a prince) or sitting on the fifty-yard line wearing a shirt that says I'M THE QUARTERBACK'S MOTHER.

BUSINESS

Enterprising #8 is attracted by the trappings of success. Concerned with her image, she dresses to impress and doesn't hesitate to spend what it takes to have an eye-catching logo designed for her business cards and stationery. With the vision and imagination of a potential tycoon, the #8 WOMAN dreams of fame and fortune in technicolor.

An administrative ace, #8 has the foresight to plan on a large scale. Her systems are brilliant, only overshadowed by her ability to persuade others to work as hard as she does.

Keeping her nose to the grindstone and her ear to the ground, #8 senses the undercurrents in the business community. She instinctively forms advantageous alliances that strengthen her position and propel her into the driver's seat.

BOSS

A natural-born executive, ambitious #8 probably started in the basement and developed a crick in her neck eyeing the executive suite. She didn't get to the top on her "dress-for-success" wardrobe alone; #8 paid her dues.

She wrote the book on organization; large-scale projects are her specialty. The #8 WOMAN knows how to manage and delegate; she's fair, but directs her support teams with an iron hand.

She's frank and honest, sometimes to the point of being blunt. If a key employee decides to cruise the Caribbean during the company's busy season, a #8 BOSS will give him or her an ultimatum: "Shape up or ship out."

EMPLOYEE

She's a bright light in the office who always shines at full power; #8 makes the most of every working minute. Confident of her abilities, she's a self-starter who thrives on challenges. She's not afraid of anyone or anything, including hard work.

It would be a wise move to give #8 the responsibility for the company relocation. On the big day, clipboard in hand, she'll sport a button saying ASK ME. I'M IN CHARGE. Rest assured that the dollies will roll until every color-coded box turns up in the right office.

When she impresses a V. P. by reciting statistics, it's clear that #8 can manage the movers as well as move with the managers. The #8 EMPLOYEE is on her way up, and possibly out, if you fail to give her the recognition and raises she deserves.

HEALTH, DIET, EXERCISE

With her vitality and endurance, #8 has what it takes to run the average aerobics teacher right into the ground; just ask the tennis chums who have felt the fury of her state-of-the-art aluminum racquet.

When she makes up her mind to diet, the #8 WOMAN has iron willpower. Rewarding herself with svelte clothes, she makes dieting a status symbol of sorts and casually drops terms such as "nouvelle cuisine" and "pasta primavera" in her conversation.

She avoids poor health by adhering to a regime of eight hours of work, eight hours of play, followed by eight hours of sleep. If you get sick, she'll send you a dozen roses in your favorite color and organize your friends to bring in dinners for a week.

TRAVEL

On-the-go #8 likes to do things right, as in "do" New England in the fall and "do" the Riviera in the spring. Regarding herself as part of the upper crust, she gravitates to their playgrounds, avoiding the flakes at the stale resorts.

The #8 WOMAN will instruct her travel agent to reserve her favorite seat on the plane and to special-order a seafood salad so she doesn't have to dine on the usual chicken and mixed vegetables a la hand cream. While en route, she keeps in touch by using the air-to-ground credit card phone.

Efficient #8 rolls her coordinated wardrobe in plastic bags to prevent wrinkles and makes sure to include the lint brush and a dark slip for her favorite black skirt.

The letter she sends on her five-star hotel stationery indicates that she has "arrived." Also note that she has underlined the hour of her return; if you can't be there on time, your driver will do.

GIFTS

The #8 WOMAN is dropping a hint when she hums "Diamonds Are a Girl's Best Friend" for a whole month before her big day. Subtle as a train wreck, she has definite ideas about what she wants. In fact, the gift registry was the brainchild of #8, who can't bear the thought of receiving flowered towels for her Art Deco bathroom.

Always interested in making a positive impression, the #8 WOMAN would like a blind embosser to mark her stationery, or anything personalized or monogrammed.

When planning a celebration for her, roll out the red carpet from her door to the stretch limo. Rent space on the marquee so she can see her name up in lights when you arrive for the performance. For the grand finale, have #8's friends toast her with rave reviews at the splashy late supper after the show.

THE NAME #8 CHILD

A #8 BABY puts you on his (or her) schedule and keeps the whole family busy waiting on him; who can resist the look of expectation in the commanding eyes of this little delegator?

A #8 CHILD has a system for everything: chores, storing his baseball equipment, memorizing history dates, the Gettysburg Address, and multiplication tables.

His (or her) most productve schemes are the ones that earn him money; don't be surprised if #8 has all of his friends working for him. Posting lookouts at every intersection on the steepest street, a #8 CHILD will charge the neighborhood kids 25 cents each for a thrilling ride on his go-cart. As #8's daredevil customers shriek "Look, Ma, no brakes!" the big spenders can be spotted by the smoking rubber on their tennis shoes and the accompanying skid marks on the pavement.

Leave your calculator at home when you go grocery shopping with #8; he'll figure the unit prices, spot all the bargains, and talk you into investing in his next enterprise with the money he saved you.

In school he's the peer that exerts the pressure. A ringleader, #8 is often elected to office and may mobilize the student body to fight for off-campus lunch privileges or start a student store.

Your #8 CHILD will make his mark on the world and want you to share in his success. Give in when he begs you to play Monopoly day and night; one day #8 will own Boardwalk and Park Place for real.

THE NAME #9 MAN

Phrases such as "brotherly love" and "peace on earth" have real meaning in the daily life of humanitarian #9. He gives without remembering and takes without forgetting. Philanthropic organizations, as well as family and friends, appreciate his charity.

An expert in human nature, the #9 MAN is quick to comment on the merit of others' ideas; he sees the beauty and potential in everyone and everything.

An optimist, he lives in the present and lets go of the past. By coming to terms with the ups and downs in his own life, he's able to relate to others with compassion and tolerance. In his enthusiasm to make the world a better place, he often shares his philosophical viewpoint with others.

HOME

The #9 MAN is a Pied Piper who encourages the world to beat a path to his door. When he says "drop in," he means it. Don't hesitate to ring the Chinese gong at his door; it's music to his ears.

#9's home is a melting pot of international friends and flavors. When he entertains, he brings his guests into the act of dipping cubes of bread in the fondue or concocting their own Mongolian hot pot dinner.

A dedicated community volunteer, he offers his home to groups and charity events. Ask any kid on the block where #9 lives; he's the nice man who always buys Little League raffle tickets and peanuts for the summer camp fund.

FRIEND

#9 counts friends as his wealth and considers himself a rich man. If you're his friend, you're among diverse company; #9 knows everyone from the butcher to the Indian chief. Forget ethnic jokes when you're around him; there isn't a prejudicial bone in his body.

A cum laude graduate of the school of hard knocks, he's won his share of uphill battles. Rely on him to help you fight your own.

When he takes you to the Italian restaurant where waiters double as opera singers, don't choke on your ravioli as the #9 FRIEND pops up to sing his well-rehearsed shower aria. Give him the applause he loves, and scream bravo as you pass the Parmesan cheese.

LOVER

Emotional, uninhibited #9 is a resting volcano waiting to erupt. He immerses himself totally in his love interest. Not exactly a soft touch, he is a bit gullible and easily taken in at times.

The generous #9 LOVER agrees that charity begins at home

and will make deposits directly to your account; your interest will compound nightly.

He understands your every need and is willing to extend himself to please you. He loves to put you on his pedestal and will leave a lasting impression. Instead of sending him a trophy engraved with WORLD'S GREATEST LOVER, immortalize your #9 MAN by displaying his image in stone—just like the Washington Monument.

FATHER

Generous is not just another word in his vocabulary; the #9 Dad lives by the Golden Rule. It's hard to say who benefits most when his youth group delivers handmade planters to the elderly—the proud kids or the grateful seniors.

Before dishing out any punishment, the impartial #9 FATHER presides over a session of the family council to hear the case. And when it's time for school elections, he educates his future class president on how to appeal to all successfully. A landslide victory is guaranteed with his suggestions for snappy slogans and eye-catching posters.

When Junior decides to form a rock group, music-loving #9 doesn't hesitate to spring for a set of drums. To pacify Mom and the neighbors, he soundproofs the garage with the condition that Little Sis can have equal time to practice her tap dancing.

BUSINESS

In touch with the human angle and able to visualize concepts on a grand scale, the #9 MAN has the ability to reach the masses. Before he makes liberal use of the media for publicity, he'll support his recommendations with careful research.

Charismatic #9 brings together diverse groups in the business community. Because he inspires trust, he succeeds where others fail. He recognizes the potential in his clients' suggestions, and colleagues respect his integrity and influence.

In his book, material success and philanthropy go hand in hand; the good he gives always comes back.

BOSS

The #9 BOSS was an equal opportunity employer long before it was a law; he runs his operation without prejudices of any kind.

There are no nameless faces in his department. He values the contributions of every member of his staff, from the mail-room clerk to his administrative assistant. When you've burned the midnight oil helping him with a report, he may not put your name on it, but your input will be noted and praised publicly.

While the rule-abiding #9 BOSS sets a good example by taking regulation forty-five-minute lunches, he also counsels his employees about choosing a health plan that best suits their needs, and encourages them to take maximum advantage of the benefits.

EMPLOYEE

#9 is a tolerant employee who can work in any capacity, as long as he knows he's appreciated. His ability to see the big picture may come in handy when it's time to make projections or determine the thrust of an ad campaign.

He works easily with all kinds of people; in fact, he's especially helpful to new recruits or co-workers experiencing difficulties. Concerned with the welfare of others, the #9 EMPLOYEE makes an ideal company representative for United Way. His own generosity is contagious and it's hard to say no to such a nice guy. Foreign clients respond to #9 when he makes attempts to speak their language and learn their customs and culture.

HEALTH, DIET, EXERCISE

As he travels the charity dinner circuit, the #9 MAN loses weight by paying more attention to his interesting dinner mate than his dinner plate.

Forget solo pursuits; #9 likes a group activity. From baseball to volleyball, he can play any position. Compassionate, he often gets additional exercise by teaching the disabled to swim.

Outgoing #9 requires proper rest to keep up with his full schedule. If he is ill he may need to block out some time to recharge his batteries. When you are sick, he'll fill your room with laughter and soothe you with his presence.

TRAVEL

A globe-trotting goodwill ambassador, #9 travels to broaden his horizons. Lured by the offbeat and unknown, the #9 MAN likes to get as close as he can to the daily life of the native people.

When he mentions a salmon bake upstream, he may neglect to tell you that the tour bus is a two-man kayak, and that instead of singing for your supper, you'll have to catch it.

Try not to laugh when you meet him at the airport; he's the one wearing the kimono and the zori on his feet, bowing in your direction. When you interrupt his "arigato" to ask why his suitcase is so light that it flies out of your hand, he'll explain that he gave away all his Western clothes and continue to tell you all about his grandiose plans to make Nagasaki a sister city. This one-man Peace Corps contributes to world understanding wherever he goes.

GIFTS

When the #9 MAN talks about reviving his high-school French, present him with a set of language tapes and a leather passport case for his next sojourn.

Tickets to the symphony or a compact disk of Dixieland jazz would please this eclectic music lover.

To celebrate his birthday, plan a fan club party for the actor in #9. Send press passes for invitations; ask the men to masquerade as paparazzi with their flash cameras, and the women to come as groupies. Provide eight-by-ten glossies for #9 to autograph and decorate the room with poster-size enlargements of the star.

THE NAME #9 WOMAN

An "A"-type person, the #9 WOMAN is *all* things to *all* people. She's the salt of the earth with power to influence the individuals she attracts from all walks of life.

Ruled by her emotions, the #9 WOMAN is a free spirit with a live-and-let-live philosophy. Able to see the overview, she is wise as a result of having overcome disappointments.

Charming #9 has a zest for living. With her dramatic flair and love of art and music, she's a one-woman show that captures the social spotlight.

Generous to a fault, the selfless #9 WOMAN sees the best in people. Always the first to build a bridge over troubled waters, her theme is "Let there be peace on earth and let it begin with me."

HOME

The #9 WOMAN has the best-swept house on the block because she can't say no to the broom salesman. Her welcome mat speaks many languages. From drop-in company to displaced relatives, there is always room for one more.

Although #9's home is her universe, it contains evidence that she contributes to the community at large and loves to travel. Displayed with her service awards and recognition plaques are mementos such as a camel saddle, a shiny brass samovar, and a nest of Russian dolls.

A #9 WOMAN's parties reflect her international tastes and her desire to involve her guests in the festivities. Greeted by luminarias lining the driveway, partygoers munch on nachos and sip margaritas before they make their own tostadas and dance to the music of the mariachis.

FRIEND

A #9 FRIEND has great depth of understanding. You may have to take a number and stand in line because many others seek her warmth and wisdom.

No stranger to disappointment, she's an expert when it comes to empathy. Nonjudgmental #9 believes that the brave forgive and the wise forget.

She gives the best of herself and gives credit to others when credit is due. If she helps you run the silent auction at your club fund-raiser, be sure to voice the recognition she needs and deserves.

When you walk into her favorite sushi bar at the appointed hour and your #9 FRIEND is nowhere in sight, be patient; she's been delayed visiting a sick friend or helping her neighbor deliver a litter of kittens.

LOVER

Amorous #9 is in love with love; she desires deep affection, even if only short-lived.

The #9 WOMAN likes to travel around the world, but her favorite spot is near the equator, where it's hot and humid.

Romantic as well as artistic, she may suggest body painting, followed by a candlelit bubble bath. Yield to humanitarian #9 when she wants to play doctor. She's an uninhibited healer who asks little and gives much. Not wanting to see you suffer, she'll do whatever it takes to put you out of your misery. She's great with endings and always finishes with a flourish.

MOTHER

The dedicated #9 MOTHER believes the hand that rocks the cradle rules the world. She rewards good behavior, and her children are easy to spot by the little gold stars she pastes on their foreheads.

Her home is a popular hangout. Always welcome, neighborhood kids know this #9 MOM is good for a snack and some sound advice. She's short on lectures and long on constructive fun. Game for a taffy pull, she's got the sugar and won't come unglued when there are several pairs of shoes temporarily stuck to her floor.

At school, future starlets needing help with costumes and sound effects come to #9, who can also paint the backdrops. At home, she makes a dull chapter in the history textbook come alive when she reads aloud with the appropriate accent.

BUSINESS

A student of human nature, #9 picks up the pulse of the public. Sensing a need, she has the ability to fill it. A natural in sales, she can sell any product that passes her tests for quality and performance.

The #9 WOMAN has great influence with her colleagues; they respect her ability to see the potential in an idea and trust her recommendations. She's a role model whose reputation for playing by the rules is respected in the business world.

Humanitarian #9 recognizes the sources of her business success by making contributions to the community; she not only enhances her company's image, but improves lives.

BOSS

The democratic #9 BOSS sees herself as part of the team, not solely an authority figure. Never at a loss for words, she speaks out when the work isn't up to snuff and encourages her staff to provide her with feedback. She trusts her employees and establishes a climate of mutual respect.

Instead of sweltering in the heat when the air conditioning fails, she considerately sends everyone home. Faced with the prospect of retiling the rest rooms, she takes a vote on the color choices.

A #9 BOSS sees the potential in every employee and forgives an occasional off-day. Count on her to back you up when you're in a tight spot and give you credit for a job well done.

EMPLOYEE

The #9 EMPLOYEE will put forth her efforts in any capacity for a boss who shows his or her respect and appreciation. Able to work with all kinds of people, she stays out of office politics.

When she sees a need to keep track of a sales trend, she pursues the project on her own and stays with it until she has some meaningful statistics to present to her boss. In charge of the Recognition Award dinner, she can produce an evening that reflects the essence of commitment found in each honoree.

If you can't attend the soroptimist luncheon, send your #9 EMPLOYEE. When she returns, she'll announce that she volunteered you to head the membership committee, and counter your objections with an immediate offer to help you.

HEALTH, DIET, EXERCISE

Attracted to beautiful food and unusual flavors, the #9 WOMAN is often tempted to indulge. She can't bring herself to decline the preparations of a gracious hostess or turn down a cute little girl scout selling cookies at her door.

Folk dancing is an ideal activity for sociable, musical #9. She makes exercise a part of her life, not an end in itself.

When her friends tease her about practicing medicine without a license, she counters by saying that she sees her doctor all the time—at parties. If you're sick, she'll bring you chicken soup and Guatemalan worry dolls, guaranteed to take the load off your mind. When she is under the weather, she bounces back quickly because duty calls and her home remedies really work!

TRAVEL

Faraway places with strange-sounding names appeal to the #9 WOMAN. With wheels on her suitcase, she's ready to roll.

Give her authentic settings with real people; she wants to sleep in a teepee and grind corn with the Indians or shear sheep and spin yarn in the backcountry of Australia.

When your #9 traveling companion suggests a shopping expedition, be prepared to rub elbows with the natives and their chickens on a bumpy bus. At the central market, smile when she asks you to pose for a picture in the produce stalls, and hold the microphone right next to the marimba so she can record the local music.

When she cables to request a mini-van to meet her at the airport, beware! She's either returning with a foreign delegation or a carved writing desk from Hong Kong that she simply couldn't pass up.

GIFTS

Music and theater appeal to the #9 WOMAN, so tickets to a performance are a welcome gift. To double her pleasure, order a gift from the catalog of her favorite charity or make an outright donation in her name.

Replace friendly #9's bulging address book with a giant leather expandable version, and offer to keep her company while she fills it.

To celebrate her special day, honor your vagabond #9 with a "tacky tourist" party. Munch on box lunches as you gawk at the local sights from a rented tour bus. Give a prize for the most garish costume; award extra points for plaid walking shorts, flowered shirts, and plastic tote bags with city names spelled out in rhinestones.

THE NAME #9 CHILD

Drifting into peaceful slumber to the tune of a lullaby, the #9 BABY dreams of exploring the world. You may have to send the search parties out sooner than you think. The #9 TODDLER ventures forth early in life to share his (or her) cookies and follow his star.

Friendly and outgoing, the #9 CHILD brings home all his (or her) friends, along with every stray animal in the neighborhood. Hold your tongue when he offers alternate licks on his ice cream cone to the dog, and pack an extra sandwich in his lunch because he likes to share that, too.

A regular teacher's little helper, obedient #9 never gets his name on the board unless he's the pencil monitor with blisters to prove it.

At the end of the year he may not bring home his sweaters because he gave them away, but he does bring home the high-point school service award for saving newspapers and collecting canned goods.

A geography buff, the #9 CHILD stacks his *National Geographic*s with his comic books and has a wall-size map of the world with color-coded flags marking all the places he wants to visit. The #9 CHILD makes an ideal tutor for the non-English-speaking student. His lessons include rules of all sports so that the new kid will be picked when the other children choose up sides for a game.

By the time you are old and gray, you will have the satisfaction of knowing that your #9 CHILD has made this world a better place.

PERSONALITY NUMBERS

Your PERSONALITY NUMBER is determined by the consonants in your name and describes the impression you make on other people. Instructions for calculating your PERSONALITY NUMBER begin on page 13.

PERSONALITY #1

■ You give the impression of being so dynamic a leader that you appear to outshine any competition.

■ In single-minded fashion you seem to take control and accomplish a great deal in a short amount of time.

■ You assume center stage with apparent ease and seem very self-sufficient.

■ Operating independently, you're a daring pioneer who's seemingly unaffected by opposition.

■ Your original approach to ordinary situations amazes people.

PERSONALITY #2

■ People find you open, friendly, and easy to talk to.

■ You always seem to say the right thing at the right time to put people at ease.

■ Your tact and sensitivity are often praised.

■ You seem to foster agreement among diverse groups and contribute to the spirit of cooperation.

■ People are attracted by your inspirational qualities.

■ In partnerships and group settings, you appear to defer to others.

■ Occasionally you seem to hesitate when making decisions, vacillating between two valid choices.

PERSONALITY #3

■ You project a toast-of-the-town image.

■ Others see you as being youthful, even glamorous.

- People recognize your sense of humor and gift of gab.

- Your optimistic attitude opens doors; once inside, you impress people with your articulate manner and social ease.

- Perceived as a creative, imaginative whirlwind, you have a gregarious, flirtatious quality that attracts a host of followers.

- You appear to use your charm to get what you want.

PERSONALITY #4

- You impress people as an organizational genius.

- Solid as the Rock of Gibraltar, you appear to be as immovable because you are set in your ways.

- You have a reputation for being loyal and keeping your promises.

- People find you as predictable as clockwork; you are prompt to the minute and always finish what you start.

- Regarded as nobody's fool, you seem level-headed and astute.

- You are respected for your no-nonsense approach and the unobtrusive way you work in the background to keep things running smoothly.

PERSONALITY #5

- You appear to have your talented fingers in many pies.

- You seem to have the versatility and energy to keep things hopping and people guessing.

- People find you exciting and unpredictable because you appear to enjoy changing course midstream.

- Your vitality and sense of adventure draw people to you.

- At ease in social situations, you're able to converse on any subject and report the latest news.

PERSONALITY #6

■ You give the impression of being a safe harbor in life's storms; when people turn to you for support, it seems you often rescue them.

■ Your behavior and appearance are above reproach, making you the picture of decorum.

■ Others seem to count on you to make fair judgments and keep the peace.

■ Adaptable to group situations, you appear to pitch in to help others and do your fair share of the work.

■ You surround yourself with quality and comfort.

PERSONALITY #7

■ Wise and refined, you seem to have your life under control.

■ Your aristocratic air and well-groomed appearance indicate a touch of class.

■ Although not necessarily quiet, you have a guarded quality when discussing your private life; it's hard to imagine that you would ever reveal secrets about someone else.

■ Dignified under any circumstance, you seem to maintain a certain distance in social encounters.

■ Your occasional silence is rarely construed as disinterest because the comments you eventually make appear to be based on careful observation and analysis.

PERSONALITY #8

■ Even in your blue jeans, you have a certain elegance that makes a million-dollar first impression.

■ You may not strive to keep up with the Joneses, but you seem to know how to spend money on what shows.

■ You're able to wield influence over people who respond to your strength and executive presence.

■ Dignified and composed in all situations, you're admired for your natural courtesy and good manners.

PERSONALITY #9

■ You seem to have enough grace and generosity to organize an international peace movement or your own Salvation Army.

■ People respond quickly to your charismatic manner; they know you as a meeter-and-greeter who appears to be at home anywhere.

■ Surrounded by friends from many walks of life, you seem like a broad-minded soul who loves everyone.

■ It's obvious you enjoy the inevitable recognition you receive for good deeds.

HEART
NUMBERS

Your HEART NUMBER is determined
by the vowels in your name and
describes your inner feelings and
talents that motivate you.
Instructions for calculating your
HEART NUMBER begin on page 18.

HEART #1

■ You're driven by a desire for independence. Happiest when in control of a situation, you want to work alone or take the lead. You hate to take orders.

■ You see yourself as an idea person who prefers to leave the details to others.

■ In your desire to act immediately on an inspiration, you're impatient and energetic.

■ Although you can be spurred on by compliments, you won't let yourself be bought or possessed.

■ You desire respect for your agile mind rather than for your appearance.

HEART #2

■ To satisfy your need to love and be loved, you desire a special partner.

■ You have a knack for mixing with all kinds of people. In your desire to please others, you hate to say no.

■ Eager to share your wisdom, you have the talent to teach and inspire.

■ In your desire to get people on your bandwagon, you're prone to embellish the facts or cloud the truth.

■ You seek the help of trusted friends when you feel hesitant to try something new.

■ You are sensitive to criticism and require tender loving care.

■ A lover of beauty and culture, you prefer the finer things in life.

HEART #3

■ You are an artistic soul who needs outlets for self-expression.

■ Motivated by a desire to be popular, you try to be friendly and overcome your inclination to be shy.

■ Driven by a need to liven up dull situations and receive applause, you flaunt your wit and gift of gab.

■ A master flirt, you use your charm to get your own way.

■ In love with the good life and all the glamor and glitz that goes along with it, you are motivated to retain your youthful good looks.

■ An incurable romantic, you make sacrifices for your loved ones.

HEART #4

■ Thriving in an atmosphere of established routine, you are a logical thinker who has a talent for developing simplified systems.

■ With a passion for facts, you require proof before accepting a new idea.

■ Determined to get your money's worth, you strive for economy and financial security.

■ Although you are sometimes set in your ways, you're willing to work hard in order to see another's point of view.

■ You have a good eye for design and are gifted with a sense of balance and rhythm.

■ In any area of endeavor, you are prepared to work hard in order to achieve tangible results.

HEART #5

■ You are driven by a desire for personal freedom and feel suffocated without it.

■ Blessed with an ingenious mind, you have many talents and diverse interests.

■ Possessing a spirit of adventure, you seek new places and new faces, and love the challenge of unconventional experiences with people as exciting as you are.

■ You know instinctively when to let go and move on.

■ Gifted with a bright mind, you are curious to explore progressive ideas and are adept at grasping concepts quickly.

■ Restless when forced to wait, you thrive on excitement and change.

HEART #6

■ You require harmony in your relationships.

■ A born rescuer, you view responsibility as a privilege, not a duty.

■ You are a loving counselor who skillfully gives impartial advice.

■ Always fair-minded, you are compelled to right all wrongs and obtain justice for all.

■ An idealist, you are often blind to the faults of your loved ones.

■ Happiest when devoting yourself to the comfort of others, you are generous by nature.

■ A seeker of comfort and beauty, you yearn for luxury in all areas of your life.

HEART #7

■ Possessing great wisdom, you relentlessly search for the truth.

■ Since you hate to be conned, you require proof of a point or reason for a course of action.

■ Concerned with cause and effect, you rarely make a move before examining the consequences.

■ Motivated by your need for perfection, you insist on quality and refinement.

■ You sometimes feel misunderstood by others and need time alone to seek the tranquility you desire.

■ Particular about the company you keep, you are also fussy about your possessions.

■ Privacy is a precious commodity: you do not reveal privileged information.

HEART #8

■ Driven by a desire to be in control, you have the ambition to achieve high positions and material prosperity.

■ Possessing highly developed organizational skills, you have the ability to take charge as the master of all situations.

■ An impartial individual, you are fair in your dealings with others.

■ You are inspired to accept difficult challenges because you believe that risk is part of the formula for success.

■ You balance your emotions and are proud of your mental and physical stamina.

■ Equating money with power, you're generous and often extravagant.

■ Compelled to produce evidence of success, you want to surround yourself with status symbols and bask in the praise and respect of others.

HEART #9

■ Eager to make the world a better place, you are capable of understanding human nature and are sympathetic toward those less fortunate.

■ You crave appreciation for your acts of kindness.

■ You're a tolerant teacher who thrives on sharing knowledge.

■ You have a knack for appealing to the masses and the power to influence them.

■ Idealistic in love, you have the capacity to feel emotions deeply.

■ You are able to overcome disappointments and are very forgiving toward loved ones.

NAME, PERSONALITY, AND HEART NUMBER COMBINATIONS

Your NAME, PERSONALITY, and HEART NUMBERS interrelate to describe you as a total person. Since the PERSONALITY and HEART NUMBERS added together make the NAME NUMBER, there are 81 possible combinations described in the following section.

NAME #1
PERSONALITY #1
HEART #9

You are a human dynamo with a reputation as a strong leader and an original thinker. Even with all of your independence and strong-willed determination, you have a rich vein of generosity that runs very deep. Your greatest pleasure is service to others, and there is no doubt that the world is a better place, thanks to your creative contributions.

People are impressed by the energy and enthusiasm with which you pursue your goals. They admire your ambition, especially when they realize that it isn't purely personal. You use your ability to conceptualize on a grand scale so that a local business goes national under your leadership and a generous gift becomes extravagant.

No matter what you do, you make big plans and put your personal stamp on everything. Your self-confident, pioneering spirit makes you stand out in a crowd and enables you to feel at home anywhere in the world.

Naturally you're proud of your ability and achievements; taking bows is your top priority, and taking orders is at the bottom of your list.

NAME #1
PERSONALITY #2
HEART #8

Even though you appear to be easygoing and considerate, you have a mind of your own and love to get your own way. People respond to your sensitive, cooperative manner without realizing that you are actually very strong-willed and determined.

You may listen politely to others' opinions, but you stand on your own two feet when it's time to make a decision. Level-headed and not easily swayed, you live by your own code of ethics. A law unto yourself, you are the author of many unique ideas.

Leadership and organizational wizardry enable you to execute custom-made plans and turn a profit from your dreams. People are willing to do your bidding because you are a diplomat when it comes to giving directions.

Even though you can run circles around most people, you appear to be patient. In spite of the fact that you dare to be different and love the challenge of competition, you temper your pursuit of excellence and are successful at convincing others to join you on the road to achievement.

NAME #1
PERSONALITY #3
HEART #7

Although you are a sociable, entertaining companion, deep down you're a serious thinker and very strong-willed. The first impression you make does not accurately reflect your inner strengths.

Your original and up-to-date appearance gives you a distinctive image. Bright and animated in groups, you seem to enjoy everyone, but you are actually very refined and selective in your tastes and choice of close friends.

Always in search of answers to knotty questions, you can be withdrawn and introspective. When people question you too closely or become possessive, you retreat, and the party is over. At other times, you can turn on the charm to get information for your computerlike mind. By adding your own innovative ideas, you are capable of making significant improvements in your field. In the process of analyzing a subject, you enjoy expressing your opinions in a lively discussion.

If the truth were known, you are not always as confident and optimistic as you appear; others would be very surprised to know that you have a shy side underneath your jovial, outgoing personality.

NAME #1
PERSONALITY #4
HEART #6

Your primary purpose in life is to help others and to achieve loving, harmonious relationships. Even though you hate arguments and want to be fair, you tend to voice your opinions loud and clear, and like to have the last word.

You take your responsibilities to heart and have extremely honorable intentions when it comes to protecting the welfare of others. People on the receiving end of your counsel must understand that even though you come on strong and seem set in your ways, yours is the image of a solid citizen who can be trusted to keep a promise.

Blessed with a quick and creative mind, you appear very logical and prefer the prudent, conservative approach. Not one to rush into a premature decision, you select only projects with potential and always finish what you start.

Home is where your heart is. Your good eye for design and balance helps you make your surroundings beautiful and comfortable. Nothing is too good for your loved ones, and you're doubly pleased when you find quality at bargain prices.

NAME #1
PERSONALITY #5
HEART #5

You are perpetual motion personified. The only predictable thing about you is your unpredictability. You like to set an energetic pace and do things on your own time, without the restriction of an imposed routine. To your way of thinking, an outside job with variety wins over a nine-to-five position every time. Filled with creative ideas, you require the freedom to pursue them.

Original and unconventional, you are not affected by what others think; however, you can readily adapt your thinking to accommodate a new concept. Refusing to be tied down, you insist on being in the middle of the action. Flexibility is your long suit, and when things get dull, you move on wherever excitement or opportunity beckons.

Risk is important in your daily diet, and with a yen for adventure, you have the makings of a true pioneer.

NAME #1
PERSONALITY #6
HEART #4

Loyalty to family and friends is one of your top priorities, and people admire your sense of responsibility. Although you care very deeply for others, it's often difficult for you to show your emotions.

You work hard and demand a lot of yourself as well as of those around you. Strong and independent, you like to do things your own way. You can be a little stubborn or set in your ways, but you have a reputation for being fair and doing your best to keep promises.

Practical and self-sufficient, you find ways to do good deeds that also add points to your record. With the ability to shape a raw idea into a workable system, you're determined to translate it into tangible results.

It is clear to others that you are quality conscious; they respect your ability to orchestrate a smooth, economical operation. Your preference for quality extends to every aspect of your life; beauty and comfort must surround you, and you take pride in providing your loved ones with many luxuries, which you delight in buying at a good price.

NAME #1
PERSONALITY #7
HEART #3

You move through life at a fast clip, carefully selecting only activities and people that interest you. With an insatiable appetite for variety, you need many creative outlets. Unless you find kindred spirits, you are content with your own company. You have an independent streak and hate to conform or be dominated.

Although you may appear aloof and difficult to approach, your youthful vitality and attractive appearance make you very appealing. Your friendly, fun-loving side will be discovered by the admirer with the compliments to flatter you, and the energy to keep up with you.

In your constant search for self-expression, you like to spend time alone refining your act. A talented observer, you enjoy dazzling an audience with your wickedly accurate imitations.

NAME #1
PERSONALITY #8
HEART #2

You are strong and in control. To others it seems that you have the world by the tail, but underneath that self-sufficient exterior beats the heart of a true romantic who wants to love and be loved.

On the job you are aggressive and independent, but when people get to know you, they realize that you do listen and sincerely want to cooperate—even though you don't always do it. Others admire the way you execute your original ideas and they are impressed by the prosperous image you project.

In personal relationships you may let your pride get in the way of achieving the love and companionship you crave. You need lots of reassurance from an understanding mate who knows the sensitive soul behind that protective shell.

Although you sometimes take things personally, you have the strength to overcome your feelings. Directing your sensitivity toward others, you can read between the lines in the personal as well as business situation, giving you a decided edge.

NAME #1
PERSONALITY #9
HEART #1

Not one to follow the crowd, you attract it by organizing and leading your own parade. A master at persuasion, you are a meeter-and-greeter and appear to have an inspirational effect on others, especially large groups.

People are impressed by the scope of your ideas and the range of your influence. You think big and push yourself to achieve success. Inspiring trust, you have no difficulty attracting followers who subscribe to your methods and want to help promote your superior ideas.

You frequently mount campaigns or stage events that, to be sure, benefit others. Although your intentions seem totally unselfish, you further your career as well.

Just as you are motivated by competition in the work world, you enjoy the challenge of the chase in your personal relationships. Once involved, you become frustrated if you feel restricted. In response to the compliments of an attentive mate, you can be demonstrative. You are an impulsive lover who is restless; you are capable of sharing great passion with the person who can catch you long enough to tap it.

NAME #2
PERSONALITY #1
HEART #1

You are accommodating and understanding to a point. Although you listen to other people's opinions, you follow your own convictions.

Aware that resentment can build from unresolved conflicts, you're observant enough to know when to clear the air tactfully. People respect you for your ability to cooperate and stand up for your rights at the same time. They find you persuasive and are happy to follow your inspirational lead.

Depending upon your mood, you can work alone or with others, provided they move at an efficient clip. When you feel someone is trying, you can be patient. On a creative roll, you work faster alone, but will proudly share your results to make sure others are aware of your original contributions.

Although you know what you want and appear to get it, you make a concerted effort to consider all sides of an issue to resolve it in everyone's best interest.

NAME #2
PERSONALITY #2
HEART #9

If you could, you would help the whole world. You are an idealist who makes sacrifices for those you love or those in need. In return, you receive the warmth and understanding that is essential to your own happiness.

A soft touch for a hard-luck story, you are sentimental and hate to say no. In the name of love, you are able to forgive and forget your disappointments in others.

A natural student, you are also a patient teacher due to your extensive knowledge and your desire to share it. Ordinarily mild-mannered, you're the model of tolerance; to make everyone concerned happy, you carefully deliberate before offering a solution.

You might not say much, but when you are hurt the intensity of your anger surprises people. In your relationships as well as your artistic or musical endeavors, you deal with life on a deeply emotional level.

NAME #2
PERSONALITY #3
HEART #8

Others see you as sociable and charming; little do they know how strong-willed you are under that patient exterior.

Whether speaking or writing, you have a good command of language and express yourself easily. Using your sense of humor to make a good story even better, you are thrilled with attention from an appreciative audience.

Involved in many activities, you get your work done and have energy to spare because you are organized and use efficient methods. You can be either a cooperative partner or a daring, take-charge person. If work is mishandled, you find it almost impossible to sit back and watch. Compelled to jump in, you do the job right, according to your high standards.

You are a good listener who's fascinated with the intricacies of human nature. You are generous and like to do things in a grand manner. You have what it takes to make people feel special, but you also like to get your own way. Most of the time you humor people into giving it to you, though you sometimes get emotional in the process.

NAME #2
PERSONALITY #4
HEART #7

You have a reputation for always knowing the proper thing to say or do at just the right time. People don't realize how much effort you put into choosing your words and analyzing a situation. Though you can tell a lively story, your sense of propriety requires you to maintain your dignity; you would never be caught speaking out of turn. Guarded about your feelings, you decide when to join in and when to remain silent.

In your desire to keep everyone happy, you have difficulty saying no. Sensitive by nature, you sometimes feel misunderstood and require periods of solitude to sort out your feelings.

In both your surroundings and your dress, you project a conservative and coordinated image. You are irritated by little things and prefer all areas of your life to be neat and orderly.

Friends respect your honesty and integrity, and they can always count on your practical, well-considered advice. In pursuit of the truth, you exercise your intuition and keen powers of observation. Though you may not confront people with their misrepresentations, you don't let them put anything over on you.

NAME #2
PERSONALITY #5
HEART #6

Even though you love your home and all of the corresponding responsibilities, others see you as adventurous and outgoing. Varied interests and a busy schedule make you seem full of curiosity and excitement.

With a genuine concern for all kinds of people, you make a

loyal friend who harbors few prejudices. Being of service is your greatest pleasure; you give freely of your advice—even if it falls upon deaf ears.

With your enthusiasm and natural ability to promote an idea, you are able to get others on your bandwagon. Sensitive to many influences, you frequently adjust your opinions to avoid confrontations and hurt feelings. Even though you are extremely adaptable and anxious to please, you have a highly developed sense of justice and tend to make value judgments, always rooting for the underdog.

Romantic by nature, you want an honorable and understanding mate. Because peace and harmony are essential to your happiness, you work hard to maintain a loving relationship.

NAME #2
PERSONALITY #6
HEART #5

A wide circle of friends is attracted to your kind and loving personality. Responding to your warm hospitality, they think of you as someone who will help in times of trouble. Those who know you well suspect that a bit of the wanderlust lurks in your heart, and they admire your curious mind and sense of adventure.

Most people see your stable and responsible side and appreciate your adaptable, easygoing nature. Known for your ability to listen sensitively to both sides and respond with tact and diplomacy, you are often called upon to settle disputes and calm troubled waters.

Your active mind absorbs new information like a thirsty sponge. Happiest when involved in many projects at once, you have a knack for dreaming up your next ideas while still working on your current schemes.

Freedom is essential to your happiness; though you desire it, you would never pursue it at the risk of shirking your responsibilities.

NAME #2
PERSONALITY #7
HEART #4

You listen to both sides of a situation and like to help others, but it's difficult to put yourself in someone else's shoes. Selective in your friendships, you prefer small groups of down-to-earth people where you can talk one to one.

Although you are friendly, you aren't one for small talk; it takes people awhile to see beyond your pleasant but reserved hello. The one who is lucky enough to be special in your life knows that even if there is frost on your roof, there's a fire in your furnace.

Often responding emotionally, you find it hard to express your true feelings without revealing a part of yourself that you would rather not share. Instead of saying what's on your mind, which might hurt someone's feelings or ruffle your composure, you keep things to yourself and sometimes become resentful.

Demanding of yourself, you are compelled to be orderly, and are bound by a sense of duty to finish what you start. People see you as fussy about little things, but they respect you for the way you seem to have your life all worked out.

Even though you are usually prudent and economical, you prefer quality and are very generous with yourself and others on special occasions.

NAME #2
PERSONALITY #8
HEART #3

Popularity personified, you are a terrific storyteller and have a strong desire to be the life of the party. Although you may be a little sensitive and even secretly shy, you never give that impression. Loads of fun to be with, you can be hysterically funny when you "tell it like it is."

You enjoy companionship and crave attention. Using your charm and your gift of gab, you are able to get just about anything you want—from a last bite of someone's candy bar to a signature on a sales contract.

You maintain your youthful good looks and polished appearance to enhance your prosperous image. Paying careful attention to diet and health, you seem to have plenty of stamina to keep up a full social calendar and handle a million details at work.

While you seem organized and in control, you also may be quite scattered; nonetheless, you appear to be the master of your destiny.

NAME #2
PERSONALITY #9
HEART #2

You have quite a following and are a source of inspiration to many people. Possessing great knowledge in your chosen field, you are sought after for your expertise and are happiest when sharing your skills.

Although you are always gracious to others and have a wide variety of contacts, a caring and intimate relationship is essential to your happiness.

With diplomacy as your middle name, you are a patient and understanding listener who goes the last mile to help others. You are highly regarded as a student of human nature, and people are willing to accept your visions of the way things should be.

Although you are not wild about changes, you evaluate your choices and vacillate until you come to a conclusion, or rely on someone else's system as a guide.

Sensitive to the feelings of others, you're always there to do generous and thoughtful things. Preferring to leave the unpleasant tasks to someone else, you're rarely the one to bring bad news.

NAME #3
PERSONALITY #1
HEART #2

You are unusually persuasive because you put others at ease and have great facility with words. Inspired by your confidence, others see you as being capable of doing many things at once. They appreciate your sensitivity to their feelings and the way you try to avoid arguments and keep everyone happy. When asked to get on your bandwagon, people say yes because they see you as a competent driver who can take it to town.

In your lifetime you will have many choices to make. Although you appear strong and decisive, you go through a great deal of deliberation. Your mind is so filled with ideas that at times you may feel scattered and have doubts over which ones to choose.

Your love of beauty and luxury is evident in the distinctive, individualized manner of your dress. You also stand out because of your youthful enthusiasm. People of all ages, especially children, are attracted to your carefree, optimistic outlook.

Able to entertain people with your charm and good humor, you usually get what you want with a smile.

NAME #3
PERSONALITY #2
HEART #1

You lead a charmed existence because you have people wrapped around your little finger. You invented social graces, and people seek your company because of your friendly, personable manner. Wearing your diplomatic hat, you appear to go along with others when, in fact, you usually get exactly what you want.

Your daredevil pace is as legendary as your youthful exuberance and busy schedule. Somehow you make it all work because you crave outlets for your energy and creativity. Anxious to pursue your many clever ideas, you hide your impatience well and manage to accomplish a lot through other people. You have real power with words and can sell people a product or inspire them with an idea. You can talk your way into and out of anything.

You need a communicative, fun-loving partner who is willing to go roller-skating or bike riding, while at the same time is sympathetic to your need for independence. Being popular and recognized as one of a kind rank at the top of your list of priorities. Remaining young and thriving on the praise you receive, you seem to collect all the kudos while others collect all the wrinkles.

NAME #3
PERSONALITY #3
HEART #9

Using your gift of gab to promote your own ideas and to entertain others, you can charm the socks off anyone. Attracting a large audience of admirers, you make even the humdrum story exciting.

A popular host or hostess, you have a wide circle of friends who praise you for your wonderful sense of humor. The way you fluff your feathers over a compliment just adds to the show.

A big-time spender, you are generous and extravagant. When it comes to clothes, you buy the best; after all, you don't want to disappoint your fans.

Although you want to get your way, you also have a heart of gold and are very indulgent of your loved ones. Unless you have many other outlets for your creative energies, you have a tendency to be a little overprotective of those who are close to you.

Your idea of a good day is to go as far as you can and meet as many fascinating new people as you can find. Your optimistic outlook helps you spread cheer wherever you go, and you have a clear picture of the pot of gold at the end of your rainbow.

NAME #3
PERSONALITY #4
HEART #8

In spite of the flood of ideas from your fertile mind, you are a highly organized manager. You achieve goals by wisely delegating jobs, but have a reputation for being blunt in your demand for efficiency.

Your creative vision is multifaceted and farsighted. In your enthusiasm you may become distracted, but your organized, practical approach usually wins out and sees you through.

Your eloquence gives you a decided advantage when you need to convince others to see things your way. You know how to win friends and influence people. Others listen to you because they know you have the executive ability to manage your high-flying dreams.

Financial success and the respect of your colleagues are your fondest desires. As you walk the fine line from vision to reality, you have the balance of a high-wire artist.

NAME #3
PERSONALITY #5
HEART #7

Your star quality shines doubly bright in the outgoing manner you use to distract attention from your inner self. Outwardly friendly at first, you are secretly a little reserved and not so quick to warm up to strangers as others may think. Just when people begin to feel they know you, another rabbit pops out of your hat.

Your glib tongue and analytical mind combine for some non-stop monologues that cover many subjects in rapid succession. In spite of your own versatility, you are always in awe of the talents you see in others and enjoy having an idol or mentor to inspire you.

Expressing yourself well in writing, you make an excellent critic who can discriminate between the quality result and the ordinary effort. A perfectionist yourself, you keep changing hats to improve your performance.

The opposite sex finds you irresistible, but you need that special someone who can be there to fill your needs when you feel misunderstood.

NAME #3
PERSONALITY #6
HEART #6

Your tremendous personal charm attracts countless admirers. Although you love to be the center of attention, you get even more pleasure from helping others. Responsibility is your middle name, and you are generous with your advice and support.

"Father knows best" or "Super Mom" describes the way your family depends on you to show them the way. Their welfare has always influenced your personal choices. Willing to sacrifice without question, you have a history of rescues to your credit, and your famous gift of gab has saved more than one friend from a tight spot. Home is your haven, and your door is always open.

Your desire for harmony requires that you do everything in your power to make others happy and content. Your sense of justice leads you to right all wrongs. In most instances you believe your way is right and expect people to agree with you.

You are very generous and always insist on quality for yourself and others. If you can't afford the best, you wait until the luxuries are within your reach.

NAME #3
PERSONALITY #7
HEART #5

Variety is a necessity in your life; your sense of adventure and optimistic outlook drives you to try many new things. To avoid boredom, you are always on the go. Freedom to travel in the fast lane is an important requirement in any relationship; you don't ask for freedom, you take it.

A quick study and a fast talker, you are a natural promoter. Your enthusiasm is contagious, and people are often flattered by your interest and the intelligent questions you ask. Though you are curious about others, you are reluctant to reveal your own feelings.

At first glance you seem to be a perfectionist, but you have such varied interests, you may spread yourself too thin.

Although you are lighthearted, some people see you as evasive and wonder what makes you tick. Misunderstanding your secretive, analytical side, others find it hard to believe you may be shy or that you lacked self-confidence at some time in your life.

NAME #3
PERSONALITY #8
HEART #4

People see you as very successful because you appear to be in charge and have everything money can buy. Obviously your belief in hard work has paid off, and you've earned a reputation for keeping your word and upholding your responsibilities. Others admire you for your logical mind and the way you express yourself when it comes to finding practical solutions to problems.

With a keen sense of rhythm and balance, you make an art of

designing systems. Blessed with manual dexterity and the logic to analyze how things work, you can always make money with your creative ideas. You make decisions based on economics, getting the most for your dollar.

You take care to build your life on solid foundations and want to see tangible results for your efforts. Preserving family traditions and forming long-lasting relationships are top priorities, along with maintaining a youthful appearance, good health, and financial security.

Convinced that your way is best, you can turn on the charm, choosing words carefully to influence others. You often hold back your true feelings; but when you get angry you can be very blunt and call a spade a spade.

NAME #3
PERSONALITY #9
HEART #3

Never at a loss for words, you want to be seen as well as heard. You have a wide circle of friends who call you Captain Communication. A telephone is practically fixed to your ear.

You are imaginative and have the charisma to broadcast your opinions to many others. Under some circumstances you're a downright flirt who can be very entertaining. You find applause and appreciation intoxicating.

An optimist, you are generous and genuinely care for your fellow man. Your free-spending habits can lead to extravagance, especially in the matter of your wardrobe; your appearance is very important, and you love to attract attention with your outlandish outfits or hairstyles. The compliments you receive for your youthful looks encourage you to spend lavishly on treatments to maintain them.

Happiest when busy, you do best when you avoid a set nine-to-five routine and make your own hours. Often artistic or musical, you are also a good dancer. There is a gypsy in your soul and you thoroughly enjoy traveling.

NAME #4
PERSONALITY #1
HEART #3

People see you as a practical leader with a strong personality. They value the way you can harness your many creative concepts and explain them in realistic terms.

Your highly developed imagination and eye for design make you one of the most versatile combinations. You're also one of the most determined; you like to get your way.

You have the ability to balance your spontaneity with hard work because you are a master planner. An urge to express yourself sometimes causes you to spend more time than you should in the talking stages of a plan. Although you like tangible results, you may procrastinate.

In pursuit of excellence, you are cautious about revealing true feelings, often cloaking them in jest. And when you are feeling less than confident, you are apt to become defensive. Even though you feel unsure of yourself upon occasion, you hide it so well that others see you as self-sufficient and in control.

NAME #4
PERSONALITY #2
HEART #2

You are blessed with good common sense and a logical mind that absorbs facts like a sponge. When you follow your inclinations to share what you've learned, you're an inspiration to others.

People are amazed by the facility with which you develop a system out of seemingly unrelated material. While no detail escapes your eye, the general impression is that you are a reliable, hard worker who's also unusually cooperative.

You are very loyal and go out of your way to please others. Even though your methodical mind causes you to be set in your ways, your sensitive heart and winning personality help others to feel comfortable around you. Surrounded by those you love, you understand the importance of being patient and making compromises.

Gentle and peace-loving, you really care about what other people think and make an effort to listen to them. Struggling with your own sensitivity, you nurse occasional hurt feelings and hold them in to avoid conflict.

In your desire to have meaningful relationships you are willing to give of yourself. Extremely generous, you are fortunately adept at finding bargains so your money goes a long way.

NAME #4
PERSONALITY #3
HEART #1

You are as patient as the day is long and have huge reserves of determination. Keeping your goals firmly in mind, you are willing to do whatever it takes to fulfill your high expectations. Completing routine jobs is as important to you as assuming the role of a creative leader who can both charm and organize followers.

Concerned with your reputation, you make sure that any job with your name on it is done correctly. You have confidence in your own ideas and want the opportunity to develop them independently. It's no secret you hate to be rushed. Proud of your daring yet prudent approach, you promote original concepts that are also practical.

Your job satisfaction increases when you work with people who share your viewpoint and high standards. And people enjoy working with you because you are so outgoing and friendly. They also respect your strength and think twice before telling you no; they would be wise to do their homework before trying to prove you wrong.

NAME #4
PERSONALITY #4
HEART #9

You are highly organized and enjoy a reputation for being dependable and trustworthy. You play by the rules and it shows. You are also known for your talents in art or music, which go hand in hand with your sense of rhythm and design.

The welfare of others concerns you deeply, and you have strong humanitarian instincts to make the world a better place. You take a broad view of things and have a heart of gold, which you temper with your sense of logic and practicality.

Although you are set in your ways and have a history of prudent decisions, you long to do something grandiose and extravagant. Your urge to be generous is continually monitored by your equally compelling need for financial security and habits of thrift. Receiving praise for all the good deeds you perform gives you great pleasure.

When confronted with people's problems, you are patient and sympathetic. And even though you are sentimental and romantic, you share your true feelings with only a few special people in your life.

NAME #4
PERSONALITY #5
HEART #8

When you make up your mind to do something, you are a persistent go-getter. Power and prosperity are what you're after, so you work hard to enjoy a high rate of success. A born organizer, you can put your ideas into lucrative practice. Security conscious and frugal, you have the ability to budget and keep track of money.

People are surprised to discover that you are happiest when in control and like to do things your way. You seem so carefree and fun-loving in the middle of all that action. It's also surprising that you're a loyal friend with your feet on the ground, since you appear to be game for anything new. In spite of your active social life, you take great care to keep mentally and physically in balance. Your stability is apparent to anyone who knows you well.

A master of all trades, you have both the ability and the desire to offer help when you see there is a need. People appreciate your energetic approach to routine work and the way you can make order out of confusion. They can forgive your perfectionist tendencies because you are flexible.

NAME #4
PERSONALITY #6
HEART #7

You are blessed with a logical mind and a strong sense of responsibility. Paying careful attention to detail, you take a practical approach and proceed cautiously. Capable of asking pertinent questions, you like to have enough time to dig for the answers. You hate to be rushed or pressured into a decision.

You have a habit of listening rather than speaking impulsively in a discussion. You prefer to withhold your feelings or avoid making a pronouncement until you are sure. Once committed, you keep your word.

Although you are compelled to know the whys and wherefores of every situation, you hate to be questioned about yourself. People see you as a harmonizer and a loyal, trustworthy friend; they may not realize that you're affectionate only to close friends and take a long time to warm up to strangers.

It's easy to see that you've got a good eye for the finer things in life. You value the luxury money can buy and make an effort to get your money's worth.

NAME #4
PERSONALITY #7
HEART #6

Under your reserved exterior beats a heart of gold. People who know you well explain your aloofness by pointing out that you are discriminating and cautious. They value your patience and the fact that you never jump to unfair conclusions.

At your warm and loving best in the service of others, you tend to accept more than your share of work. In your desire to help, you like to give advice, even if it falls on deaf ears. You mean well, but others sometimes misunderstand your motives and take your words to the wise as criticism.

You hate to argue and will go to great lengths to avoid an unpleasant confrontation. Adapting yourself to others is sometimes hard for you, especially when you don't agree with their point of view. Put off by dishonesty or insincerity, you are critical of superficial types and shoddy workmanship. You play by the rules of integrity. People appreciate your efforts to sort out the facts and to see that justice is done. Your analytical bent also makes you a keen buyer who finds quality at the best price.

NAME #4
PERSONALITY #8
HEART #5

You have the ability to manage large groups of people and the energy to keep working right along with them until a job is done. You aren't afraid to get your capable hands dirty if that's what it takes to achieve tangible results.

Meticulous and painstaking about your work, you are your own disciplinarian. But afterhours means the freedom to enjoy an exciting social life crammed with all kinds of friends. Loyal to each one, you make sure to touch base often.

You always look great because you dress well and take good care of yourself. Friends know that your impressive wardrobe cloaks a down-to-earth, honest soul. You consistently appear in control, even if you are falling apart inside.

Because of your outer balance and inner complexity you're a bit of a puzzle; though you may seem stubborn, you can be quite flexibile when someone presents a logical reason for you to change your mind. Behind that practical, conservative face is a free spirit with a contagious case of wanderlust. People are in for a pleasant surprise when they discover the many dimensions you have.

NAME #4
PERSONALITY #9
HEART #4

You've got things down to a system. After figuring out how something works, or ought to work, you go about perfecting it. Unless someone can prove to you that there is a better way, you'll stick to the tried and true and avoid wasting time on experiments.

Demanding excellence of yourself and others, you make every effort to finish what you start. People know they can depend on you to keep to a schedule and abide by a budget. You are very methodical in your approach and always like to know where you stand with regard to others and the details of your work.

You may have been born punctual and frugal, but you were also there when they handed out musical and artistic talent. Your senses of rhythm, balance, and design all contribute to your creative spirit.

Though your emotions run deep, you may not always express them. But you show that you care by being generous within the bounds of your prudent spending habits. Charities that benefit from your contributions are those that will spend your hard-earned money wisely. You receive genuine pleasure from giving, especially when the recipients go out of their way to give you richly deserved appreciation.

NAME #5
PERSONALITY #1
HEART #4

People see you as self-sufficient and determined, a leader who can cope with a variety of situations. The fact that you meet others easily and can negotiate in such a genial manner makes you an excellent salesperson.

Your active imagination allows you to think of many clever ideas at once. Fortunately, you also have a need to be practical. In your methodical way you impose order and precision on your creative endeavors.

You are a great detective who leaves no stone unturned when researching the facts. Analyzing the data, you discard the useless and move forward with only the best information.

Because you have a strong sense of responsibility, your recreation never gets in the way of keeping a promise or meeting a deadline. Although part of you wants to throw caution to the wind and take chances, your practical streak and desire for security usually win out.

You maintain a good balance between originality and practicality. Not many people have your ability to keep their noses to the grindstone and still adapt to life's unexpected pleasures and pitfalls.

NAME #5
PERSONALITY #2
HEART #3

A master with words, you have a talent for expressing your imaginative ideas. With a versatile mind that works like lightning, you enjoy sharing your brainstorms with an audience.

While they are still trying to digest what you have just said, you are making your next point.

Easily bored and quite adaptable, you welcome change and the challenge it brings. Like your sentences, your projects sometimes remain unfinished. You have to curb the temptation to spread yourself too thin and promise more than you can deliver.

People find you charming and cooperative. In addition to being entertaining and at home in the spotlight, you are an understanding listener who weighs both sides of an issue before making a decision.

Others frequently call upon you to help negotiate a settlement or settle a disagreement. Even the most difficult parties seem to respond to your friendly manner, and members of the opposite sex find your flirtatious approach irresistible.

It's not that you can't make up your mind; you are constantly changing it. A change in direction just makes life more interesting for an optimistic person like you. With few fears to stand in your way, you play at life with enthusiasm, rarely looking back or worrying much about the future.

NAME #5
PERSONALITY #3
HEART #2

Surrounded by an adoring audience, you are quite content in the spotlight. Blessed with a natural talent for expressing yourself, you can be very entertaining. Fans dote on your every word, and customers are impressed by the way you promote yourself or your wares. When moved to share your profound insights, you can also be inspirational.

You seek companionship and group activities. Above all, you want to love and be loved. A supportive mate who is as fun-loving and flexible as you are will fill the bill nicely. Interdependence at every level describes the perfect union in your book.

You have many talents and a detail-oriented mind to pursue them all. With your fingers in many pies, you give the impression of being able to accomplish anything you've set out to do. It's hard to believe that someone as obviously sociable and confident as you can be so sensitive at times.

Behind the energy and enthusiasm you announce to the world is a little voice of caution that keeps your adventurous side from taking unnecessary risks.

NAME #5
PERSONALITY #4
HEART #1

Although you appear very traditional, you're actually a nonconformist who'd prefer not to be pinned down. People who think of you as the pillar of strength and reliability would be surprised to learn that you aren't crazy about those routines you devise, and that you would enjoy the freedom to explore new ideas.

Happiest when leading, you are able to provide direction to projects or groups. As a side benefit you can also set your own hours and vary your schedule to include physical activities so necessary for the release of your pent-up emotions.

Although you seem patient, you often feel restless because you already know what people are going to say when they start a sentence. Adaptable and preferring to move quickly, you are able to accomplish more in less time than do most people.

You appear to be loyal and have many friends, yet you need time alone and hate to be possessed. You crave independence and must have your freedom, so you gravitate toward people who respect those needs.

NAME #5
PERSONALITY #5
HEART #9

The key to your happiness is keeping busy. You require a fast

164

pace and plenty of mental stimulation. When boredom strikes, your adventurous spirit moves on without hesitation to find new fields for your quick mind to conquer.

A born teacher, even in an informal setting, you impart excitement and enthusiasm to your students. Capturing their interest requires an adaptable approach that is no different from enticing the general public with a new idea. A natural salesperson, you have a million ways to appeal to the masses.

Full of sympathy for those less fortunate, you enjoy helping others. Charitable activities take a considerable amount of your time and attention. People soon realize that the motivation for your philanthropic efforts is a kind and generous heart. When you receive the recognition and appreciation of others, you feel a deep satisfaction that makes it all worthwhile.

Full of restless energy, you yearn for the change of scenery that travel provides. Between the long trips, three-day weekends break up your busy schedule and give you R and R, which in your book is revelry and recreation.

A romantic at heart, you are in love with love. You tire quickly of the possessive type.

NAME #5
PERSONALITY #6
HEART #8

You have a good head for business and are sure to make money from one of your many lucrative ideas. The secret to your success is the way you are able to handle people. Not only are you a mastermind when it comes to organizing an efficient operation, but you also appear to be a genius when it comes to developing a compatible team.

You set a good example by being so adaptable. Although you can do many things at once and can cope with change, you need stability and organization in your life. Even though you like to do things your way, you try to be fair in your dealings with others. Admired for your sense of justice, you also have a genuine desire to help people.

In your ambitious climb to the top, you take on all challenges. Never without a project, you are constantly looking at the big picture and trying for more.

When others show their admiration and respect, you know you're on the right track. Conscious of your reputation and your image, you lead an active life with emphasis on health and fitness.

NAME #5
PERSONALITY #7
HEART #7

A born detective, you tend to investigate even the most bizarre possibilities to find the answers you want. You have an eagle eye for flaws and a nose for inconsistencies. Relentless in your search for clues, you ask the most perceptive questions to arrive at surprisingly accurate conclusions.

You're somewhat of a puzzle to others. Assuming your friendly approach is an open invitation, they make the mistake of invading your privacy. You are more comfortable asking questions than answering them. At times you feel misunderstood and wonder why other people don't think the way you do.

Blessed with a quick mind, you need new interests and plenty of intellectual stimulation to be happy. People who are willing to share their vast knowledge are the kind of company you keep.

Happiest when you are free to follow your own inclinations, you need someone in your life who is flexible and will give you some private time.

NAME #5
PERSONALITY #8
HEART #6

You have the look of a winner. Emotional strength and stability are written all over you. And no matter how busy you are, you always land on your feet.

Like a turbo-charged engine, you have that extra push that allows you to take control of a big project while simultaneously planning the next one. Your strong sense of duty ensures that you will deliver every promise on time.

Although you are restless and like a change of scene, your home and the responsibility it entails are very important to you. To satisfy your need for variety and your creative urge to beautify your surroundings, you frequently rearrange the furniture or redecorate. Your artistic flair for color naturally figures into your latest design.

People are drawn to you because you have an air of authority; they respect the way you deal fairly with others. A good friend and neighbor, you are often called upon to create harmony between varying factions.

Even though you value your freedom, you favor solid commitments and have many loyal friends.

NAME #5
PERSONALITY #9
HEART #5

Blessed with the energy required to exercise all of your talents, you are especially influential in any area dealing with the public. Because of your friendly and gracious manner you are able to gain the trust of many kinds of people.

A student of human nature, you are particularly compassionate when it comes to the problems of others. Good at character analysis and fascinated by what makes people tick, you are genuinely interested in others and like to keep up with their activities.

You are a free spirit who bristles at the thought of a schedule and runs in the opposite direction if faced with a time clock. People see you as a worldly, well-traveled adventurer who is continually on the go. They assume that you have seen it all, and they envy your life of excitement.

Somewhat impatient, you are curious and quick; before you've patented your latest invention you're off to the next. You'd rather be busy than bored.

NAME #6
PERSONALITY #1
HEART #5

Amiable and outgoing, you genuinely enjoy people. A magnet to friends when you are in the mood, you attract people because you are so protective and nurturing. As a counselor who is willing to give good advice, you have to be careful not to overdo it in your desire to help. People value you for your objective viewpoint and the effect you have on them. Applying logic to every situation, you are able to help them see their problems in perspective.

Also admired for your determination and sense of responsibility, you can be counted upon to make just decisions and to keep your word. Your personal ethics preclude your involvement in unscrupulous practices.

Even though you have a strong desire for independence and freedom, you are loving and devoted to family and friends. Within the community you are liked for your friendly attitude and are respected as a leader because you have a mind of your own and can't be pushed.

You enjoy a high degree of mental stimulation and include a wide variety of people within your circle. Your surroundings must also be first-rate. Luxury and comfort are high on your list, and you are more than willing to wait until you can afford the best.

NAME #6
PERSONALITY #2
HEART #4

Your world centers around home and those you love. Home represents peace and security, the place where you can live according to the principles of honesty and loyalty you value.

Like a magnet, your warmth and generous spirit draw people to you. With a talent for making others comfortable, you go even further to fill their emotional needs and provide counsel according to your own set of ideals. Laced with common sense, your advice may be practical to your way of thinking, but not necessarily appropriate to the person you are helping. Nevertheless, people respect your good intentions and the fact that you take your commitments seriously.

In addition to being dependable in personal relationships, you are conscientious on the job. In order to fulfill your ambitions you work hard to build a solid foundation. Honest to the core, you will not tolerate cutthroat business practices, which would undermine your security and damage your sterling reputation.

Both at work and at home you will do what it takes to maintain peaceful relationships. You hate arguments and have a generous spirit.

NAME #6
PERSONALITY #3
HEART #3

Popularity personified, you exude charm and have a gift of gab. Never at a loss for words, you can strike up a conversation with anyone; if your companion is uncommunicative, you can fill the silence with a monologue on any subject, even if it's a cursory view. When the spotlight is on, you rise to the occasion and liven up the dullest situations, bringing cheer to the most downtrodden.

In group situations, you can't stand it if people aren't getting along. Using your jovial, humorous approach, you are always successful at replacing discord with harmony. People love to have you around because your exuberance is contagious.

You attract a loyal following of people with your good cheer and optimistic outlook. They also count on you to be responsible and keep your promises. Occasionally you are overwhelmed when you have too many commitments, and worry that you can't possibly fulfill them.

Your clothes budget contributes greatly to a healthy economy. Placing importance on looks, you know how to put outfits together; your wardrobe represents an outlet for creative expression.

NAME #6
PERSONALITY #4
HEART #2

People are drawn to you because you are courteous and adaptable. Polite and well-mannered, you make a great listener. Others value the way you meticulously handle details and logically synthesize information.

A pillar in the community, you have a reputation for keeping your word. People respect your self-discipline and the no-nonsense approach that allows you to deliver consistently on your promises. Honest in your dealings, you are known for adjusting all wrongs and making things right.

In your desire to be well-liked, you go out of your way to help people and may allow them to take advantage of your kindness. You require harmony in your personal relationships, and as a supplier of affection, you have a deep need to love and be loved. Your life is worth living if you have someone to share it with.

Peace at any price is an expensive motto. Some compromises leave you feeling as if your toes have been stepped on.

Even though you are seen as practical and economical, you tend to spend lavishly for quality. Especially generous with your loved ones, you will do anything in the name of love.

NAME #6
PERSONALITY #5
HEART #1

Always willing to help others, you enjoy involving yourself in groups where you can exercise your ability and desire to lead. Happiest when in charge, you are good at dreaming up new twists and finding solutions to problems. Even if you choose the conservative approach, you are a pioneer at heart.

Idealistic and goal-oriented, you like to get credit for your innovative ideas and are pleased when your peers look to you for advice. You listen to their opinions in your desire to keep everyone happy; but you have a mind of your own and usually do things your way.

Your energy allows you to accomplish a great deal and accounts for your reputation as a busy person in the middle of the action. Because you are always up on the latest, people assume that you are a good source of new ideas.

Especially alluring to the opposite sex, you respond to a novel approach. Loyal and loving, you ask for variety and excitement in return. You are dependable, but bristle if you think you are being taken for granted. Adventurous and outgoing, you crave independence and dislike possessiveness in a mate.

NAME #6
PERSONALITY #6
HEART #9

You were born to help others. Respected and admired for your understanding of human nature, you can adjust all injustices. Solving people's problems is your specialty. Because you have survived your share of disappointments you are able to give compassionate advice.

You are a romantic at heart and make relationships a top priority. Gracious to a fault, you get along with everyone and would rather give in than fight. You are continually adapting yourself to the needs of others, especially your family's. They know they can depend on you for direction and emotional support.

Fighting for the rights of your loved ones, you may become involved in even larger causes. Politics is within your sphere of influence as you champion human rights.

You love to travel—even if it means being away from your beloved home. Your side trips often involve service to others, such as a midnight ride to the edge of town to rescue a stranded neighbor with a flat tire.

NAME #6
PERSONALITY #7
HEART #8

A complex combination, you are not always easy to understand. At times so lovable you're hard to resist, you can also keep people at a distance, holding a part of yourself in reserve. You appear poised and self-contained; the impression is that you have your life all worked out.

Ambitious and organized, you accept challenges with enthusiasm and daring. A prestigious position means the opportunity to manage large groups of people. You covet a big title and an equally impressive office—not to mention a high salary.

When delegating responsibilities, you are fair and use good judgment. The basis of your opinions is without bias. A harmonizer, you calm troubled waters to keep everyone happy.

Demanding excellence not only for yourself but for others, you seem to have everything you want. Even if you don't have an abundance of clothes, you buy only the best and always dress tastefully.

Filled with energy, you often become involved in community affairs. A chairmanship suits your take-charge talent and the ease with which you handle a busy schedule. When you try to organize your loved ones the way you line up your volunteer committee, you may meet with resistance. Fortunately, you see the folly of your ways and stop short of computerizing the family.

NAME #6
PERSONALITY #8
HEART #7

You love to help others, but you also need time to pursue your own interests. Even though you're a social animal, it takes you a while to warm up to people who come on too strong. You have to get to know them before you divulge any personal data.

You give the impression of being very strong, able to handle whatever life presents. A harmonizer, you know how to analyze a problem and work out a feasible solution. People who see you as emotionally stable would be surprised to know that there are times when you feel misunderstood.

You give well-considered advice but don't solicit it from others. In your efforts to help people, you masterfully encourage them to talk, but you don't volunteer your innermost thoughts. When pressed, you may lose your normally cool composure and bristle at the invasion of privacy.

Serious about your responsibilities, you pitch in to help others, especially when it is clear they could benefit from your assistance.

NAME #6
PERSONALITY #9
HEART #6

To reach the degree of harmony that you desire in relationships, you draw upon your ability to work in concert with others. Not content unless those around you are happy, you give without thought of yourself and make sacrifices necessary to establish a congenial atmosphere.

You are gracious and know how to meet and greet the public. With the skill to reach the hearts of all kinds of people, you are very convincing and inspire trust. Others respond to your amiable, helpful approach; you attract a wide circle of friends and contacts.

In your desire to right all wrongs, you may wear out your soapbox. Even though you have insight into human behavior, you need to curb your tendency to smother people with your advice. Your way may not be right for everyone. Most important, people realize that you want to help and regard you as a stable and loyal friend.

NAME #7
PERSONALITY #1
HEART #6

Your commanding air suggests that you are a self-sufficient leader with great determination. You also have a quiet, reserved quality that makes you seem aloof upon first meeting. Revealing only what is appropriate to a given set of circumstances, you play everything straight and close to your chest.

Regardless of how people see you, the essence of your being is a need to help others and a desire for harmony. Willing to give of yourself, you encourage others to come to you for answers. In response to the people you love and trust, your inner warmth is bound to melt that cool exterior.

Because you want to be the best at whatever you do, you set high standards of intellectual achievement and behavior. For all your efforts, you want to be loved and respected; but most of all you want to be understood.

NAME #7
PERSONALITY #2
HEART #5

You present a pleasant, friendly face to the world. People appreciate your perceptive questions and the way you listen to their answers. It is obvious that you are interested enough to analyze the details of their replies.

If you sometimes appear aloof, it's because you are concentrating on a situation and choosing your words carefully before you speak. Quick to pick up a flaw in an argument and intolerant of dishonest "slips," you avoid confrontation and file your observation away carefully for future reference.

In an effort to cooperate, you politely protect the other person's feelings as much as your own. Your patience, however, extends only so far. You lose it when people fail to respond in a manner you think is appropriate.

Choosy about friends, you are intrigued by unconventional people and like to associate with other curious minds that can keep you guessing. You like to know what makes people tick, but your own thoughts and feelings are a private treasure.

To satisfy your curiosity about life, you are willing to take calculated risks. You'll try a new restaurant, bet on a long shot, and go along with your partner's impulse.

NAME #7
PERSONALITY #3
HEART #4

Responsibility is deeply ingrained in you from the analytical way in which you handle money to your desire to be depended upon by others. Sentimental when it comes to love, you make a patient, loyal mate for a reliable, practical partner.

Demanding a great deal from yourself and others, you maintain one standard of excellence. Perfection is your goal, and to that end you are methodical and precise in your approach to life. New ideas must pass your tests and prove their reliability before you accept them.

You are traditional in your tastes and very refined. Socially at ease, you have a clever sense of humor and are generally expressive. However, you draw the line at revealing too much of yourself and are careful about what you say.

An independent thinker, you sometimes believe that no one else understands life the way you do. When you are feeling introspective, you need time alone to figure things out. During these periods you enjoy communing with nature or working with your hands, perfecting your own designs.

NAME #7
PERSONALITY #4
HEART #3

People depend upon you because you are a pillar of strength. You offer solid advice and work hard to excel in your specialty. To ensure the recognition you enjoy you may overcommit yourself and end up burning the candle at both ends.

An optimist at heart, you have big dreams and a great imagination. Your talent expresses itself in many ways, but a facility with words is your specialty. Given the opportunity and an audience, you can be quite entertaining. Be glad that you make a practice of thinking before you speak; otherwise, in your enthusiasm, you might talk too much.

Although you are charming and enjoy social contacts, you can also be shy. Reluctant to reveal your true feelings, you select friends who understand that you need time alone.

Appearances are important to you; turned off by flash and trash, you dress tastefully.

Influenced by a strong sense of loyalty, you are capable of making sacrifices for others. Honest and proud of it, you expect a lot of yourself and those around you.

NAME #7
PERSONALITY #5
HEART #2

You appear to be the impulsive type, pursuing numerous interests with the frenzy of a whirling dervish. However, there is method to your madness: a busy, up-to-date image is a useful ploy to distract people from your shy, sensitive inner self. And in spite of your obvious energy, you are refined and mannerly.

To a casual acquaintance you don't seem to need people; but your true friends know otherwise. They also understand that you pride yourself on being tactful and diplomatic.

In your efforts to gather facts and sort out problems, you retreat to a calm center within yourself. Analyzing information and reading between the lines, you allow your intuition free rein. In order to make a decision you need absolute proof, otherwise you may vacillate until you are sure or can call in a trusted advisor.

A specialist in spite of your many talents, you are a fine teacher. People find you inspirational and look to you for wisdom and approval.

NAME #7
PERSONALITY #6
HEART #1

You're a class act—beautifully groomed, tastefully dressed, and always well-coordinated! You analyze your purchases carefully and like to be first with a new style.

People regard you as a dependable friend whom they can call upon often for wise counsel. Although you are warm and loving, you never gush. Naturally reserved, you like to test the water and give careful consideration to everything you say.

You avoid pushy, possessive types and can spot a phony a mile away. To be included on your select list, a person must keep his (or her) word and do his fair share.

You like to be in control, maintaining the freedom to follow your hunches and do your own thing. Such self-sufficiency can make you impatient with others who may not understand your approach. After all, why should you have to justify your stand when it makes sense to you? People may think of you as a loner, but you actually desire praise and appreciation more than most.

NAME #7
PERSONALITY #7
HEART #9

A perfectionist, you are discriminating in all your choices—from associates to possessions. Coarse or crude does not fit into your picture of dignity and refinement.

Although honest, you withhold your true feelings out of fear that you might hurt someone else's or be misunderstood. Speaking out only when you are sure of your position, you are especially reticent unless you know someone well. You require close friends and loved ones whom you can trust. On the surface you may seem aloof, but at heart you empathize with others and inspire large numbers of people with your humanitarian message.

The inner workings of a complex issue fascinate you. A natural at research, you examine everything to obtain proof and you are able to scrutinize details to determine their patterns and abstract meanings. Always concerned with the whys and wherefores, you listen with an intuitive ear for clues to the answers you seek.

NAME #7
PERSONALITY #8
HEART #8

You strive for a tasteful appearance and achieve a million-dollar look. To maintain it you are finicky about your possessions and buy only the best. Selective in your choice of friends as well, you are an elitist who prefers to relate to people on your social level or higher.

Careful about how much personal information you reveal, you can be secretive when asked probing questions. You are self-sufficient and like to have time alone to size up a situation. Problems are puzzles to be solved, and in your search for the truth you refuse to take no for an answer.

Demanding high standards of achievement from yourself and others, you qualify as a workaholic. With a clear sense of the big picture, you have the organizational skills to set up a system and administer it efficiently. You're also a superior manager who's made the art of delegating a science.

Ambitious to the point of daring, you aspire to a position of power and influence. Your planning ability, which allows you to get to the bottom of things more quickly than anyone else, will surely propel you to the top.

NAME #7
PERSONALITY #9
HEART #7

The picture of refinement, you are poised and in control. Your dress and behavior are always within the bounds of good taste. Enjoying the finer things in life, you accept only the best and are finicky about your possessions.

A seeker of knowledge, you are drawn to the mysteries of life. You also require time alone, often in the tranquility of nature, to deal with the mental challenges you set for yourself.

Respected for your great powers of observation and your astute mind, you need to see the veracity of a concept before you embrace it. Once you have discovered the answers, you inspire others with your knowledge. Spreading your wise words, you have the ability to reach the masses. In your capacity to meet the public, you have a gracious quality and acting ability that allows you to mask your real desire to be alone or with friends of your choice. In your book, intellectual stimulation wins out over superficial company every time.

Your desire for perfection leads you to demand a great deal from yourself, as well as from others. You insist upon honesty, but frequently withhold your true feelings to preserve your privacy. You can be trusted with others' secrets and are equally guarded about your own, revealing them only when you find someone equally trustworthy.

NAME #8
PERSONALITY #1
HEART #7

People see you as an independent leader who has the courage to act upon his (or her) ideas. Initially aware of your strong will, they begin to realize that you are an ambitious, able administrator who can analyze the requirements of any situation and manage people efficiently to get the job done. You like to be your own boss and work better alone, without someone breathing down your neck. Given the choice, you would rather give orders than take them.

You are career-oriented but your skills are apparent in any setting you choose, from home to volunteer organizations. With the force of your strong personality and your knack for asking penetrating questions, you approach challenging problems with obvious pleasure.

Your Midas touch allows you to turn a profit in almost every project you encounter. A prosperous future and a prestigious position are within your reach because you have the emotionally balanced makeup and determination to play for big stakes and succeed.

A private person, you reveal your inner feelings only to those you trust. You also respect other people's privacy and can be trusted not to reveal their secrets. You are a deep thinker and use both your powers of observation and your keen intuition to arrive at sound conclusions.

NAME #8
PERSONALITY #2
HEART #6

Ambitious and strong-willed, you are an efficient leader with a surprisingly soft heart. Even though you like to be in charge, you want people around you to get along and be happy. You listen with great understanding to others' ideas and genuinely care about their feelings. You often become involved in community projects—organizing committees, delegating jobs, and handing out advice. You are particularly talented at managing successful fund-raisers.

Adept at making people feel comfortable, you are frequently asked to mediate when misunderstandings occur. If you had your way, there would be peace and justice for all. Even though you are blessed with common sense, you must not allow your feelings to get in the way of making intelligent decisions.

Family is important to you. In creating a stable atmosphere for your loved ones, you expect them to accept your help and become credits to you. You are exceedingly responsible and enjoy having people depend on you. If for some reason others cannot do their fair share, you will step in. Fortunately, you are able to speak up in a nice way if you feel they have taken advantage of your kindness.

NAME #8
PERSONALITY #3
HEART #5

You thrive on change and are happiest when involved with many different projects at once. Somehow you manage to keep your life organized in the midst of a hectic schedule. In keeping with your flexible style you like to set your own hours and make your own rules.

You have a curious, versatile mind capable of generating original ideas that are often unconventional. Quick to size up situations or grasp concepts, you make instant decisions. Striking while the iron is hot, you rely on your friendly, articulate manner to involve people in your business ventures. You love competition and welcome challenges, particularly in business, where the stakes are high and there is money to be made. You never pass up a chance to make a contact or take advantage of an opportunity.

The opposite sex finds you attractive because of your humor and the excitement generated by your energy. Happiest when you have as many admirers as you have moods, you hate to be tied down; you want no obstacles in your path as you pursue personal freedom (and the almighty dollar!).

NAME #8
PERSONALITY #4
HEART #4

You lead a disciplined life and make your hours and days count. Thanks to your ambitious approach you accomplish a great deal. Sound business judgment and a logical mind make you an organizational genius. When you set up the perfect system and delegate the jobs, you expect people to produce. You don't like to make changes and are happiest when everyone adheres to your precise instructions.

Willing to work hard, you take commitments seriously and expect the same of others. Economical by nature, you want quality for your hard-earned money but never make extravagant purchases. Financial security is more important to you than ostentatious displays of material success.

Devoted to your loved ones, you desire deep, meaningful relationships. If you discover that your mate falls short of your high ideals, you will speak your mind. On the other hand, you are capable of holding in your feelings when the situation calls for it.

NAME #8
PERSONALITY #5
HEART #3

An optimist at heart, you work hard at keeping things light so you won't give in to the worries that come with a busy schedule like yours. You maintain a pace that would prove impossible for most; your organizational ability carries you through as long as you have the freedom to set your own hours and make your own rules.

Blessed with the ability to spread joy, you are welcome wherever you go. Your gift of gab and love of the spotlight make you a natural entertainer. In your own inimitable style you can charm people into giving you whatever you want.

Socially adept, you are attractive and have a knack for making important contacts. In your travels you notice the latest trends and make an effort to keep your appearance up-to-date and youthful. With careful attention to good mental and physical health, you are able to relieve the stress and maintain the energy needed to satisfy your restless pursuit of many projects.

With every passing birthday you become more confident as you move closer toward your goal of position and power.

NAME #8
PERSONALITY #6
HEART #2

Happiest when in love, you make a devoted mate who wants a partner to pamper. Filled with a desire to give, you need affection in return. Easily hurt, you may be crushed when your lover wants more space.

Your thoughtful and understanding nature makes you a wonderful friend or co-worker. As patient as the day is long, you go out of your way to be courteous and cooperative. You don't just support people, you rescue them, giving them credit in return when they help you. A natural harmonizer, you are adaptable and live by your motto: peace at any price.

To further your ambitions, you are willing to meet challenges and accept responsibility. An able facilitator, you work effectively to unite factions within groups. Your expert handling of details and skill at directing others make you a dependable manager.

When sentiments are involved, you find it difficult to make decisions. Ordinarily the one to do the convincing, you become the easy mark because you see both sides and consider people's feelings. When pressed, you tend to overlook the rules and allow your heart to rule your head. In your effort to be fair, you may ride an emotional roller coaster and notice the corresponding ups and downs on your bathroom scale.

NAME #8
PERSONALITY #7
HEART #1

A bundle of energy, you're always on the go and headed to the top. The prestige of an important position inspires you to work hard. Impressed with the power of money and what it can buy, you want only the best, and plenty of it.

Because you are content to be alone, you don't seem to need many people in your life. Although others find you pleasant and dignified, they may find you hard to get to know.

It's difficult to draw the line between your working and nonworking hours. You never miss an opportunity to follow up a lead or make a favorable impression on a potential contact. And you know all the right places to be seen, the company to keep to get ahead socially and professionally.

With the confidence to make an original impression, you like the status of being a trendsetter but you don't need the approval of others. A trim, well-groomed appearance is important to you, so you find time in your schedule to exercise regularly. You like the competition of a sport and the stress reduction it affords, not to mention the business opportunities it presents.

Your independent streak makes you better at giving orders than taking them; under no circumstances could you tolerate someone breathing down your neck. Though you like your own way of doing things, you delegate well. You may be impatient with slow or lazy types, but you do listen to comments from others. Though quickly formulated, your decisions reflect input from your associates.

NAME #8
PERSONALITY #8
HEART #9

In your ambition to make a meaningful contribution to the world, you establish high goals that are matched only by your determination to achieve them. Idealistic and broad-minded, you have the ability to see the big picture and appeal to the masses.

Your air of authority gives you great power and influence. A natural executive, you not only give the impression of being in charge, you give the orders to back it up. Organized and efficient, you work well with large groups of people and accomplish a great deal. Travel, often a necessary but enjoyable part of your work, satisfies your need for freedom.

Caught up in your career or charitable endeavor, you give it your all and are respected greatly for your accomplishments. Although you are hard to get to know, people admire you, and it seems that you have everything that money can buy and are willing to share it generously with those you love.

Although you are independent and won't let others push you around, you are a softhearted romantic. There isn't anything you won't do for your loved ones, especially when they show their appreciation.

NAME #8
PERSONALITY #9
HEART #8

A source of inspiration to many, you have the poise and elegance of gracious authority. You pride yourself in knowing all the right people; a catalyst in your community, you mingle with the social lions and seem to accomplish worthwhile projects through compassion and understanding. People appreciate your ability to see the big picture and communicate it to the public. They respect your business sense and know you can be trusted. Nobody's fool, you never let anyone take advantage of you.

You like to be in control of a situation. Insistent upon your own system, you use your executive ability and your high level of energy to accomplish a great deal. Even though you tend to leave the details to others, your long hours on the job qualify you as a workaholic. As a result of taking your responsibilities very seriously, you may not take off much time for recreation.

Because of your excellent taste and beautiful clothes, you achieve a million-dollar look that is a reflection of your attraction to money and power.

NAME #9
PERSONALITY #1
HEART #8

Anything is possible since you have the will to meet any challenge. Exercising your executive ability, you throw yourself into a project with energy and enthusiasm. You're not one to stand back; you want power.

People are in awe of your ambitious schemes and the daring with which you implement innovative solutions to problems. Projecting a larger-than-life image, you are able to reach the masses, using your influence where others may have failed. People accept your take-charge attitude and follow your orders because you have a reputation for being tolerant and broad-minded. They also trust you because of your compassion and charitable motives.

In sharing your expertise to help others, you always seem to make money. Spurred on by the financial rewards for your efforts, you also require public appreciation. The individual or group that forgets to express thanks will not benefit from your charity a second time.

NAME #9
PERSONALITY #2
HEART #7

Although you seem cooperative and sensitive to the feelings of others, you do all you can to avoid small talk and superficial company. Requiring mental stimulation, you are fussy about your choice of friends and prefer your own company a good bit of the time.

You are deeply concerned for the welfare of large segments of the population and, if necessary, can deal easily with all kinds of people. In your desire to help others you will go along with anyone who appeals to your sense of logic and presents a good case. You are perceptive in the analysis of information and have great success when you follow your hunches. Quietly taking it all in, you never speak until you are sure of your stance.

People are often confused by your sympathy for public causes and the intensely private side of your character. Add to your mixed messages an apparent reluctance to state an opinion and you remain a mystery to most casual observers.

Those who know you well understand that your impeccable manners are sometimes in conflict with your insatiable curiosity. Though politeness is your policy, you are compelled to ask questions in your pursuit of knowledge.

NAME #9
PERSONALITY #3
HEART #6

Regarding home as your haven, you open your door wide and attract people with your optimism and warm hospitality. Happiest when those around you are comfortable and well-cared for, you enjoy shouldering responsibility for others.

Your devotion extends to those close to you, as well as to mankind at large. In your idealistic desire to promote justice and right all wrongs, you are often involved in charitable causes. Giving freely of yourself, your home, and your talents, you often make contributions in the area of art or music. Your talent for self-expression is also evident in the way you make people laugh, and in the conscientious manner you give advice.

Generous with your loved ones, you spend lavishly and buy only the finest. Your family, as well as your home, make a beautiful statement of your good taste.

NAME #9
PERSONALITY #4
HEART #5

As a humanitarian, you share yourself and your many talents with the world. A student of human nature, you can appeal to the masses.

A progressive thinker, you excel at problem solving and are quick to grasp ideas. And because you are able to cope with many types of people and situations, you compete effectively in all of life's challenges.

Although you have a live-and-let-live philosophy, you give others the impression that you lead a very disciplined life. Seeing the results of your hard work, not many realize that you have the energy to play just as hard.

To relieve stress, you are a firm believer in exercise. Always looking for ways to kill two birds with one stone, you are the kind of person who will pack the golf clubs or tennis racquet and combine business with pleasure and travel. Since you thrive on adventure, the world is your playground; you are willing to search its far corners for unexplored territories.

Your family, however, is the center of your universe. No material sacrifice is too large to ensure their security and comfort. A pillar of strength, you give generously of your knowledge to make their lives better.

NAME #9
PERSONALITY #5
HEART #4

Although you appear to be the bon vivant, you are actually quite conservative and set in your ways. Honesty is your middle name, and you are respected for high principles.

You have the ability to think things through clearly, coming up with practical solutions to problems. After planning carefully, you work hard until you achieve tangible results. Others applaud you for being able to cope well with a variety of situations.

Though you are generous, prudent spending and financial security are important to you. You avoid wasteful practices and go out of your way to get top value for your dollar. With an obvious taste for the finer things in life, you realize that everything has its price; if what you want contributes to the comfort and beauty of your surroundings, you are willing to pay for it.

On the go and right in the middle of the action, you seem to have many social contacts. You live the good life, enjoy travel, and cultivate your interest in the arts.

At heart you desire meaningful relationships. Although you feel deep affection, you often have difficulty expressing it. However, there isn't anything in the world, short of something dishonest, that you wouldn't do to help the ones you love.

NAME #9
PERSONALITY #6
HEART #3

Friendly and outgoing, you seem to be the center of attention; you can talk to anybody about anything. People claim that your youthful enthusiasm is contagious; they are happier just being around you.

Convinced that you are a responsible, solid citizen, people would be surprised to know that you sometimes take on too much in your desire to find outlets for creative expression. Free with your time as well as your money, you have been known to make generous gestures that border on the extravagant.

Sharing your many talents with the world, you excel before large groups. A kind and compassionate teacher, you like to climb on your soapbox to inspire people. When others depend on you and show respect for your advice, you've earned your gold star.

A youthful appearance is important to you. To look your best, you may spend a small fortune on clothes and personal grooming.

NAME #9
PERSONALITY #7
HEART #2

You have an aristocratic air that says you're in control. Even though you may appear aloof, you're a sensitive soul. In your desire to love and be loved, you make overtures that are sometimes misunderstood. Can you help it if you care so deeply that you sometimes come on too strong? Occasionally, you soft pedal your own feelings, apprehensive of what others might think.

Happiest when working with groups, you encourage people to have confidence in your vision. And since you are able to embellish the facts, you can paint a convincing picture.

You have many friends from all walks of life. Knowing that you want peace and harmony at any price, people sometimes try to take advantage of your kindness. Generous to a fault, you will give the shirt off your back to anyone you feel is deserving; in return you naturally require appreciation.

You have a wide variety of interests, including art, music, and travel. Compelled to have beautiful surroundings, you collect things of quality.

NAME #9
PERSONALITY #8
HEART #1

You are an energetic go-getter who is happiest when in charge. Impressed by your air of authority, others respect your confident approach to challenges.

With the vision to see the most efficient way to accomplish your goals, you like to start on projects as soon as you get the idea. Best at handling the main issues, you are a true executive who delegates the details to a staff.

A pioneer in the field of philanthropy, you think of original and inventive ways to raise money. Though you care deeply for the work you do to benefit others, you look out for yourself. You always seem to succeed in improving your position in the scheme of things, since you're able to see the big picture. You always manage to look as if you have everything money can buy.

Apparently in control of your destiny and most certainly your staff, you have the world by the tail. A free spirit, you refuse to be dominated; you crave independence and like to set your own hours.

With the know-how to appeal to the masses you are able to broadcast your theories and philosophies. Proud of your inspirational effect on others, you enjoy their adulation.

NAME #9
PERSONALITY #9
HEART #9

Your mission in life is to help others. You share not only your-self, but your talents, with the world. You offer generously, with-out expecting to receive in return; however, you do love appreciation for your good deeds.

Using a convincing line, you manage to meet all those who in-terest you. Not bound by prejudice, you have unusual friends from all walks of life. You are trusted by others because of your compassionate, broad-minded outlook.

In love with love, you are ruled by your heart and have had your share of disappointments. You have strong emotions, which can tear you apart if you let them.

Even though you have a heart of gold and will do just about anything for a friend, you are a free spirit who bristles when too closely bound by commitments. You don't mean to hurt anyone, but you need the freedom to pursue your many interests. Your good intentions and tolerance make you able to forgive and for-get.

Filled with high-flying plans and big dreams, you like to deal with grand concepts, inspire others, and leave the petty tasks to someone else. You want to touch the hearts of many and would divulge your trade secrets to anyone you thought was truly in-terested. In your desire to help, it is important that you don't let people take advantage of you.

With a talent for music or art, you have a need for harmony and beauty in your personal surroundings. In fact, you hate the unlovely anywhere in the world.

NAME
NUMBER
RELATIONSHIPS

THE NAME #1 MAN
AND THE NAME #1 WOMAN

A pair of inventive #1s generate enough electricity to light a city block. The powerful #1 MAN is impressed when he meets his match in an equally intense #1 WOMAN. As if looking in a mirror, he sees his strength of character reflected in her. She, in turn, sees a man who won't be threatened by her self-reliance and tenacity.

Getting together is a challenge. Since she's always on the go, he has to court her on the run, which is right up her alley.

Her definition of original is pretty far out, but he won't have trouble coming up with some bizarre versions of the traditional flowers-and-candy routine. A century plant proclaims his undying love, and a lifetime supply of macadamias should get the message across that he's nuts about her.

Once past the initial courtship, their relationship has no pattern at all. These nonconformists enjoy playing one-upmanship with activities that appeal to their pioneering spirits.

While they may not stand still, they both enjoy stopping long enough to play. Not limited to the bedroom, their sex life will be as exotic as this pair is resourceful; they'll try anything once.

He's used to being on top in most situations and so is she; they may have to keep the chiropractor on call to untangle them from time to time. Challenging positions in daring places describes most of their unions: a couple of upwardly mobile #1s started the Mile High Club when they couldn't find time to get together on the ground. A pair of self-sufficient #1s won't rely totally on each other for amusement. To make sure their paths cross frequently enough, they must keep a joint calendar. When scheduling conflicts arise because one forgot to tell the other, they can both be very stubborn.

Just as they share strengths, the #1 MAN and #1 WOMAN also share faults. They both want their way and neither will give in without a fight. The ensuing argument may generate as many sparks as their lovemaking. One of their egos is bound to be bruised, since he's used to being a leader and she's never followed anyone in her life. But if they can end the shouting match before one of them changes the locks and throws the other's clothes on the lawn, making up should be fun.

The #1 pair can maintain a high level of excitement by egging each other on to pursue challenges they both enjoy. As soon as they realize that they must feed each other's ego, they are well on the way to a satisfying life together. Fifty years later, they'll be candidates for the record books, having survived the most tempestuous relationship in history.

THE NAME #1 MAN AND THE NAME #2 WOMAN

In the game of life opposites attract; that's the secret of this relationship. The macho #1 MAN, who quickly orders his double shot straight up, impresses the indecisive #2 WOMAN, who can let half the evening go by before deciding between the strawberry or peach margarita. But when he sends over a frozen Daiquiri instead, her appreciative response satisfies his need to be admired.

Later, when the waitress spills a drink on her and he starts to fly off the handle, he has to admire the diplomatic way the #2 WOMAN touches his arm and accepts the waitress's offer to have the house pick up the tab and the cleaning bill.

Off to a good start, he will be successful with the #2 lady if he puts on his best behavior and acts like a gentleman. She, in turn, will land her #1 MAN if she admires his self-reliance and take-charge ability.

This cooperative woman is likely to go along on any activity he arranges, and their romance will blossom as long as she can abide whatever he may decide. She may have to swallow her fear from time to time; his escapades are seldom in the realm of the ordinary. When the #1 MAN wants to discover uncharted territory alone, the #2 WOMAN is happy to turn to her hobbies and wait patiently by the phone.

The #1 MAN won't take no for an answer; nor will he hear it from the ready-to-please #2 WOMAN. Occasionally, she will refuse gently, in a way that leaves her man with an unbruised ego and just as persistent the next time.

His originality in the bedroom, along with her memory for his all-time great performances and preferences, will keep them both coming back for more. He's likely to make love in any setting and the accommodating #2 will bend over backwards to keep him satisfied; and when he appeals to sentimental #2 with posies on her pillow, her delight will keep him up all night.

He can call all the shots in this relationship as long as he doesn't hurt her tender feelings. A #2 WOMAN can put up with a lot and still keep smiling, but beware the calm before the storm. When pushed too far she comes out swinging, and the resulting explosion can stop even the strongest #1 MAN.

Knowing that she's responsive to romantic gestures, he can save the day by making a sincere apology. It's a foregone conclusion that her anger will melt even before he's said "I'm sorry."

As long as she's willing to play Follow the Leader and remembers to praise him as her one-of-a-kind lover, this romance will flourish. They can learn a lot from each other. She can develop a little of his independence while he's off doing his thing, and he can add some of her sensitivity to balance his strong will. The level of intoxication remains high if she continues to accept his decisions with the same receptive smile that attracted him in the first place.

THE NAME #1 WOMAN AND THE NAME #2 MAN

Fulfilling each other's needs and complimenting each other's temperaments, the #1 WOMAN and the #2 MAN are bound to have a promising relationship. The #2 MAN is excited by the energy and intensity of the #1 WOMAN; she's attracted to his sensitivity and attentiveness.

Studious #2 makes the perfect teacher's pet for the #1 school mistress. She loves it when he spends hours at her feet and hangs on her every word. No detail escapes a #2 MAN, who bestows personal gifts and thoughtful remembrances on every occasion. When he opens doors, holds chairs, and drapes her coat gently over her shoulder, it's clear that he can pass every test in the manners department.

Out of school he'll soon learn that impressing this impressive lady takes some doing. The first time he offers to carry her things to the car and hesitates about asking her out, she asks him. He's quick to pick up on the fact that she's used to being first with the best. However, even a strong #1 WOMAN needs a shoulder to lean on occasionally, and a sympathetic ear to bend instead of just an audience. He will indulge her with long walks and talks, and treat her as if she's the only one in his life.

As their relationship develops, they settle into their roles. He researches the Sunday paper's calendar for exciting field trips; she makes the final decision. He may have to reach to come up with something she hasn't already seen or done. When she decides to exercise her independence, he resorts to hobbies and friends to satisfy his need for companionship.

In bed he follows instructions to the letter. Although the #2 MAN is willing to learn new tricks, he is concerned about what people think. Extra homework is okay; it's the extracurricular assignments that get him down.

As long as she doesn't overdo her commands or neglect him because of her independent study, he'll want to stay in her class and make the grade. Accusations may fly if teacher's pet becomes teacher's errand boy. Even a strong-willed #1 WOMAN may be stopped in her tracks by the unexpected fury of a #2 MAN's pent-up anger.

In order to pacify her pupil, she may have to swallow her pride. If she makes a genuine apology for taking advantage of his kindness and puts him first for a change, he'll forgive and forget.

To keep their relationship exciting, they should trade places more frequently; she can't be on top all the time.

THE NAME #1 MAN AND THE NAME #3 WOMAN

Looking every bit the master in his toga, the #1 MAN projects a commanding presence at a costume party. Enter the #3 WOMAN dripping flowers and wearing flowing robes. Quickly surrounded by her friends, she is the center of attention. These two stars will inevitably meet in their quest for the spotlight. Initially fascinated by each other, they are really very different.

The #3 WOMAN will let her #1 MAN know that she enjoys basking in his reflected glory. Creative herself, she appreciates his original ideas and lets him know by crowning him with laurels and promoting his talents to anyone who will listen. Fairly bursting with pride, he is naturally taken by her flirtatious ways.

Whether or not they are good for each other depends on how they manage their considerable differences. The single-minded #1 MAN can be serious, while the versatile #3 WOMAN bubbles over with cheer and optimism. Her happy-go-lucky attitude will either drive him nuts or provide a necessary balance to his hard-driving approach. His intensity and determination may put a damper on her effervescent spirit.

Both given to imaginative flights of fancy, they can amuse each other with an endless array of erotic pastimes, should their costume party become intimate. A perfect slave to her #1 master, #3 can entertain him with endless chatter. Happily peeling grapes with great abandon, she's fine until he threatens to use them to silence her. Much later, grapes forgotten and #3 speechless with delight, #1 prides himself that he was able to make her focus on nonverbal romantic pleasures long enough to get his best word in edgewise.

Besides costume parties, this pair will enjoy a wide range of activities, from his daredevil pursuits to her favorite artistic endeavors. When he asserts his independence, she'll have all her friends to fall back on. As long as his exploits give her something to talk about, she'll tolerate his absence.

Though they are willing to share center stage for a time, neither one likes it when the other claims exclusive use of the spotlight. He gets that superior look and she pouts. Her whining may send him out the door, but she won't carry on for long. If she's smart she'll cut her complaining and jolly him out of his anger before he gets miffed enough to leave. Experience will teach her that the more he pushes the more she should relax, lie back, and enjoy it.

Overpowering to be sure, a #1 MAN may be too strong for a shy #3 who tries to live in his shadow. When he keeps moving, she has to hustle to keep within his protection.

But when they are in sync, their life is the continual party she craves, and he can have the vocal admiration he adores.

THE NAME #1 WOMAN
AND THE NAME #3 MAN

The professional #1 WOMAN may have to abandon her plans to work on the airplane when she's seated next to a talkative #3 MAN. Given to flights of fantasy, he is about to discover the dominant woman of his dreams, at least his dreams of submission.

It's a good thing he's optimistic, because she's determined to get through her paper work; only a charming #3 MAN could persuade her to put it aside. The more she protests, the greater is his desire to claim her strong will in a romantic hold.

Once he gets her to laugh, which isn't hard for an entertaining #3, he has it made. It's not only his humor and youthful good looks that attract her; his refreshing, lighthearted manner is a welcome contrast to her serious mood. Not impressed by the same old lines, the #1 WOMAN appreciates his novel approach and is flattered by his attention.

They discover a mutual interest in exploring new cities and begin to realize they are kindred spirits—energetic and adventuresome. The more they talk, the more she realizes how creative he is. It occurs to her that he should focus on a few of his better ideas; he is realizing how great she would be at helping him zero in on his brainstorms.

Off to a high-flying start, this romance is not likely to come down for quite a while; these two will quickly land in bed, at his silver-tongued suggestion.

Determined to corral his talents, the resolute #1 WOMAN plays right into his fantasy. Submitting to her romantic directives as well, the pleasure-seeking #3 MAN succumbs with delight. Only a #3 MAN would go along with some of her more bizarre ideas and have the restorative powers to keep up with her.

When they come down off their emotional high, their first disagreement will be based on their differences. Prone to providing a continuous performance, he may not like it when she announces that the party is over, even temporarily. When they both want their way, he will pout and she will berate his frivolity.

To remedy the situation, she's likely to issue him orders to snap out of it and remind him of the potential he's wasting. If he makes the first move, it will be an outlandish bid for her attention; the irresistible #3 MAN never stays down for long. When their good intentions replace an argument with a flattering match, the problem is solved and their super egos are soothed.

The #3 MAN and the #1 WOMAN will never lack for new ideas to keep their relationship exciting. They may have to look farther afield for new places to meet, but they will never exhaust each other. As long as she laughs at his jokes and he gives in to her demands, they should be very happy. Toss in a few spotlights and mirrors, and they could frolic forever.

THE NAME #1 MAN
AND THE NAME #4 WOMAN

Counting respirations and taking her pulse at the proper intervals, the #4 WOMAN perseveres in her morning workout. With the concentration of a serious athlete, she runs her laps rain or shine.

The #1 MAN can't help but notice her steady progress and the way she begins each session with stretching exercises. He, on the other hand, starts running immediately, striding easily at first; then, as if he could chase the wind and win the race, he works his way through the other runners to lead the pack. This #1 trailblazer can't escape #4's notice.

Is it any wonder that #1 and #4 are attracted? So different, they secretly envy each other's style. The road to romance, however, may not be as smooth as the track. A creative nonconformist, he is likely to suggest a cross-country run on the spur of the moment. Taking a conservative approach, she replies that she couldn't possibly change her plans on such short notice. Full of practical reasons why his idea won't work, she may put a few hurdles on the course of true love. If they jostle and bump their way to a second date, they've made great strides in resolving their differences.

If he marvels at her endurance on the track, he'll love her record performances in bed. He's aware of her fleet feet, but he didn't bargain for the added surprise of her manual dexterity. A great one for following directions to the letter, #4 will enjoy carrying #1's creative ideas through to completion. She's open to a new technique if he can prove it works and he gives her plenty of time to perfect it.

They make a balanced team: he runs the sprints while she runs the distance races. Patient, practical #4 keeps her impulsive #1 MAN on the track in his many pursuits. He, on the other hand, can lead her down a path more adventurous than she might have chosen.

Both #1 and #4 can be stubborn. There is a limit to her patience and a limit to the number of times he will curtail his freedom. They may fight about money: she saves it, he spends it. When she worries what the neighbors think and he replies "Who cares?", she's likely to bristle. To convert her to his point of view, he must appeal to her sense of logic. To win his apology she must appeal to his ego and be more tolerant of his independent streak.

Keeping their relationship more exciting is easy for #1; the challenge for #4 is to bite her tongue when every bone in her conservative body wants to resist his wild ideas. They need to give in to each other when it counts, and cheer each other on as they each run a good race.

THE NAME #1 WOMAN AND THE NAME #4 MAN

The competitive #1 WOMAN is teed off. It's absolutely maddening; after dozens of private lessons with the best pro, she still can't hit that golf ball with the accuracy of the self-taught #4 MAN.

With incredible concentration and superb technique, he swings with just as much determination as #1, but his ball seldom veers from the straight and narrow. (He owes it all to the golf manual he found on sale after months of searching.) It's obvious to him that she needs to follow his system instead of her pro's.

Quick to size up a situation, decisive #1 will add other games to their courting repertoire. There isn't much future in games where there is only one winner, particularly if it isn't #1. Once they resolve who gets to make the first move, #1 and #4 will find that making love is a sport they can both enjoy.

When creative #1 thinks up a new love game for two, she'll go along with #4, who insists that practice makes perfect, and will keep it up until he gets it right. Their only problem in bed may be his tendency to stick to rules-and-regulation equipment. She'll need all her wiles to lure him into more unconventional contests—unless he's assured of scoring some points.

Single-minded #1 and tenacious #4 can be persistent when it comes to settling an argument. Overtime may go on indefinitely until one of them decides to apologize, and they may need the help of a referee to decide between #4's favorite haunt and #1's latest suggestion. She complains of boredom, while he insists that she lacks consistency.

Impulsive #1 can learn from practical #4. He can keep her inventive ideas from crashing down around both of them. She, in turn, can keep him from being too stodgy.

To keep their relationship exciting he needs to be more experimental. While she's praising him for his efforts, she needs to devise more clever ways to encourage his spontaneity. As long as they throw out the score card, they can play out the course of their relationship in harmony.

THE NAME #1 MAN AND THE NAME #5 WOMAN

He can't help noticing her; there's no one else on the slopes moving that fast. The rest of the skiers respond cautiously as they see her streak by in fluorescent yellow. What amazes #1 is that she's been at it all morning and shows no sign of slowing her pace. It looks as if she's skiied every run on the mountain for starters and is still raring to go.

She's spotted him, too. It's hard to overlook perfection in red. He attacks each run as if he owned it and is obviously determined to be the best skier on the mountain. Keeping him in the corner of her eye, #5 isn't surprised when he appears suddenly in the lift line, making the snow fly in a rooster tail to announce his arrival. When she moves forward to claim one seat on the double chair and the lift operator calls out "Single," who should appear but #1, fairly crowing with delight.

For the rest of the day she's happy to follow his lead and he's delighted to find that she can keep up. Putting on a show for the crowd on the sun deck, he's in his element with a fearless partner in pursuit. Curious to know him better, the #5 WOMAN leads him on a merry chase through a series of après-ski spots until they're the last ones in the hot tub. Was it his idea or hers to make this an all-night test of endurance? Maybe she read his mind and suggested it to save him the trouble.

No snow bunny on the slopes, the #5 WOMAN is as adventurous by night as by day. She was all over the mountain, now she's all over him. Anxious for one new run after another, she keeps even innovative #1 on his toes.

Though it drives him wild with delight in bed, her restless spirit can also drive him to distraction. Her continual search for new places and new faces can leave him feeling neglected. He prefers riding *à deux* to sharing his gregarious lady with a whole gondola of skiers.

When their skis cross, she's wise to remember that he likes to be treated like #1. And he may have to give her more freedom. To keep their relationship exciting, #5 will rely on her slalom-racing instincts and vary the course. She'll also figure out a way to end a cold day on a warm note. The #1 MAN is a downhill racer; he'll keep his #5 lady interested by continually beating out the competition.

THE NAME #1 WOMAN AND THE NAME #5 MAN

The action-loving #5 MAN is easy to spot at the company picnic; he's the running-back on the football team. Leaping to catch a pass, he darts from side to side as he carries the ball toward the goal. If there is a determined #1 WOMAN on the team to run interference and call the plays, he'll score a touchdown every time.

It's no wonder that the #5 MAN and the #1 WOMAN make a winning pair; they are both predisposed to perpetual motion and famous for their spirit of adventure. No matter who wins the coin flip for openers, their courtship will get off to a fast start.

A spur-of-the-moment kind of guy, he'll call at the last minute or just show up with several ideas in mind. Quick on the uptake, she'll jump at the chance to decide for both of them. It won't take them long to discover that they are a couple of nonconformists. There isn't a pass he can throw that she won't intercept. And they won't get their signals crossed because they can practically read each other's minds.

She's a no-nonsense kind of woman who goes after what she wants. When he thinks he's pulling a quarterback sneak into her end zone, she'll be ready for him. Not afraid to tackle him below the belt, she should be glad there's no referee around to call holding.

#1 likes to win, and that's okay with easily distracted #5. She may toss a flag down on one of his plays when it looks like he's picked another player to receive his pass. If his #1 lady intercepts the ball that she thinks he's intended for someone else, he's in for trouble.

Adaptable #5 can call a time-out to explain his strategy and assure his proud #1 lady that she's misread his signals. She'll call off her threat to give him a penalty for backfield in motion and they can resume their game.

To keep things exciting, the #1 WOMAN can change the rules of the game to keep her #5 MAN interested; he thrives on sudden change. In turn, the #5 MAN can find new ways to show his lady that she's #1 on his team.

THE NAME #1 MAN AND THE NAME #6 WOMAN

If he can't shoot his own lion-skin rug from Africa, the #1 MAN will settle for color close-ups of the king of the jungle, proving his courage on the trigger of a camera. Determined to go first class, he chooses a deluxe photo safari, hoping to experience the exhilaration of the hunt without threatening the endangered species.

Enter the highly principled #6 WOMAN, a charter member of Save the Animals. Deciding to rough it in a two-room tent with fresh linen daily and four-course meals, she's assured of all the comforts of home.

It's love at first sight; he is attracted by her genuine concern for a good cause and her classy appearance; she admires his enthusiasm and daring disregard for the obvious dangers of the jungle.

While #1 fantasizes about how he can save vulnerable #6 from peril, #6 starts a mental list of ways to rescue her hero from his long day behind the camera. Always dressed to kill, she can get her man without setting foot in the jungle. To set the mood, #1 plays right into her hands; all he really wants is her devoted attention when he regales her with his daring exploits.

He will forgive the #6 homebody if she doesn't want to swing through the jungle on his vine. Content to swing in her tent at night, #1 finds her attention positively therapeutic.

Her smothering techniques may interfere with his independence. When #1 balks at her unwanted advice, adaptable #6 will back off because she hates arguments.

In her need to center her life around someone she loves, #6 will make #1 her top priority. She keeps the home fires burning and nurtures her man so he can go out in the world and bring back the excitement to her. If he remembers to ply her with the luxury she loves, he will keep her fire glowing.

THE NAME #1 WOMAN AND THE NAME #6 MAN

The #6 MAN's style harks back to the chivalry of yore; when other little boys were wearing dirty sneakers, there was #6, robed and crowned. His adult life has been a continual search for a worthy princess to share his castle.

Enter regal #1, an enchantress who exudes an air of sophistication. Is it possible he's found her at last, the stately consort of his dreams?

Though the produce section of the supermarket seems an unlikely spot to meet a Princess Charming, #6 has learned to spot quality when he sees it; just because his manners are stuck in another century, doesn't mean his brain is backward.

Smitten by her strength of purpose and decisive demeanor, #6 rushes to rescue her from an avalanche of Chinese peas. Even though he's left his scepter at home, she can tell he's someone special; what ordinary man would offer to help her dig through a pile of peas for the plumpest and most green? Obviously, quality is as important to him as it is to her; only the best will do.

Entranced, he follows the princess and her peas from produce to pasta, offering to push her cart and majestically plucking her heart's desire from the highest shelves. So attentive and considerate is he that their romance has begun by the time they reach the check-out counter.

Instead of a quick cup of coffee, he suggests they become better acquainted at his place over Café Royale flambé; igniting more than her brandy, he causes #1 to melt in the process. As the romance progresses, his courtly approach includes other domestic dates. Following her on her daily rounds, he holds the door at the cleaners and reads poetry to her at the Laundromat.

In sexual pleasures, as in other diversions, #1 likes to give the commands. Bowing to her pleasure, #6 devotedly follows her lead. It's a good thing he turned out to be a king instead of a knight. Once a king, always a king; once a night is not enough.

Since gallant #6 can't abide arguments in any form, he'll give in to her whims. When she wants to be alone, he will gather his legions of friends and pass the time until she returns. Always thinking of others, he is willing to adjust. Only when he hands out the heavy-handed advice will there be trouble. Even a #6 king cannot entirely rule a #1 princess.

In order to keep their kingdom as enchanting as Camelot, he needs to catch her off guard and insist on some surprises of his own.

THE NAME #1 MAN AND THE NAME #7 WOMAN

Even for a self-assured #1 MAN, it's difficult to make small talk with an introspective #7 WOMAN. They've been riding the same train morning and night for weeks, but he knows no more about her than he did when they first nodded "good morning." Refined and aloof, she has piqued his curiosity and exhausted his repertoire of opening lines. True to his #1 NAME, he is intrigued by the challenge of the uncommunicative #7 WOMAN.

Analytical and reserved, she may very well be interested in this powerful #1 MAN. But she's not ready to open up until she's chosen the right words and selected the perfect moment. Opposites in nearly every way, the thorough #7 and the impulsive #1 may pass each other by without getting to know one another because their styles are so diverse.

In a stroke of creative genius, determined #1 decides to stay on the train beyond his stop, bidding her "good day" as she gets off the train. That evening it's a different lady who shares the outbound ride. She wants to know all about him: Has he changed jobs? Did he forget his stop? Where did he go? Clever #1 has hit the jackpot in his shrewd appeal to her natural curiosity. It's clear she likes a mystery to solve and he has finally presented a subject worth discussing.

As much as she likes to ask questions, answering them is another matter. Private to the core, #7 won't even tell her best friend who she's dating or where they go. A married #1 could carry on an affair with her for years without fear of an indiscreet slip on her part. Nor will she reveal what she does on the nights when they're not together.

Once their relationship develops beyond the train station, they discover a shared taste for the finer things. #1 and #7 enjoy dinners at the best restaurants and front-row center seats at the theater.

Resourceful and persistent, aggressive #1 will eventually woo his discriminating #7 lady commuter into his bed. Beneath her reserved surface lies a kinky streak; he'll get the clue when she starts to cry, "All aboard!"

It's only natural that he'll want to know where he stands with her, and her reticence can lead to problems. He likes to know all, but she's not one to be possessed. Preferring to investigate and wait, she could easily be annoyed by his impulsiveness. In the heat of battle, she'll head off his brilliant frontal attacks with her highly analytical reasoning.

Making up may be a slow process as these two lovers retreat to lick their wounds. She may take her own sweet time to emerge, but she'll finally assure him that he's still #1. Lapping up her compliments, he'll be only too happy to reestablish their daily routines.

These fellow travelers may be waylaid on different sidings occasionally, but they have what it takes to stay on track for a long and satisfying journey.

THE NAME #1 WOMAN
AND THE NAME #7 MAN

Head bent in deep concentration, the #7 MAN stares at the museum display. Suspended from wires, exotic balls of varying sizes form an abstract pattern he has yet to decipher.

With her usual authority, the #1 WOMAN marches up and pushes the magic button. As the spheres begin to dance around the central orb, he looks at her astounded; was it really that simple? While he was lost in thought, she impulsively hit the switch.

Delighted by his obvious amazement, she takes the lead and asks him to join her as they tour the display of executive toys. The curtain of his typical #7 reserve is momentarily lifted and he happily gives her a mini-lecture on the ant farm exhibit. She is fascinated by his knowledge and ready to find out more about scientific #7.

Dallying at the last table, he sensuously fingers the sand beneath the pendulum and suggests they adjourn to a quieter spot. She knows just the place, and they are soon sharing their philosophies of life over a bottle of wine. Actually he's asking penetrating questions and she's doing most of the talking. Later, when she can't remember what he said, she will realize that he gave little information about himself.

Tucked into her mailbox the next evening is a dinner invitation written across the front of the toy catalog. When she calls to accept, he's only too happy to accept her choice of restaurants; like #1, he appreciates first-rate establishments.

In sensual pleasures, their tastes are also in tune. Though aloof and refined in public, #7 drops his reserve in the bedroom. Discovering his sexual eccentricities is a worthy challenge, even for an innovative #1. Their first meeting was obviously not his first exposure to toys; his storehouse of games and gadgets promises unlimited enjoyment.

Sure in the thought that he will keep their little secrets, she is all the more free to express herself. She relishes his romantic subtleties; he loves her direct approach. They love spending time alone, though she is never sure what he does when they are apart.

He may want to take his toys and go home when she gets too bossy; she will be furious when he neglects her. And if she gets impatient because he spends so much time plotting and planning, he will retreat to his own world, feeling miserable and misunderstood.

When it comes time to make up, stubborn #1 may have to give in. Finding it difficult to forgive and forget, #7 has the patience for a long, cold war. There's hope as long as #1 always tells #7 the truth; one lie and it's over.

THE NAME #1 MAN
AND THE NAME #8 WOMAN

#1 and #8 tend to gravitate toward each other, even in crowds. Self-confident, powerful #1 is drawn to a take-charge, efficient #8 with an irresistible urge to discover her secrets and meet her challenge.

He sees himself in her, right down to the commanding presence, self-reliance, and drive. She, in turn, admires in him all the qualities she seeks to nurture in herself: leadership, decisiveness, and ambition.

They would make a perfect pair if only they could find time away from their desks. Once the #1 MAN puts his mind to meeting the #8 WOMAN, he'll realize that this health-conscious lady undoubtedly goes to the gym every night on her way home from the office. Sure enough, there she is doing twice as many leg lifts as anyone else.

If #1 plans to pursue this iron-willed, iron-pumping executive, he should check his credit rating and prepare to use it—to the hilt. Winning the heart of a #8 doesn't come cheap, nor will it be easy. In order to get a time slot in her schedule, he'll have to impress her at least as much as she impresses him.

Their courtship will be a whirlwind of the latest restaurants, theater offerings, and serious shopping. #1's creativity will be tested severely when it comes to selecting gifts for #8; what is there to buy that she doesn't already have? Baskets of flowers, the splashier the better, may be the ultimate choice. No single orchids for this woman when dozens of sprays make a showier display.

A matched set when it comes to energy, #1 and #8 can amuse each other endlessly in the bedroom. Lithe and limber from their hours in the gym, they can endure an amazing amount of erotic exercise. Into repetitions and peak performance, these two up-scale lovers should glow with good health and satisfaction.

Two goal-oriented powerhouses under one roof will survive if their objectives are compatible. They are better off not competing in the same field because neither one will appreciate living in the other's shadow. The power struggle between them can become a tug-of-war: she wants control and tends to get emotional; he makes pronouncements and walks out. Fortunately, persuasive #8 can usually get her #1 MAN to give in long enough to reach a compromise.

To keep things exciting after a hard day's work, they reward themselves with first-class recreation.

THE NAME #1 WOMAN AND THE NAME #8 MAN

When the #1 WOMAN spots a #8 MAN in the pre-game crowd, she knows instantly that she's found the league she wants to join. She's impressed by his impeccably tailored appearance and classy car, and she's thrilled by the challenge of meeting him. As she beats another car to a parking place and neatly zips into the tight spot, he can't help but admire her assertive behavior; her performance has all the earmarks of a resourceful, strong-willed #1. Disappointed when she loses sight of him, #1 turns to get out of her car and finds him standing beside her, ready to shake her hand for a job well-done.

Taking control of the situation, #8 insists that she join him on the fifty-yard line unless she'd rather sit with her friends in the end zone. It's lucky that she brought a couple of pewter mugs for the beer; he hates plastic cups, too. When he produces imported mustard for the hot dogs and a pocket TV for the replays, #1 senses she's arrived.

She knows it's true love when the messenger delivers a tiny gold football on a delicate chain. #8 is quick to pick up that no ordinary flowers or candy will do for his one-of-a-kind football fan. Preferring to state his intentions with the permanence of 18 karats, #8 has big plans. Leaving the details to his secretary, he maps out a whirlwind courtship, alternating between the trendy restaurants he loves and the more unconventional pleasures she enjoys. He may not share her taste for modern opera, but he's happy as long as they have box seats.

Competitive by nature, these two lovers stage a contest in the bedroom to see who ends up on top. She loves his firm control and he's fascinated by her independent streak, which makes the chase all the more fun. They set standards of behavior in and out of the bedroom that are challenging to meet. Both success-oriented, they push each other to greater heights.

When their goals diverge, a power struggle can ensue as each partner tries to convince the other of the superiority of his or her own particular target. #8 uses his executive abilities to negotiate a settlement, while creative #1 will be more devious in her approach to a solution. Not even a #8 can keep his mind on the issues when #1 goes to work using her diversionary tactics. Since they both need to win, they should define their territories to avoid competing with another.

Playing one-upmanship for high stakes should keep their life interesting. Outdoing each other in the extravagant gift department, they'll never get tired of pleasing each other, no matter how many anniversary diamonds her little gold football acquires.

THE NAME #1 MAN AND THE NAME #9 WOMAN

The whole world loves a #9 WOMAN, and the feeling is mutual. Frequently involved in charitable activities, she exudes warmth and caring. Since the #1 MAN wants this lovable creature all to himself, he must come up with another one of his imaginative ploys to spirit her away from the crowd.

Inspired by the challenge of a #9 WOMAN, he appeals to her need for appreciation by staging a private banquet, complete with a speech and a trophy. She realizes he's the kind of man who goes first class and pays him the ultimate compliment by praising his originality.

After a delectable dessert created and named for her by the chef, #1 suggests they get to know each other better. Thrilled to have her all to himself, he reminds her that charity begins at home.

She quickly understands that he loves to be aggressive, and is willing to follow his lead. Inspiring trust, she encourages his every move and leads him to new levels of awareness. As a helpmate, #9 knows no peers, and her giving ways excite him.

Her broader view of the world helps him to widen his horizons. Intrigued by her unconventional social life, he is drawn to her eclectic mix of friends. She, on the other hand, is delighted to follow him on a round of his one-of-a-kind evenings. He can show her how to be more aggressive, while she teaches him how to show compassion for others.

When their differences erupt into a quarrel, it won't last for long. #9 will understand #1's pride and be the first to apologize. His challenge is to avoid being jealous of the many recipients of her attention, while she must be tolerant of his self-centered attitudes.

As long as she's willing to follow his lead and save time for him alone, this pair will be happy. He can ensure her unlimited generosity if he remembers to show his appreciation with an annual awards banquet for two.

THE NAME #1 WOMAN AND THE NAME #9 MAN

Adjusting the tray table in front of her, the #1 WOMAN raises her glass and smiles as she proposes a toast to her #9 seat mate: "Here's to a great trip." Between his job with an international news organization and extensive personal traveling, he's been all over the world. She can tell that he is at home anywhere. The #9 MAN is impressed by her plans to do northern Italy; she's doing more in her first trip than he did in his first three. Now that they have agreed to dinner in ten days when their paths cross, he toasts, "To a better dinner in Milan." . . . And to breakfast, he thinks to himself.

As they touch down in Rome several hours and much conversation later, #1 makes an impulsive suggestion in her usual direct manner. They drive off together in a rented car heading north.

He's in love and she's found the key to Italy, so why wait ten days?

On the outskirts of the city, he pulls up at his friend's restaurant. They eat marvelous fettuccine Eduardo and #9 buys her a painting by a friend of a friend. Little does she know that this generous man, who had eyes only for her on the plane, does indeed know half the people between Rome and Milan. As the trip progresses, she realizes that the only time they are alone is in the car. He begins to notice a decided chill the farther north they drive, and it's not the weather.

It's become clear that time alone with him is at a premium; #1 has to stake her claim on #9 very assertively, beating off his groupies with a stick. On the other hand, he's confused by her alternate needs to explore the countryside independently and to have him all to herself when she wants his undivided attention.

Once alone behind closed doors, #1 and #9 forget their differences and become the pair who invented the lost weekend. A jug of good local wine, a loaf of bread, and a picturesque villa to themselves are all they need. The passionate #9 Romeo lets his creative #1 Juliet write a new scenario. She can take all she wants and he holds nothing back. Basking in the warm glow of his attentions, #1 feels as if she's the most important woman in his universe. As far as she's concerned, she would willingly go around the world with him, indefinitely.

On future trips, she may be alarmed at his generous gestures toward friends, especially when he pays more than full price for those paintings. Their battles are fueled by her inability to understand his selfless extravagances and his observations of her self-centered attitudes. Ordinarily tolerant, #9 can forgive and forget; fortunately, it's easy for him to apologize. #1 is so stubborn she might not come forward to make up.

To keep things exciting, he must remember to put #1 at the head of his list. She can contribute to their relationship by spiriting #9 away from his fans for more lost weekends.

THE NAME #2 MAN
AND THE NAME #2 WOMAN

It's easy to spot the refined #2 MAN in a crowded lobby. He's the one who not only allows the women and children to enter the elevator first, but ushers in the old men and stray dogs before entering himself. It isn't that he's claustrophobic or wants to be near the front; he's so polite he doesn't want to offend anyone by appearing to be pushy.

If there is also a gracious #2 WOMAN near the door, they can be there all day waiting to see who goes first. Eventually the doors close and the #2 pair are left in the lobby to get acquainted.

Chances are they will have plenty of time to get to know each other. As crowds continue to arrive, they keep urging them through the elevator doors. Finally, when a stranger offers a tip for their assistance, they realize that it's time to stop standing on ceremony. By the time these #2s arrive at their floor, they are old friends planning further encounters. It's easy to build a relationship when you can read each other's mind.

He invites her to a lecture and she suggests they take in a collector's show. Natural partners with an aversion to being alone, a pair of #2s gravitate to one another in pursuit of the pleasures they both enjoy. Sharing friends, hobbies, and responsibilities, they are the model of cooperation. With a distinct desire for the finer things, they both strive to maintain a high degree of culture and refinement in their lives.

Considerate of one another's feelings, a pair of #2 lovers form a mutual admiration society. Neither wants to offend the other by making a new move without first asking permission. Their lovemaking resembles their lengthy wait in the elevator lobby; each one patiently takes the time to please the other. Full of more ups than downs, their relationship is sensual and loving because they share imaginative fantasies and push all the right buttons in a playful, gentle manner.

Trust builds up quickly between this pair. They reinforce each other's good qualities, such as patience and kindness, and are protective of each other's weaknesses, especially their sensitivity to criticism.

Neither of them vents anger and, as a result, the pressure

builds. Explosions are infrequent but so devastating to civilized #2s that they avoid fights at all costs. Quick to give in, neither one wants to risk disruption of their normally peaceful relationship. Some of the anger comes from indecisiveness. To keep their relationship on the up and up, they should help each other make decisions and express negative feelings.

By pursuing their hobbies independently, they can avoid forming a closed corporation that would eventually prevent them from growing as individuals. At the risk of hurting the other's feelings, each #2 must cast aside any fears or misgivings and take the lead to initiate a new round of fun and games. Since they both wear kid gloves, it won't hurt a bit; the results can be instrumental in getting their romance off the ground floor.

THE NAME #2 MAN AND THE NAME #3 WOMAN

The outgoing #3 WOMAN makes a good match for the organized, diplomatic #2 MAN. While she is in the front of the class teaching public speaking, #2 is madly writing down questions to ask his charming teacher after the lecture. The student, as well as the man in him, hangs on her every word; she can't help noticing how attentive he is as he smiles from the second row.

She is flattered by his after-class questions, especially the one he saves for last. Of course she would love to discuss good introductions over coffee. Quick with a comeback, fun-loving #3 tells him he already has a great opening line and thinks to herself that she'd rather have cocktails with this sensual man at her favorite afterhours spot.

Reading between the lines, perceptive #2 lets her choose their destination and she gets her way after all; they wind up at a booth for two in full view of the room. She loves the spotlight, and a smitten #2 MAN makes a wonderful audience. Not one to quibble when someone else, especially his speech instructor, makes a decision, #2 is happy with her choice.

This teacher's pet knows how to polish the apple and he pleases #3 with lively entertainments that have enough class to satisfy his sense of good taste and decorum. He's understanding when she's running late and tolerant of her penchant for talking the night away; he doesn't mind when they are the last ones to leave a party or close a restaurant. While he's more attuned to one-on-one discussions, she prefers to socialize with everyone within shouting distance. He rationalizes her behavior by telling people she's a speech expert who's exercising her voice projection.

Romantic #2 loves to shower #3 with flowers and candy. She playfully licks her lips and tells him the sweet, soft centers remind her of him. Never at a loss for words, she praises him constantly for his thoughtfulness. Playful in bed, #3 can dream up zany love games to teach her willing, but more sedate #2 lover. Happy to oblige her, he relishes his role as a partner. Only an imaginative, diplomatic #2 would think of a way to get talkative #3 to reach new heights of nonverbal communication.

A good balance for her, #2 can roll his eyes over her bizarre behavior or bring her back into line when she's slightly blue. She, in turn, can jolly him along when he worries about what other people think.

The course of true love may not go smoothly for #2 and #3. His love of detailed lists and scripts may run headlong into her off-the-cuff approach to speeches and to life. A classic #3 sulking session is inevitable when he reminds her of a trifle she overlooked. Since it takes a lot to prompt his anger, she's safe with a little pouting. A lot of childish behavior will drive him over the edge, and she is well-advised to keep her distance until the big explosion subsides.

When he cools down, #2 will be more patient than ever and ready to give #3 her way. It wouldn't hurt for her to share the spotlight occasionally; she could also stop talking long enough to listen to him the way he listens to her. She can take advantage of his kindness for only so long before he rebels.

Their key to success as a couple is the creativity they share; they're bound to coauthor a happily-ever-after life script.

THE NAME #2 WOMAN AND THE NAME #3 MAN

Taking tests is easy for the #2 WOMAN; in command of the facts, she's also organized in her thinking. Cooling her heels while the game-show contestant coordinators grade the papers is harder. She's usually patient and doesn't mind waiting, but today is different; she's never tried out for a game show before and isn't quite sure what to expect.

On the other side of the room, talking nonstop, is a #3 MAN with youthful good looks. Also a potential contestant, he obviously loves being the center of attention. She can't help overhearing him optimistically reassure the other hopefuls that they will all pass the test. His enthusiasm is contagious; he's convinced them that instant riches and stardom are just around the corner.

The first pair is summoned for the oral interview, and #2 finds herself entering the assistant producer's office with none other than Mr. Verbal. How will she ever get a word in edgewise? Momentarily torn between fear and escape, #2 feels a sudden excitement at the touch of an encouraging hand on her shoulder; the decision is made as #3 guides her through the door. With a blinding smile, he introduces himself and gives her shoulder a good luck squeeze. As her knees begin to feel weak, she isn't sure whether it's her anxiety over the impending interview or her involuntary reaction to this electric man.

Outwardly proud, she settles herself for what's to come next. While the producer explains the game and questions #2, loquacious #3 bites his tongue and observes #2 in action. Impressed by what he sees, #3 realizes that she has turned the tables and is putting the producer at ease. Full of the details of her most embarrassing moment, she's a delightful creature. By the time she explains why she wants to be on the show, both the producer and #3 are convinced. After eloquent #3 makes the grade, too, he suggests a cup of coffee while they wait to play their trial game. Captivated #2, who by now knows all about him, agrees, and their romance has begun.

Suggesting some practice sessions before their tape date, he engineers an exchange of phone numbers before they leave the studio. After ten days of intensive study during which he eases her fear and she builds his self-confidence, the big day arrives. To mark the occasion, thoughtful #2 has a good luck horseshoe of flowers sent to his office. When they meet at the studio, clever #3 presents her with one made of silver for her key ring.

Waiting to go on the air, they continue to practice and drill one another, though not always with the show in mind. This creative pair has found some new games to try and new depths to explore. He brings a playful imagination to their encounters, while she remembers to pay attention to the important little details, making their intimate moments last round after round. Always eager to try something new, he's inspired by her gentle prodding to achieve new heights. A couple of winners, no matter what game they're playing, #2 and #3 make a championship team. They will both enjoy spending the money they win.

He may fail to score points with her when she questions his impetuous decisions and tactfully chides his youthful exuberance. On the other hand, she may lose a round with him because she won't make a decision.

Their fights will be quiet ones rather than noisy arguments. Each tending a fragile ego, he may sulk and she will nurse hurt feelings. Requiring an attentive partner, #2 may be jealous of gregarious #3 and his flirtations.

To ensure mutual satisfaction in the game of life, they must remember not to contest each other. By playing as a team they can bring home the grand prize.

THE NAME #2 MAN AND THE NAME #4 WOMAN

Dancing in the dark, the #2 MAN and the #4 WOMAN fairly float to the music. They move as one perfectly synchronized unit of beauty in motion.

He noticed her sense of rhythm on the first night of class, so he asked her to be his partner. Responding to his gentle lead, she found him to be a cooperative partner right away. Later she came to appreciate the way he listened to the instructor as carefully as she did. It was fun to be the first pair in the class to execute a step correctly.

#2 could have adapted to any partner, but he was fortunate to find #4. No other woman in the class was as prompt or faithful in attendance as she; no one else would have brought such concentration and diligence to the task of learning each complicated step.

After a particularly challenging lesson, he tactfully suggested extra practice, to which she heartily agreed. As he got to know her, he realized that even though this woman was light on her feet she really had her feet on the ground.

Neither one was given to flamboyance; even though their rhumbas were as reserved as their sambas were subdued, every step was perfection. They eventually danced their way to a collection of prizes, which he kept at his place until they got married.

Now she lines up their trophies the way she lines up their lives. Super organized, she's cataloged all his other collections. When he can't decide where they should go for dinner, she helps him choose the restaurant and makes sure the prices fit their budget.

He's learned to curb his generous spending habits to please her thrifty streak. Instead of an extravagant gift, he puts a tender note on her pillow. As synchronized in bed as they learned to be on the dance floor, this pair has all the right moves down to a science. She's still happy to follow his lead, and what she lacks in originality, she more than makes up for in her willingness to repeat a basic move until they get it right. With his patience and her perseverance they will eventually trip the light fantastic in their own private ballroom.

A pair of sentimental lovers, they will never trade partners; loyal to the end, they choreograph their lives carefully and deliberate the pros and cons of each new move. They rarely step on each other's toes; he hates to fight, and she's so practical that she's devised foolproof systems to avoid potential missteps in every aspect of their lives.

Money may trip them up. When frugal #4 bluntly expresses her honest displeasure at #2's purchase of yet another pair of dancing shoes, his tender feelings may be hurt. She may stubbornly refuse to change her mind even though he's tried to make her see both sides of the argument. Unless #2 can prove to #4 that he needs new shoes and that they are a good buy, he's out of luck.

The resulting misunderstanding will lead to silence rather than shouting. Too civilized to raise their voices, #2 and #4 will dance to their separate tunes until #2, who expects her to read his mind, is pacified by #4's personal touch. They have too many basic values in common to stay apart long.

They can add excitement to their lives by learning a new step; the challenge of a more complicated routine will keep them moving together. Dancing in the dark is guaranteed to produce its own reward.

THE NAME #2 WOMAN
AND THE NAME #4 MAN

Even though his vacation is a year away, organized #4 decides to visit the travel agency because it's never too early to start planning. Standing on the other side of the brochure rack is an attractive #2 WOMAN, obviously doing careful research on a future vacation. He can't help but notice her choices and admire the practical questions she's asking about airfares and tours. With her kind permission, he joins in the conversation, and soon they are both quizzing the travel agent.

While #4 takes notes, #2 picks up his system and jots down reference numbers on the brochures they are collecting. Excited by the instant partnership they have formed, she is impressed by the clever ways he has spotted to save money and see more cities. As they begin to discuss their destinations, the travel agent is soon forgotten. Absorbing #4's comments like a sponge, #2 asks questions to keep the conversation going. Quick to sense his needs, she happily shares the information she's gleaned and relates the pros and cons of each tour.

Color pamphlets in hand, they leave the agency at closing time to continue their research. More convinced by the moment that their paths were meant to cross, #2 sees in #4 a man she could trust, a faithful partner. Completely at ease with her, #4 appreciates her obvious good taste and dignified behavior. Before long they've put more than their heads together, and two trips for one have become one trip for two.

Though she is less concerned than he about getting the most for her money, she's delighted to leave the final choice to practical #4. Having renewed passports in plenty of time and purchased tickets well in advance to take advantage of the lowest fares, the dependable pair meticulously check off their lists every step of the way.

With the travel plans proceeding on automatic, they can get down to some serious work on their relationship. Quiet evenings poring over detailed maps turn into quiet evenings conducting studies of each other's topography. Technically perfect, he drives her to a frenzy by systematically investigating her byways. With slow, steady progress and attention to detail, he doesn't miss a single side attraction; their erotic trips are always successful. Thanks to #2's more vivid imagination, they may take some exciting detours; #4 always brings her sojourns to a satisfying conclusion.

These two are so neat and orderly that they seldom fight about everyday things. Only her tendency to accumulate possessions will cause him to balk. Petty jealousy isn't a problem either, because they each have what it takes to form a stable, loyal partnership. Sharp words over finances reveal a general inflexibility on his part, which will require all her ingenuity to overcome.

As quick to forgive and forget as she is to cry, #2 will gladly give in to keep the peace. #4 contributes to their reconciliation by making one of his sentimental gestures. As they travel through life together, a favorable wind will be at their backs if she can diplomatically lead him down new and exciting paths, and he gives in to his gentle traveling companion.

THE NAME #2 MAN AND THE NAME #5 WOMAN

Watching his energetic #5 WOMAN from a shaded cabana on the beach, the patient #2 MAN waits breathlessly for her to finish the sailboard lesson in one piece. It was her idea to try it. Cautious #2 would hear none of her arguments for giving it a whirl by herself. Used to experimenting, #5 was curious about the possibility of harnessing the wind and the waves. Why pay for a lesson if she didn't like it? His answer was to inquire about every instructor on the island and get her the best. #2 knows he did the right thing.

Suddenly she's covering him with saltwater kisses, raving about the sailboard and how far she went and how fast. Impressed by his daring pupil, her proud instructor says she's accomplished more in one lesson than most people learn in a week. As she dashes to the room to change for lunch, #2 wonders whether he should set up another lesson for the same time tomorrow; for all he knows, impulsive #5 will have moved on to scuba diving by then. Undecided, he takes the instructor's card and dashes off to get his telephoto shots of the lesson developed quickly.

Later, as they dig into their crab salads, the pictures are delivered to their table per his special request. Overwhelmed by his thoughtfulness, she more than repays him by devouring each picture enthusiastically. She recounts each glorious moment, the feel of the wind, the sound of the waves, and the joy of the ride. Reminded of the reasons he loves his #5 WOMAN, #2 marvels at the way she dives into all of life.

There is just time to grab a final gulp of coffee and a handful of mints for quick energy as they start on a full afternoon of activities. Happy to attend the class he chose on tropical flora and fauna, she's glad when it's over and they can go shopping. While she checks out all the shops in the hotel, he heads for the one that carries the shells he needs for his collection. Later, when she's off inquiring about helicopter rides to the falls, he'll go back to one of the shops she showed him and buy her a present. Her enthusiastic reaction to his gifts always gives him new incentive to find an even better surprise the next time.

As inventive and daring by night as she is by day, the #5 WOMAN inspires her #2 lover to give her everything he's got. Even though some of her erotic adventures stretch his limits of understanding, he hates to say no. When satisfying her urge to smell the night-blooming flowers leads to satisfying her sudden desire to bed down in the garden, he worries about what other people will think.

#5 is occasionally stifled by #2's concern for propriety. In reaction to his thousand reasons why she shouldn't do something, she's likely to dash out the door tossing a rude remark over her shoulder. He can beg all he wants; she will rarely sit still for long-range planning. When she can't understand his inability to make a snap decision the way she does, he will retreat with a severe case of hurt feelings.

This sensual pair can't stay angry very long. She is so flexible that one look at his sad face and a whiff of his aftershave will send her back into his arms. And he's so determined to keep her happy, he will say something sweet and sentimental to patch things up.

For years to come, emotional, togetherness-oriented #2 and sensual, free-spirited #5 can provide constant stimulation for one another. As long as #2 can watch, he'll let #5 go anywhere.

THE NAME #2 WOMAN
AND THE NAME #5 MAN

Settled in her seat at the track, the #2 WOMAN has made it in time for the daily double. Even though she's studied the racing form, she can't make up her mind which horses to pick, much less whether to bet win, place, or show. Next to her the #5 MAN impulsively scans the form. Picking a couple of horses by the appeal of their names, he checks the field and changes his mind when he sees their colors. When he finally makes up his mind, he dashes off to place his bet before the race starts. When he returns, it's obvious that he waited too long.

Impatient for the third race to start, he decides to strike up a conversation with #2. The discussion turns to strategy, and he can't believe his ears; she's missing all the fun. Why do all that homework? She's even considering a horse's trainer and owner in addition to its statistics.

She marvels at how he can watch the odds change, make a snap decision, and race off to the window to place a bet. What an education! Calling her his good luck charm, he flashes the cash he's won and invites her out to dinner, but not before he buys her something in the gift shop for her collection.

Off to an unexpected start, their romance flourishes, thanks to #5. #2 can't believe she'd pick up a perfect stranger at the track, but she couldn't say no. She admires his adventurous pace, which leaves her breathlessly running to catch up. A cooperative and willing partner, #2 loves to tell her friends about curious #5's escapades; it doesn't take much embellishment on her part to make each one a marvelous story.

A few good times around the track and it's a good bet they'll land in bed. Agreeable #2 doesn't care whether her fast-paced #5 wins, places, or shows in their race for pleasure, as long as she can go along for the ride. The odds are that she will finish with him if she can hang on and use a light rein.

Freedom-loving #5 is a high-strung racehorse who likes a fast track. If #2 tries to cut him out of the herd and retire with him to the pasture, she's out of luck.

In constant search of variety, #5 is good for cautious, conservative #2. However, this major difference can lead to trouble. It's one thing to agree on a $2 bet, it's another to plan a lifetime's financial strategy. When disagreement turns into a battle, expect #2 to give in before #5 walks out. Forgive and forget is their motto; #2 forgives because she's so understanding, and #5 forgets because he's on to something else.

Thanks to the activities of a restless #5, the relationship should remain exciting enough for both of them. Patient #2 mustn't let #5's flexibility throw her. The secret is to keep the door open; that way they'll both end up in the winner's circle.

THE NAME #2 MAN
AND THE NAME #6 WOMAN

There's nothing mysterious about how the #2 MAN and the #6 WOMAN find each other amidst the hundreds of passengers on a multideck cruise ship. Images of refinement, they both stand out in a crowd. Since the brochure stated formal dress for dinner, he packed his tuxedo, and she brought a wardrobe of gowns.

After an introduction engineered by tactful #2, it's clear sailing as they fall into a pattern of romantic moonlight trysts and daily shopping excursions. No burrito lunch on the run for this pair. #2 lets her decide between the terrace of the grandest hotel or an intimate booth in the country club bar. Inveterate spenders, they both sport well-used credit cards and a devoted following of native craftsmen. #2 and #6 accept no shoddy workmanship however quaint the design, and #2 is patient when #6 holds out for the best.

After the second expedition, they use his cabin to store their voluminous purchases and hers for their love nest. It's an obvious choice: #6 booked the owner's suite and has made it as homey as she can with daily supplies of #2's favorite snacks.

They may encounter rough water when she goes overboard giving him advice. The #2 MAN enjoys having his #6 WOMAN make some decisions and will bite his tongue most of the time to keep peace. But just let her swamp him with orders and he'll get his feelings hurt. He might even blow a gasket if the pressure builds; peace-loving #6 will see it coming and adjust her course to ensure a smooth passage.

Once in home port, this friendly pair may have to do some maneuvering to keep their combined families and friends from taking advantage of their generous hospitality. #2, who is everyone's favorite listener, will have to take the phone off the hook, and #6, a one-woman rescue team, will have to turn off the porch light. Alone at last, they cater to each other in loving harmony; he will be patient and sensitive, while she adapts to his every wish. Content to make waves in their waterbed, they love to remember how they first rocked the boat.

Between her desire for a family and happy home, and his need to have a loving partner, they have the makings for an enduring relationship. No stormy passages are predicted for this pair. They maintain such a considerate climate that their life should provide continued smooth sailing. As long as the money holds out, they'll keep their love for luxury afloat.

THE NAME #2 WOMAN AND THE NAME #6 MAN

The #2 WOMAN has had her eye on a silver tea service for at least a month. Still undecided, she pays her weekly visit to the antiques store to admire the set. This week there is an additional attraction, an impressive gentleman who's telling the dealer that the fumed oak sideboard is just what he's been waiting for.

#2 approves of his taste; the piece is the best she's seen and has a price tag to match. He, in turn, comments on the quality of the tea set and advises her to buy it. He's flattered by the way she listens to his appraisal, and she's buoyed by his encouragement. Striking a deal, they negotiate a good price on both items with the antiques dealer.

To celebrate their good fortune, #6 suggests high tea at the stately old hotel around the corner, a sentimental occasion that will be repeated many times in the course of their courtship. Before long her silver resides on his sideboard and they're having high tea in luxurious comfort at home.

Their lovemaking tends to be leisurely and loving. He takes on all the responsibility until she gently reminds him that she likes to express herself and take the lead occasionally. Though not usually given to athletic contests in bed, their intimate moments are fulfilling and tender.

#6 is a protective mate who is perfect for cautious, sensitive #2. Because neither likes to fight or hurt the other's feelings, they may avoid expressing their true emotions. #2 collects her complaints and blasts him with an uncharacteristic explosion. #6 may be tempted to recount all the times he's showered her with advice, only to have her accept someone else's opinion. Devastated by disharmony in their home, they will make up quickly. Tactful #2 will beg his forgiveness and #6 will be fair enough to accept criticism or kind enough to accept an apology.

They can keep the relationship fresh by bravely asserting themselves before little problems become big ones. And as long as they can afford to indulge themselves with luxuries, their relationship should become more treasured as time goes by.

THE NAME #2 MAN AND THE NAME #7 WOMAN

The #2 MAN and #7 WOMAN have sat next to each other every Wednesday evening for five weeks. While the creative writing class focuses on the short story, he has been focusing on getting her beyond the coffee-after-class stage. Intrigued by her elusive behavior as well as her obvious writing talent, #2 does most of the talking while she listens. Seldom revealing her thoughts except through her short stories, #7 seems to enjoy his tendency to embellish and tell all.

If he would exercise his ability to read her secretive mind, he'd realize that she's as attracted to him as he is to her. It's not in her nature to express her feelings until she's sure, and more than one suitor has already given up.

Assuming that she will respond to his sensitive, thoughtful gestures, patient #2 proceeds to work magic. An inveterate gift giver, he presents her with an out-of-print book she's mentioned. She's touched by his thoughtfulness and accepts the book as well as a date. It may still take some time before they become a steady duo, but at least he has broken the ice.

#7's cool reserve keeps patient #2 platonically pecking at her cheek far longer than would most modern-day fiction characters. But their intimate relationship is well worth waiting for; it's as torrid as their courtship was cool. #7 may spend a long time contemplating her actions, but once she's committed she finishes what she starts.

Beneath the analytical exterior of a #7 WOMAN lies a sensual soul with a wild streak. Pampering her requires every inch of #2's fertile imagination. In and out of the bedroom, they are sensitive to each other's feelings. She understands his need for a social life beyond their intimate circle, and he understands her periodic need to retreat for solitude. Allowing each other to pursue individual interests enhances their relationship.

Whatever fights they may have will be quiet disputes, since neither one likes to shout. Resembling a cold war, their disagreements will crush them both. The best way for them to make up is to leave each other alone until their hurt feelings subside. In time, trust can be rebuilt and life will get back to normal.

He'll sustain this exciting relationship with creative romantic interludes. And by not revealing everything about herself, #7 will keep the mystery alive.

THE NAME #2 WOMAN AND THE NAME #7 MAN

Does she like the new exhibit in the Sea Life Park better than the old one? The #2 WOMAN can't make up her mind. As she watches the dolphins before going to the gift shop, her main concern is whether she should limit her collections to whales or include dolphins as well.

Standing a few feet away, the #7 MAN is oblivious to everything but the dolphins. He wonders which of their playful movements represent sexual contact and pictures himself making a pass at a watery nymph. They could glide around one another for hours in effortless ecstasy if they didn't have to come up for air. Turning to leave, he is still caught up in the fantasy—his vision becomes a collision as he sends #2 sprawling. The perfect gentleman, #7 guides her to a bench and questions her thoroughly to detect any injuries.

Assuring him that she's fine, #2 puts him at ease. She senses his reluctance to make small talk and fills the void by telling him the purpose of her visit. Reluctant to let him go, she gives him a few more details about her collection; she just can't decide if she should pursue this mysterious man.

Once he's analyzed the situation and assured himself that she isn't the kind to use him, he moves their relationship forward. He suggests a trial run to the gift shop to see how she's feeling, and she graciously agrees to let him buy her a porcelain dolphin. He urges her to take the time to choose just which one she wants, but she's unable to decide between two. Their eyes meet as he tells her to take both, because a pair like that shouldn't be separated. Catching his drift, she's suddenly sure she's made the right decision about him.

#2 knows intuitively that her #7 MAN needs to trust her before he warms up, so she turns on the charm. Beneath his cool exterior she discovers an insatiable lover whose expressive body speaks volumes. As communicative as the pair of dolphins, they leave no doubt about the erotic content of their body language. A willing partner in his fantasies, she soon has him whispering his secrets in her ear.

Ripples on the calm surface of their relationship appear when #7 hurts #2's feelings by going off on his own too often. Feeling misunderstood, #7 insists that he didn't mean to neglect her.

These two tend to let small problems become large ones. Normally cooperative #2 says yes when she really means no and explodes in a torrent of fearful accusations; #7 responds by slamming the door.

#2 makes up with a diplomatic gesture; she knows how important it is to tell #7 she sees his side. He comes up with an in-depth analysis of their problem and provides the logical solution.

They have the capacity to amaze each other continually. #2 pampers #7 with a stream of thoughtful gifts, while secretive #7 masterminds fantastic surprises.

THE NAME #2 MAN
AND THE NAME #8 WOMAN

The #2 MAN needs someone to tell him how to implement his new packaging idea. After extensive detective work he turns up a #8 WOMAN who owns her own market research company.

He decides to observe her in action at the next chamber of commerce meeting. Marveling at the energetic way she moves from committee to committee to give directions, he thinks she may be too busy for him. When she comes to his table at last, #2 graciously offers his chair. Obviously at the end of her rope, she bristles at the group's lack of cooperation. The #2 MAN counteracts her blunt stance by charming the members into at least listening to her request and together they persuade the members to comply.

Thanking him at the end of the meeting, she agrees to consult on his packaging idea. #2 is sensitive to the fact that she's had enough for the day, so he suggests that he take her away from it all. They could escape to any quiet spot she names and discuss business or pleasure, whatever she prefers.

The #8 WOMAN is fascinated by a man who seems to take over while at the same time letting her have her way. As he helps her into the driver's seat of her car with a flourish, she suddenly realizes how exciting it will be to have him all to herself this evening. To heck with the work she had planned!

He reads her mind, sees to her every comfort, and mixes well with her friends. On the arm of her gallant partner the #8 WOMAN not only looks like a million, she's ready to earn it. She finds the money and manpower to develop his great idea. When the profits roll in, the whole town knows they've made it by the time #8 gets through. Their public celebration leaves them feeling pleased and anxious to go home to one of their private celebrations.

The #2 MAN is a gentle giant who loves to inspire his savvy partner. Eager for her to achieve success, he is completely unselfish and ready to try it her way. Intense #8 visualizes his romantic ideas even better than his commercial ventures, and they truly enjoy getting down to business together.

It's highly unlikely that she'll get tired of making the decisions for both of them; however, he may get tired of having her take advantage of his kindness. In almost every case he will try to use tact and diplomacy with her, but when that fails she'd better watch out; when #2 has had it he can be forceful, and she may wish she hadn't been so blunt. Realizing she's hurt his feelings, the fair-minded #8 WOMAN will see the error of her ways; though sure she's right, she'll see the advantage of making up.

To maintain the peace he requires, the #2 MAN uses his sensitivity to keep #8 on an even keel; plying her with dozens of long-stemmed roses and the current status-symbol gifts, he knows he can keep her happy. She shows her appreciation for his tender loving care by taking time away from work just for the two of them.

THE NAME #2 WOMAN AND THE NAME #8 MAN

Speed-skating around the rink, the #8 MAN wishes he could go on the public address system to tell all the skaters how to use the space more efficiently. It infuriates him to see people skating every which way; the cautious #2 WOMAN he's noticed over by the rail will be in for trouble if she gets mixed up with the hot-doggers.

The music changes, and she ventures out into the mainstream of traffic. Taking charge, #8 arrives at her side just in time to guide her through a maze of disorderly skaters. Thrilled by his strength, gentle #2 soon finds herself in his arms, gliding easily around the ice.

#8's quick to see what a cooperative partner he's found, and puts his plans in motion. Off to a fast start, their relationship flourishes because he's so good at giving directions and she's quite happy to follow them. Everywhere they go he takes the lead; he loves to be seen in all the better places and she's delighted to wear the fashionable clothes he selects.

While his tastes are extravagant, her gestures are sentimental. Even in bed he does everything in a big way. His voracious appetite is matched only by his stamina. She loves the upfront way he expresses his needs and never says no. Inspired by his every move, supportive #2 is more than willing to add the finishing touches to bring every one of his plans to completion.

Since he seldom leaves time in his busy schedule for a romantic encounter, diplomatic #2 makes an ideal partner because she can always come up with a good time for him to squeeze it in.

Emotions run high with this pair; #8's assertive approach may overpower sensitive #2. #8 works off his steam with an exercise program and can't understand why she should waste time crying. #2 has the choice of giving in to an argument (which she does so well) or waiting until #8 moves on to the next compelling item on his agenda and forgets all about the fight.

If he takes her for granted, she must show anger, for a change, to recapture his interest and prove she's not a pushover. He can stay off thin ice with her by planning more time together. There is no denying that #8 needs his one-woman cheering section; she'll follow him anywhere and make him feel like a champ.

THE NAME #2 MAN AND THE NAME #9 WOMAN

The #9 WOMAN's latest trip to Africa has sparked her interest in native dancers. So she's gathered some friends and headed for the folk-dancing class run by the local adult education center. A perpetual student, the #2 MAN is there because he's already taken the other courses offered on the same night.

As the music starts, she's the only one in her group without a partner. At her side in an instant, #2 knows exactly what's happened; she has taken care of the others first. One dance into the evening and he's sure she's the partner he's always wanted.

Obviously a favorite with her friends, she's already making converts of perfect strangers to her fan club. With extravagant gestures and an aura of happiness, she transforms the activity room into a party that #2 never wants to end.

Outside of class, #2 and #9 fall into a round of concerts, art gallery visits, charitable functions, and even an occasional peace rally. Giving of their time as well as their worldly goods, they are prone to help whenever asked. Her causes become his; they share the need to work for the betterment of their fellow man.

Not one to give anonymously, #9 loves to receive any form of recognition for her efforts, and #2 is the perfect person to lead the applause. And she loves it when an occasional gift is directed to her.

When they break away from the masses to spend time alone, their romantic life can be marvelous. Capable of an intimate two-step as synchronized as the folk dance they mastered, this pair has potential for great sexual satisfaction. She can follow any new moves he imagines, and he delights in her extravagant displays of affection.

Unless they make some attempt to curb their generosity toward others, they may deplete their resources. Dancing out of time and money for themselves is detrimental to their relationship. A constant flow of fascinating friends, from business leaders to out-of-work actors, may be stimulating, but not as a steady diet.

The #9 WOMAN is the one who may devote too much attention to outside friends. Needing companionship, #2 may feel hurt and decide to put his foot down. Once she reaffirms his primary place in her life and lets him talk out his feelings, they'll be in step again.

To keep things exciting they should give in to their love of travel. Globe-trotting #9 wants to mingle with the natives, while #2 wants to find handmade treasures for his collections. When his cache of worldly goods threatens to overtake their home, she's only too happy to call in the local charity truck.

Since both love to give credit where credit is due, they will find it easy to show each other well-deserved appreciation. Given a trust fund or steady income to supplement their generous ways, this pair can dance through life in perfect harmony.

THE NAME #2 WOMAN AND THE NAME #9 MAN

The #2 WOMAN loves to give presents and is on a first-name basis with the staff of every gift-wrap desk in town. She can't help noticing the #9 MAN ahead of her in line at her favorite store. The clerks are also calling him by name.

Giving him a pleasant smile, she asks his opinion on the kind of paper to choose for her ten-year-old nephew. Before the wrapping is done, she's discovered that his four "kids" are children he supports in foreign countries where business frequently takes him. He tries to visit them at least once a year and sends them sweaters and coats for the winter.

Discovering that they both have toys to buy, #2 and #9 set a shopping date for the next evening. He helps her decide on purchases, and she expresses admiration for his generosity toward his "kids." #2 sees she's hit a receptive chord in #9; before the night's over, they are joking about his offer to help her have a foreign child of her own. Perhaps they should become better acquainted!

Both are adored by their many friends. Charitable at home as well, they ply one another with tokens of love. Their intimate moments represent an unselfish surrender to each other. More than happy to meet each other halfway, they perform many acts of kindness together. He knows firsthand that her heart's in the right place, and she knows for a fact that he's willing to be of service.

Trouble can brew in Xanadu when he wants to comfort the world and she wants to comfort those a little closer to home. Envious of his mass appeal, she may strike him as clingy and narrow in her thinking. She may also object to the procession of derelicts and do-gooders that parade through their lives. When she wants him to join her in an intimate tête-à-tête on their couch, and he's offered it to a down-and-out friend, she may lose her ordinarily infinite patience.

Since they both love harmony, their serious fights will be as infrequent as harsh words that tear them apart. The focus of the disagreement is usually his need to be part of a larger group and her desire for an intimate partnership. This naturally loving pair has no difficulty making up. She is diplomatic and sensitive in her apology, and he forgives and forgets.

To keep things exciting, they must concentrate on each other and make sure that charity begins at home.

THE NAME #3 MAN
AND THE NAME #3 WOMAN

It's definitely some enchanted evening when two #3s see each other across the crowded room of a party. A couple of fun-loving flirts, they have enough twinkle in their eyes and music in their laughter to entertain all night long. If the center-stage position has enough room for two, they'll be sharing it together by the time the buffet line starts moving. Swapping jokes and playing like a couple of kids, this pair is off to an exuberant start in keeping with their enthusiastic approach to life.

The next day, when a messenger delivers a giant lollipop and a note saying "I'm a sucker for you!", he'll know exactly who sent it. She'll be touched by his stuffed koala and card: "I can't bear it when we're apart."

Their answering machines may be better acquainted at first than they are. Always on the go, they both need these gadgets to stay in touch with all their friends. A large appointment book or a social secretary would help if either #3 would accept the necessity of planning ahead.

Having fun is their primary objective; since they can have a ball with something as mundane as taking out the garbage, they'll have a lot of alternatives. From shopping for clothes to entertaining friends, they gear their lives to amusing pursuits.

Once they remember to use their whistles to call time out on their nonstop social life, the imaginative #3 pair make playful lovers. Fond of bright lights that show off their youthful appearance, they are just the kind to have mirrors installed on the ceiling. Basking in the reflection of their athletic antics, they might even go so far as to videotape one of their more impassioned performances for an inspirational rerun.

Their lack of discipline will be a recurring problem—unless one of them steps out of character to establish a method to their madness. Content to play around the clock, these two will eventually feel the effects of an unbalanced checkbook; their lavish tastes may also cause some anxious moments on the edge of bankruptcy.

When his flirting gets out of hand or she talks too much, there is likely to be a tantrum or at least a good pout staged by the injured party. Punctuated by the stamping of angry feet and the slamming of doors, their fights will be noisy but short-lived, especially when it ceases to be fun.

As long as they keep their creative juices flowing to make life exciting, these two have a rosy future. With good accountants and a patient housekeeper, these showboaters can go on indefinitely.

THE NAME #3 MAN
AND THE NAME #4 WOMAN

A high-speed collision seems an unfortunate circumstance for a first meeting. And if it weren't for charming #3, #4 would not see the positive side of the encounter. Minding her own business, #4 came to the park to get in her mile of speed walking around the baseball field. Playful #3 brought his kite to take advantage of the brisk wind and the bright sunshine. Oblivious to the fact that he is about to intersect her well-worn path, he runs full tilt into incredulous #4, who is sure she has the right of way.

Normally patient and dignified, #4 loses her cool and becomes even more furious at #3's profuse apologies. Rising to the occasion faster than he can rise to his feet, he turns on the charm and soon has her smiling. Lying back on the grass, he makes her look at the sky and the clouds instead of her skinned knees. Later she can't resist his offer to carry her to her car where she has a well-stocked first-aid kit.

As far as he's concerned, their romance is off the ground. Like his kite, #3 is always sky high, darting here and there. What he admires in #4 is that she has her feet firmly planted on the ground and will hang on tight to keep him from flying out of control.

When he plans evenings that are long on dreams and short on realistic expectations, methodical #4 calls to make reservations and checks to see if they have gas in the car. In response to his extravagant gestures, she checks the budget and often races to the grocery store to buy the ingredients for coq au vin plus candles, to satisfy them both.

He gets the message fast to buy only gifts they can afford; she returns the ones that break the bank. She indulges him with adult toys, to a point, choosing a gadget that will help him balance his checkbook or get him to appointments on time.

Barring further collisions in their practical life, they can do some high flying in the bedroom. She can hang on to more than his kite string to get him down to her level, while her exacting memory for what he likes will keep him up all night. Her down-to-earth performances balance his off-the-wall fantasies; while he creates their bedroom games, she can keep score. Squeaky clean by nature, she encourages interludes in the tub that will leave them both gasping for air, while the toweling-off process will stimulate them right back into a cold shower.

Even though she's his most loyal fan, she may get sick of his jokes. Keeping his stories straight may not be her idea of a good time. His lack of routine and aversion to schedules can also test her patience severely. The point at which she becomes tired of assuming all the mundane responsibilities may pose a serious threat to their happy home.

When he pouts or has a temper tantrum, she'll think he's childish and out of control. He will find her logical recitation of the facts maddening, especially since she's usually right. Since stubborn #4 finds it hard to give in, lighthearted #3 will be the one to apologize. He may succeed by appealing to her logic, and she might return the favor by cajoling him with a few compliments.

Exuberant #3 and sedate #4 can open new vistas to each other. Until he comes along, she may not know the fun of eating pie for breakfast or the wonderful feeling of playing hookey. And he may not realize the pleasure of a secure home and future until a loyal, level-headed #4 crosses his path. As long as they learn to view their strengths as more important than their weaknesses, they'll be happy together.

THE NAME #3 WOMAN AND THE NAME #4 MAN

With her pile of chips scattered all over the table, the #3 WOMAN constantly needs to ask what number is point. Shooting craps certainly requires more concentration than dropping nickels into slot machines, and this gambler at heart is having trouble paying attention. She's distracted by the adorable man at the other end of the table who is calmly placing his bets without missing a beat. The more she watches #4, the more she wants to move closer to see exactly what he's doing.

Clutching her purse and chips in one hand, she nearly spills her drink as she slips in beside him. When there's a break in the action, #4 is suddenly aware of #3 and blinded by her smile. He is soon helping #3 place bets, and she is chattering nonstop until even the #4 strategy master finds himself losing track of the numbers. Encouraged by her obvious interest in him, #4 decides to abandon the game in favor of a more private spot where they can talk—without attracting more angry stares from the other players.

As different as day and night, the animated #3 WOMAN and the serious #4 MAN make a curious couple. While he is satisfied to figure out his game plan in a quiet corner, she is an impulsive gambler who loves the limelight. Optimistic #3 is sure she deserves credit for bringing him luck. Deliberate #4 insists that while she's the prettiest charm to grace his arm at the crap table, he won as a result of his system.

When cooperative #4 grows tired of the casino scene, he'll be delighted when innovative #3 comes up with a private little game of strip poker. No matter who loses, they both win. Settled in for an evening of play, she'll provide provocative gambling attire and refreshments to keep up their strength.

When she distracts him with her constant babbling and it dawns on him that she's quiet only when her mouth is full, he'll do his best to keep her occupied. Used to established routines, he'll find her spontaneity disarming. Fortunately for both of them, even a #3 likes some rigid structure from time to time.

As their relationship grows, they will have to make compromises. He may think she's silly and disorganized, and she may find him boring and overly responsible. When they fight, she will throw a tantrum and stamp her feet to get her way, and he will become silently determined to get his. If he's smart he'll walk away. Deprived of her audience, the #3 WOMAN usually comes around.

By allowing each other equal time, they can have a lasting love affair. She can let him work out his system in the casino while she gets a beauty treatment, and he can quietly cheer her on while she shines at a party.

THE NAME #3 MAN
AND THE NAME #5 WOMAN

Talkative #3 and curious #5 are telephone junkies. Searching for the latest in communication gadgetry, they meet at a local phone store. When #3 decides on an automatic dialer, he notices that she is looking at cellular models for her car. By the time they reach the cashier, they've admitted to a mutual addiction to Alexander Graham Bell's invention.

With a knowing look, flirtatious #3 tells her he likes to reach out and touch people; #5 responds that she likes to do it on the run. As they dash out the door, they agree to call each other as soon as their new toys are operational.

The first time he calls, he pushes the right buttons because she agrees that they should check out each other's equipment. She offers to take him around the block, and he invites her to his apartment to see that she's the first number on his automatic dialer.

Romancing by phone, they ring each other's bells morning and night. He never gets a busy signal from #5 because she works him into her already active life. She loves his spontaneous sense of humor and he understands her restless energy. Fond of parties, this popular couple are on constant call for the social circuit.

Their mutual passion for pleasure isn't limited to partying with friends. Able to find time alone only by unplugging their phones or turning on their answering machines, they are never at a loss for entertainment. Nowhere is their sense of adventure more evident than in the bedroom. She has an unlimited number of erotic delights to amuse #3, and he dares her with sexy messages.

The static on their line comes from both parties neglecting to slow down long enough to organize their lives or finish a project. When the phone goes dead there will be a huge argument over who didn't pay the bill. In the midst of #3's wordy tirade, #5 may hang up on him and take off for a much-needed change. Off the hook momentarily, she'll return when she's ready to give him the attention he demands.

Making up is easy if #5 understands that her spotlight-loving #3 MAN needs to be flattered; she can bring him around with a little sweet talk that turns into an all-night conversation.

244

THE NAME #3 WOMAN
AND THE NAME #5 MAN

Operating on overdrive, #5 nearly flattens #3 as he rushes into the deli to place an order for an impromptu party of twenty. Uncharacteristically silent, #3 has to catch her breath before she lets him have it. Just as she is about to launch a verbal assault, he apologizes profusely for his rudeness. Explaining his situation, he takes note of her trendy appearance and charming smile. Where has this irresistible creature been all his life?

Amused by her lighthearted repartee with the counterman about how lucky they are that she isn't suing for great bodily harm, #5 is unable to resist the impulse to invite her to his party. As crazy as it sounds, this is just the sort of invitation #3 loves; an optimist at heart, she figures the deli owner knows this #5 MAN. And with twenty other guests, she can look over the situation and leave if it isn't to her liking. As impulsive as he, she accepts, and their history has begun.

Charmed by the eclectic decor of his home, she asks about the various art objects he has collected on his travels and expresses her delight at the unconventional way in which they're arranged. Her gift of gab goes a long way to make the party a success, and she naturally falls into the role of hostess.

He's captivated by the way she lights up the group, and finally pulls her away from the crowd long enough to discuss their immediate future. How soon is it polite to tell people to go home so they can be alone?

His deli dish turns out to satisfy his taste for a little of this and a little of that. Focusing on her completely, he finds her to be a real delicacy in bed. Impatient with anything routine, #3 and #5 frolic from room to room playing imaginative games. Insatiable in his appetite for sensual pleasures, #5 puts #3's considerable vitality to the test and silences her for a second time in one day. Never at a loss for words, #3 knows that her speechless reaction is a profound sign of her deep attraction to #5.

Sharing a love of laughter and a cheery outlook, they make excellent goodwill ambassadors wherever they go. Ready to travel at the drop of a hat, #5 teaches #3 to keep their bags packed. A couple of freewheelers, they never plan and don't care if they get the last room in town.

As alike in their faults as they are in their strengths, neither one can stick to a deadline or complete a plan. They believe in playing first and doing everything else later, including doing the laundry and writing the rent check. If one can't take the responsibility to bring order into their lives, they'll have to hire a good accountant and a housekeeper.

When they have time to fight, it will involve their lack of control over the practical matters in their lives. After #3 pouts a while, her optimism will take over to minimize the severity of the crisis. #5 will suggest a major change in the way they do things to avoid repeating the mistake. They both look forward to kissing and making up; it's so much more fun than fighting.

Easily distracted, the #3/#5 couple is not one to set your watch by; they live in their own time zone, and it's the secret of their success. If they can take turns keeping each other focused on reality as well as they take turns entertaining each other, they are an unbeatable combination. Keeping a schedule is a small price to pay for unlimited laughs they are sure to enjoy.

THE NAME #3 MAN AND THE NAME #6 WOMAN

The whole is even better than the parts when the responsible #6 WOMAN and the entertaining #3 MAN join forces; their strengths complement one another in an uncanny way. She loves to give advice; he would rather have someone else give him the salient facts so he doesn't have to bother with them. She is full of common sense; he is full of clever ideas. Content to let him have his full share of the limelight, adaptable #6 willingly takes a back seat.

First attracted to each other by their love of luxurious things, they tend to extravagant or romantic gifts. Although they are tasteful in their selections, #6 may have to work on #3 until he understands that she wants a few small gems rather than dozens of spectacular paste copies. Romantic to the core, he'll order the perfect long-stemmed roses she likes and add balloons for his own satisfaction.

At home in the kitchen, she prefers to cook perfectly prepared scampi to going out for mass-produced lobster. With her added touch of soft lights and music, he'll agree that few restaurants can hold a candle to his capable #6, and he'll offer to take her out dancing for dessert.

From the day they first met at the health spa, fitness has dominated their relationship. Sharing saunas and jumping into whirlpools, they have toned their muscles as well as their relationship.

Popular with a variety of people, they find it difficult to make time for each other. At his best with an audience, #3 has plenty of attention from loyal, loving #6. Willing to follow him anywhere, she regards his every wish as her command; when he wants to be with her, she'll happily lock the doors and concentrate only on him. Anointing him with the wonderful oils they bought at the spa, she'll arouse his tenderest feelings. Inspired by her touch, he can massage her every muscle to ultimate relaxation.

By flattering his ego and adjusting to his imaginative lifestyle, #6 can keep their relationship solid. As long as she curtails her tendency to give too much advice, the smitten #3 will idolize his dependable mate.

Anxious to avoid arguments at any price, she will give in to most of his whims and resort to harsh words only when she feels he's not being fair. Even when he avoids his responsibilities in favor of recreation, she'll rationalize his behavior rather than scream and shout. When they do have their rare arguments, #6 will give in to #3's pouting.

The key to improving their relationship is better communication; talkative #3 may have to tape up his mouth from time to time and pay attention to what #6 is saying.

Rendezvous at the health spa can keep their romance bursting with vim and vigor, taking massage classes together will give them ideas for endless amusement. Keeping a full stock of scented oils on hand, and using them often, can keep their romance in motion even when their bones begin to creak from old age.

THE NAME #3 WOMAN
AND THE NAME #6 MAN

The social butterfly of the artsy set, the #3 WOMAN is a sought-after guest at gallery openings. At the center of his own attentive circle, the #6 MAN is the loyal friend who provided the artist many a meal during his lean years. Even from opposite ends of the exhibit, #3 and #6 noticed each other right away. He's taken by her animated personality and youthful good looks, while she's drawn to his warmhearted, caring manner.

Catching her eye, #6 has a hard time breaking away from his friends who, as usual, want his advice. Finally able to make his move, he rescues #3 with a glass of champagne. Although she loves the spotlight in a group, she's flattered when he singles her out. Her dazzling smile and animated chatter are hard to resist. Proposing a toast to the success of their artist friend, he gets a word in when she drinks to his sentiments.

Amused by his stale line, #3 nevertheless accepts #6's invitation to see his extensive collection of paintings from their artist friend's early years. Not content to see only the artwork, she's intrigued by the good taste displayed throughout his home. Obviously a lover of beauty and quality, #6 has made his home as comfortable as it is artistic.

Flattered by #3's sincere compliments, #6 courts her with caviar and candlelight and is only too happy to let electric #3 set the pace. With her creative fingers she introduces him to the joys of dabbling with body paint. Posing for fantasy paintings, #3 is in her element. #6 faces the challenge of getting her to hold her pose long enough to complete his picture. Only a #6 could adapt his brushstrokes so well to her every whim.

When insatiable #3 wants even more attention than he already gives, nurturing #6 will go out of his way to comply. With his champagne tastes and her penchant for parties, their lives will never lack fun and excitement. Both look for the best in each other and are determined to please. Home-loving #6 fills their nest with fun and games to keep her by the fire, while optimistic #3 adds sunshine and beauty to his life.

Arguments will occur when #3 fails to keep commitments or talks too much. If #6 tells her a picture is worth a million words, she'd better listen; it takes a lot of pent-up anger to elicit harsh words from #6. Neither can tolerate hostility, so they work hard to mend a rift. Flattering each other into a quick compromise, they'll rush to put on their artist's smocks for a rousing session with the brushes.

Still posing for each other when they're old and gray, this couple can have a long and harmonious romance. He'll always lure her with his etchings, and she'll charm his smock off year after happy year.

THE NAME #3 MAN
AND THE NAME #7 WOMAN

The analytical #7 WOMAN has resolved to test the waterbeds thoroughly before buying one. There she is, flat on her back, gently undulating in full view of the salesman and a gathering crowd of customers. As soon as she's satisfied with the comfort for one occupant, she realizes the need for a partner to make the test valid.

The outgoing #3 MAN would love to share her bed. As he removes his tie with a flourish, he announces how flattered he is that she chose him. Enjoying the attention from the other customers, he plays his role to the hilt while #7 calmly asks the salesman a few more questions and places her order.

Intrigued by the lengths to which she is going to qualify her purchase, #3 is attracted by the possibility of introducing an element of fun into her serious pursuit. He floats through life on youthful good looks and charm, and his act-first-think-later style is in direct contrast to her methodical manner.

When he tells her that the least she can do is have dinner with him now that they've slept together, she rewards him with a smile. Off to an auspicious beginning, they exit the store on a wave of applause from the customers.

The courtship of this discriminating pair takes them from one elegant spot to another, with a few cultural events thrown in for good measure. Not one to reveal her true feelings, she keeps him guessing while thoroughly enjoying his entertaining monologues. He learns quickly that she is finicky about her possessions and keys his gifts to fit her refined tastes.

Able to jolly her out of her quiet moods, the #3 MAN discovers she's a nature lover with a passion not solely limited to the study of science. More straightforward than her public persona, her private side is very sensual. Still waters run deep, and impulsive #3 is only too happy to take the plunge.

When it's time to redecorate, he dreams of a luxurious display. Full of ideas, he brings home the samples only to have her choose the most refined colors and patterns and request plants for a natural touch. He may also have trouble understanding her need for privacy while she may have problems with his open-door policy.

Their differences over his many friends and her preference for a select group may also cause arguments. The angrier she becomes, the more silent she is; #3 noisily shows his displeasure, then enters a period of sulking. Giving her time alone proves the most reasonable road to reconciliation. The cure for #3's poor humor is distracting him with an activity that offers more excitement.

#7 must learn to speak without analyzing every word in order to hold her own against chatty #3. To please her, he has to concentrate on being more practical and less extravagant. Better communication and strict reliance on the truth are the secrets to maintaining this relationship.

THE NAME #3 WOMAN AND THE NAME #7 MAN

Eyeing the ADULTS ONLY shelf at the video rental store while ordering a couple of PG-rated movies, the gregarious #3 WOMAN can't go anywhere without attracting attention. She's just noticed a #7 MAN who's quietly ordering by number several X-rated tapes from the counter catalog. Without thinking, she blurts out, "So that's how you do it!" Amused at her candor and turned on by her obvious interest in his selections, he explains that there's nothing to it. Heads together, they spend several minutes going over the titles.

Never at a loss for words, #3 quickly admits that the titles alone don't tell you much. She wonders how you can tell which ones you want to see without reading the blurb on the cover. After telling her that they're all alike, he takes her gently by the hand and leads her to "the" shelf. When she objects, he offers the alternative of having a private conference over a cup of coffee. Rolling her eyes, impulsive #3 agrees.

Razzle-dazzle #3 and analytical #7 are proof that opposites attract. It's no accident that their X-rated tastes bring them together. Spotlight-loving #3 has found the perfect partner in #7, who can adjust the lights with scientific precision so that her best side always shows and she's the center of attention. Leaving not one word unspoken or feeling unexpressed, she provides enough gaiety for them both while #7 observes from the sidelines and keeps his thoughts to himself. It's hard to imagine aloof #7 losing his cool—even with the exuberant, outrageous #3 company he keeps.

Deep and mysterious, his sensual side is as imaginative as fun-loving #3's. When it comes to collaborating on their own X-rated plot, some of his intimate scenarios may shock even the unflappable #3. An elaborate planner, he can conjure up fantasies that will magically render her speechless. He always finishes what he starts and manages to keep something in reserve. Able to live up to all her exaggerations, the #7 MAN may use bizarre techniques to elicit her deliciously illicit behavior.

Her noise often destroys his quiet, and her penchant for crowds doesn't fit in with his desire for a few select companions. Particularly maddening for #7 is impulsive #3's disregard for his carefully laid plans. When the power of their opposite personalities works against them, #7 may turn on the silent treatment, to which #3 must respond by biting her tongue. When #3 throws a temper tantrum and pouts, #7 should give up trying to analyze her and rely on the one thing they have in common. A quiet evening at home with a few inspirational movies should do wonders to restore his #3 video star to her sensual self.

THE NAME #3 MAN AND THE NAME #8 WOMAN

The #3 MAN's idea of the perfect ski weekend is catching the high mountain rays on the sun deck by day and exercising his elbow over hot buttered rum by night. The #8 WOMAN is a serious competitor on the slopes, pushing herself harder and faster on each run. Dressed in the latest and the best, she's the center of attention when she enters the lodge to warm up at the end of the day.

#3 is used to the spotlight himself, but is only too happy to move over for the attractive #8 WOMAN. Aroused by his enthusiastic invitation and sense of repartee, she agrees to join him by the fire. Their first impressions are favorable; show-stopping #3 and striking #8 are immediately aware of the stunning picture they make together.

A master with words, #3 works his magic on #8, who flatters him with attention and an invitation to join her on the slopes the next day. So long as she varies the runs for him, and they have a chance to chat and get acquainted in the lift lines, #3 is delighted to pursue her and his tan. Though he prefers the camaraderie and physical comfort of the hot tub to strenuous skiing, he has the vitality and versatility to meet any challenge #8 can offer.

With a tendency to gad about and scatter his energy, #3 benefits from the stable influence of #8. In particular, during intimate moments her powers of concentration can keep him on the right track. Willing to struggle against obstacles to achieve a goal, she finds a willing partner in #3, who will happily put a few bumps on her path and see to it that downhill progress is interrupted with a good-sized tree here and there. A lighthearted lover, #3 can vary his game plan to keep #8 challenged for hours.

Both like to spend money to enhance their image; they live at a fashionable address and drive the "right" cars, a classy one for #8 and a flashy one for #3. They also wear the "right" clothes, thanks to designers who use their logos conspicuously.

When she works too hard and wears herself out, he can convince her not to take things so seriously; #3 believes that all work and no play makes life dull. Occasionally finding #3's behavior frivolous, #8 may chide him for his vain and childish antics. Once displayed, her anger is short-lived. Clever #3 will win the day if he can appeal to #8's logic, and #8 will soothe his wounds with a few well-placed compliments.

Their endless store of new ideas will keep the relationship exciting, and their willingness to focus on each other's needs will help their romance survive the avalanche of time.

THE NAME #3 WOMAN
AND THE NAME #8 MAN

Excited by the sound and speed of the cars, the #3 WOMAN is thoroughly enjoying a day at the races with a group of auto enthusiasts. On the lookout for the #8 driver, she's heard that he's got it all—money, power, and success. A corporate executive, he's a health and exercise nut who enjoys the challenge of controlling the fastest machine he can find.

When her friends decide to go to the restaurant where the drivers and mechanics eat after the race, #3 enters with her usual burst of glory in hopes of attracting #8's attention. In control of the situation from the moment she cracks her first joke, he is aware of her presence and her attempt to engineer a casual meeting. Her sense of style and tasteful designer-sportswear touch a familiar, status-conscious chord in #8. Despite his attraction to his eye-catching fan, he decides to play hard to get.

From the starting flag to every satisfying finish, he's in the driver's seat. She loves being a part of his social scene as much as he enjoys having a fun-loving fashion plate on his arm. Adorable, impulsive #3 is at her best with an audience and the hit of every party. Even though she's busy herself, she sees to it that workaholic #8 takes time to play.

Their intimate moments are a test of his athletic skills and her creativity. Admiring each other's finely tuned engines and stopping only to refuel, these racy lovers enjoy lap after lap of record performances. Since they both like to get their way, they may have to take turns in the driver's seat.

Well-suited to each other, they can turn their attraction into a long-lasting partnership. Her social skills benefit his business, and his management technique can turn her creative ideas into money-making endeavors.

The last of the big-time spenders, they buy whatever they want; he directs his dollar toward status symbols such as cars and jewelry, while she buys faddish items that he thinks are silly. Another sore point is her constant use of the phone. Her best bet is to humor him when she wants to get her way.

Keeping their romance alive requires a few rejuvenating trips to the spa, where she can maintain her youthful appearance and he can improve his already impressive physique. Limited only by their financial resources, this couple has nothing but miles of straight track ahead of them.

THE NAME #3 MAN
AND THE NAME #9 WOMAN

Appearing back to back on a TV talk show, the outgoing #3 MAN and the inspirational #9 WOMAN first meet in the studio's "green room." Scheduled to make an appeal for an international relief organization, she wants to meet #3 because she's heard he's doing a super job promoting a local fund-raiser. Taken by his boyish charm, she watches him chatting with the makeup artist. Little does she know that #3 spotted her long before, when she greeted her friends in the studio with a flurry of hugs and kisses.

On the air, his innovative ideas inspire #9 to see her job in a new light, while he's moved by her sincerity. After the taping they explore the similarity of their interests. Long on dreams and short on practicality, they both love art, music, and traveling. He shares her bent toward the extravagant and proves it by sending an elaborate arrangement of flowers with a note asking her for a date. Easily impressed, #9 is completely taken by #3's flamboyant style and his silver tongue.

Their social life is a whirlwind of charity balls, board meetings, and art openings. Entertaining #3 shines socially with #9's large, diverse group of friends as his audience. When they are alone at last, he's only too happy to continue his show because she's such an admiring fan.

Never has he met a more giving woman; selfless in her desire to please, #9 sees to his every comfort. He eats up the attention and is very good at telling her just what he wants and how good it feels. Fortunately for him, she's a perfectionist who is willing to keep trying until she achieves results. With only the slightest encouragement, she'll give until she drops.

Their arguments will center on the fact that she falls prey to everyone's requests. Compassionate #9 may deplete her reserves long before she gets home; envious of her contacts and jealous of the time she spends on them, #3 may get tired of laughing off the evenings she cancels in order to recuperate. He goes along with her universal approach as long as he's the center of it when they are together.

When he complains, she may be tempted to point out the wide gulf between his selfish posture and her magnanimity. Their tearful arguments will be full of high drama and emotional speeches. Understanding #9 will give in when #3 insists upon getting his way. #9 is so forgiving, and #3 is such an optimist, that neither of them holds a grudge.

To keep him happy, #9 must cancel a few meetings when #3 gets the urge to play; knowing that he adores her public displays of affection, she can always set the right mood by showing the whole world how much she loves him. In return, he must show that he not only treasures her loving nature, but also admires her altruism.

In a relationship where there is so much love and the innate ability to express it, there can be much happiness and fulfillment.

THE NAME #3 WOMAN AND THE NAME #9 MAN

The #3 WOMAN really wanted to learn *parler Français* when she signed up for the class. But now her attention has shifted to parlaying her presence into a romantic relationship with her gallant #9 classmate. Distracted by her admiring glances, he's having trouble keeping his tenses straight, although learning the feminine forms of adjectives has never been easier. *Belle* this and *bonne* that make him daydream about her, and the electricity that flies across the room could light the Eiffel Tower.

A law-abiding type, he abandons the idea of breaking into her bedroom and forcing her to study with him all night. An offer for café au lait after class would be much more civil. She accepts enthusiastically, and they're soon discussing French culture at the bistro. The next thing he knows, he's explaining the origin of French kissing and suggesting they do some homework at his place.

Coy in class, #3 is more demonstrative in public; she hangs on his arm and every word as they move in his social circle. Fascinated by #9's unusual mix of friends, #3 enjoys the way #9 expands her horizons.

Convincing her that she shouldn't limit her French to what is available in class, he liberally shares his knowledge of worldly ways in the boudoir. An enthusiastic participant in his tutoring session, she is soon able to wrap her tongue around the most difficult syllables. Speechless with delight over his conjugation of verbs in a conjugal setting, #3 passionately moves from one action verb to another and matches him superlative for superlative.

#9 seems to comprehend the intimate workings of #3's mind. He's sympathetic to her need for attention and only too happy to let his fellow pupil shine in class. A generous man, he attracts many others who'd like to improve their skills; sharing him may be more than #3 bargained for.

When she doesn't get her way, a loud argument may ensue. Vociferous #3 and verbal #9 are capable of a shouting match, but it won't last long. Quick to forgive and forget, #9 is always the first to give in; he can't stand to see his beloved pout over lack of attention.

Though she may never completely understand his humanitarian motives, she must accept them if the relationship is to continue. To keep her happy, #9 must reserve time for private instruction on a regular basis.

THE NAME #4 MAN AND THE NAME #4 WOMAN

In the office parking lot, the #4 MAN counts on seeing the #4 WOMAN every day. At precisely 8:15 A.M. she drives her economy car into the spot next to his and carefully records her mileage. He admires her well-groomed, conservative appearance and her obvious respect for routine.

In the habit of checking their appointment books in the elevator, they seldom do more than nod. Once he finally resolves to offer a noncommittal "good morning," her enthusiastic response prompts him to ask her for a date. Taken by his equally sedate appearance and punctual habits, she enjoys the attention of this #4 MAN. Consulting her calendar, she says she's booked up with her regular Wednesday evening grocery shopping and other week-night routines. Fortunately, Friday is free for both of them.

Once written into both calendars, their romance progresses rapidly. Compatible right down to the kind of detergent they use, the #4 pair soon fall into a comfortable routine of weeknight dates at the Laundromat and Saturdays cleaning their cars.

These do-it-yourselfers enjoy helping each other paint and paper their new apartments. Attending the local swap meets for bargain pieces to refinish is the highlight of their weekend. From one practical project to the next, their love and respect for each other grow.

The #4 approach to sexual pleasure is as orderly as the rest of their lives, with emphasis on the conventional. Seldom impulsive and never irresponsible, they make up for it by stressing a steady venture of technically outstanding performances. Mutual satisfaction is their common goal; neither ever forgets what pleases the other most.

Building their relationship on a firm foundation of high standards and a desire to achieve tangible results, #4s are usually very content. They agree on the need to do things the right way and to finish projects on time. Since thrift is also a common goal, they never argue about repairing or replacing a household item.

With unforeseen differences accounted for in their master plan, fights that disrupt their schedule are rare. Usually over petty things such as misplaced twist ties and dirty screens, these differences are difficult for logical, stubborn #4s to resolve. Comparing their lists on the salient points of the argument, each relents only when sure the other has learned a valuable lesson.

They make their relationship work by carving out areas of responsibility. Taking occasional detours to keep themselves from getting into a rut is imperative, even if it requires some checking beforehand to see if the side road is a worthy path.

THE NAME #4 MAN AND THE NAME #5 WOMAN

Always in a rush, the #5 WOMAN enters the post office with a pile of Christmas presents stacked dangerously high in her arms.

She's the picture of disorganization as she gathers overnight delivery forms and moves from line to line. In desperation, #5 asks the first man she sees to watch her pile so she can retrieve her checkbook from under the front seat of the car. Even though he's already bought his out-of-town gifts through a discount catalog and is only checking his post office box, the patient #4 MAN agrees to hold her place in line.

Curious to see the outcome of her melodrama, he stays around to help her fill out her forms. A tiny part of him admires a free spirit who can live off the cuff, though he is the exact opposite. When she thanks him profusely and insists that he join her for pie and coffee next door, he is flattered and fascinated by her spontaneous approach. From #5's point of view, this #4 MAN is like nothing she's ever experienced; he's a model of meticulous order. Convinced that she can't make it across the street without him, #4 decides to pursue #5 for her own safety and consults his pocket calender for a date.

Arriving on time, #4 proudly presents a flabbergasted #5 with her very own ZIP code directory (she'd expected flowers or wine). Carefully stacking the newspapers and magazines she's scattered on the couch, he makes a space to sit down while she finishes getting ready. What a challenge her apartment presents to a systems man like #4; he's already making detailed plans.

Content to work her way into his schedule, the #5 WOMAN is delighted by the prospect of bringing some variety into his life. She treats him to picnic dinners at his office when he works late, and surprises him at the Laundromat with an ice cream cone.

Public displays of affection or extravagant spending habits aren't #4's style. He prefers quiet evenings to expensive meals at ostentatious restaurants.

#5 is flexible and will try anything once. The fact that she provides the diversion his life has been lacking is nowhere more important than in bed. Still shaking his head over some of the new games she instigates, he has to agree she has what it takes to shake him out of his rut. As bored with the same old routine as he was bound to it, she reminds him of their first meeting and says it's only fair if she teaches him some new ways to play post office.

Balancing their strengths, she learns to make lists, and he tries to be more flexible. The problems occur when she loses the lists and he gets a pain in the neck from having to bend too much. Set in his ways, he tends to argue about money and everything else his scattered #5 misplaces. When he gets stubborn, she tries to distract him. When she goes off on a tangent, he tries to use logic.

Agreeing to disagree, they must appreciate the positive influence they exert on each other. If she can be content to surprise him by staying on schedule, and he can block out periods of unplanned time for "spontaneous activity," their relationship has a future. Eventually she will figure out how to minimize the frequency of the emergencies he's always prepared for. They need each other so much, they are bound to be happy.

THE NAME #4 WOMAN
AND THE NAME #5 MAN

The only man in his shirt sleeves, fumbling with the tire chains, has to be a #5. He left the desert floor for the mountains without listening to the weather forecast. Now that it's snowing, he congratulates himself that at least he had chains in the car.

Unlike #5, the #4 WOMAN is prepared for any emergency; not only does she have chains, she has gloves and is wearing overalls over her cold-weather duds. She's good with her hands and squares away her car in a flash. Taking pity on him, she looks over his situation and explains at length why nothing will work. In a moment of brilliance, #5 assures her that he's relatively harmless, suggests that she frisk him for a concealed weapon, and begs for a ride up the hill. When he promises her everything from a hot buttered rum to his firstborn son, she decides for once in her life to take a chance; off they go in her car up the snowy mountain.

Never again will making a date be so easy. His schedule is always frenzied and hers is cast in concrete. Dashing into the hotel bar late as usual, #5 is carrying the biggest bunch of fresh flowers he could find on such short notice. Completely taken by the vision of #4 without her overalls, he sets out to woo her. Suddenly feeling almost giddy with excitement, cautious #4 is completely swept off her feet by impulsive #5.

Romancing their way from dawn to dawn, extravagant #5 and frugal #4 strike the first of many compromises. She stops him from buying her every bauble he sees, and he convinces her to shop at the gourmet takeout when she insists on packing picnic lunches herself.

Their evenings are the most romantic she has ever known. His creativity and zest for varied sexual pleasures tests even her legendary endurance. When he reminds her that it was chains that brought them together, she takes him seriously, but only for a moment.

They will argue about priorities; fun's at the top of his list, while hard work heads hers. And his need for variety will run head on into her aversion to change. He may succeed in proving to her that a different approach is in order, but she'll never convince him that keeping his nose to the grindstone beats having a good time.

#5 has it in him to keep their relationship exciting, while #4 maintains its stability. As long as she sees the value of his adventurous spirit, and he is appreciative when she bails him out, they should be happy.

THE NAME #4 MAN AND THE NAME #6 WOMAN

The #6 WOMAN stops at the village bakery to buy fresh bread twice a week. Treating herself to pastry and a cup of coffee she wonders about the attractive man who comes in every Thursday.

Sure enough, the #4 MAN arrives on schedule, list in hand. Annoyed when the clerk tells him the cinnamon buns aren't ready, he glances at his watch impatiently. To placate him, the clerk offers coffee while he waits. He agrees, but only if he can use the phone to call the office about the change in his timetable.

Delighted at the prospect of making his acquaintance, #6 offers advice about the most comfortable place to sit and suggests that he try the same pastry she's eating. Between bites they discuss the merits of the bakery's confections; she stresses their quality ingredients while he notes the fair prices.

When his order is ready, she's intrigued by his explanation of the precise assortment. Certain pastries are for immediate use since they are best eaten fresh; others that take well to freezing can be heated in the microwave during the week. Still others are day-old bargains he couldn't resist. It's obvious to #6 that this orderly man lives alone, and her heart goes out to him.

Flattered by her solicitous manner, #4 congratulates himself on a few minutes well-spent. He makes a mental note to escalate the relationship, ensuring their next meeting with a "See you next Thursday at the crack of dawn." From the drift of her conversation he deduces that she's a connoisseur of art as well as food, so he plans to invite her to use his museum guest pass on Saturday.

#4 is further impressed after their date; why, she's able to identify more paintings than he is. While he decorates his walls with a succession of prints borrowed from the library, she is making monthly payments on an original oil because she prefers one good item of quality to several of lesser worth.

The dinner she cooks him is proof of the pudding, and the freshly squeezed orange juice and pastry she bakes the next morning are equally perfect. Only the incessant phone intrudes on their idyllic tryst; obviously she has many friends whom she nurtures with practical advice.

Efficient #4 and responsible, charismatic #6 form a unique partnership from their first meeting in the bakery. Loyal to family and friends, they are equally loyal to each other. She loves to please, and he has an unnerving memory for every little squeeze she requires. Dependable lovers, each one seeks to satisfy the other; he fills her needs with first-quality ingredients, and there is nothing flaky about her consistent response.

#6 can adjust to #4's meticulous ways, but #4 has a hard time putting up with #6's constant stream of needy friends. The cost of her nonstop entertaining and her penchant for luxury causes budget-conscious #4 to complain. She hates disharmony and will give in to his requests by barring their door to visitors temporarily and agreeing to attic insulation as a cost-saving measure. He will give in to her desire for new furniture only if she can prove to him that re-covering the old is almost as expensive as buying new.

She can try to keep things exciting by planning a wine-and-cheese-tasting evening alone by the fire. If #4 can take a break from his normal routine to savor the moment and not choke over the price of the wine, the romantic interlude will be a success. Their best bet is a bakery treat shared in bed—provided #4 doesn't object to the crumbs.

THE NAME #4 WOMAN
AND THE NAME #6 MAN

The #6 MAN is standing in line to do some banking for a sick friend. It isn't even his bank, but how could he say no to a friend. The #4 WOMAN is anxious to reinvest her CDs and be on her way in no more than thirty minutes, otherwise her afternoon errand schedule will be ruined.

Sensing her obvious impatience, #6 decides to come to her rescue. It looks like a long wait; he suggests that if she says "yes" they could probably celebrate their first anniversary by the time they reach the teller. Rewarding him with a lovely smile, #4 gratefully accepts his proposal . . . to chat while they pass the time.

A few minutes into their conversation she decides that getting to know this obviously nice man is more worthwhile than picking up her only silk dress at the cleaners. And if he asks her out to dinner, it won't make any difference if she doesn't get to the supermarket. The way their conversation is progressing, she can tell he's an upright, responsible type. By the time the line ends they've traded life histories and made a date for dinner.

A lover of home and family, #6 makes good on his estimate, a short courtship. He smiles when she protests that a plant would be more practical than the dozen roses he brings. Telling her she deserves the long-stemmed beauties, he continues to do everything he can to give her the best.

She's the tidiest housekeeper he's ever seen, and he actually enjoys letting her loose in his coveted kitchen. Given the passing parade of his family and friends, she's never sure whether to prepare dinner for two or twenty. While he may be a more creative cook, she is a competent one who can work circles around him.

Finding something to do after dinner is usually not a problem for sensual #6; he can't wait to usher their guests out the door to have time alone with his #4 WOMAN. She loves to make his romantic investments pay big dividends by putting herself in a high-yield position.

Loyal to each other, both of them want a stable, long-lasting relationship. The #6 MAN will do anything to avoid an argument, which can make him physically ill. He tries hard to adjust to #4's ways to keep peace. When trouble brews, he appeals to her sense of logic in an effort to change her mind. He knows that if he can prove to her that he's right, she will try to see things his way. She may be stubborn, but he's fair-minded and will give her the benefit of the doubt. In order to make up to him, #4 may apologize with a sentimental gift, even if it strains her budget.

These two are basically kind and responsible, which are two qualities that make for a stable relationship. They both want the best for each other and are willing to work hard to keep each other happy.

THE NAME #4 MAN AND THE NAME #7 WOMAN

To the inquisitive #7 WOMAN a bookstore is bliss on a rainy Saturday afternoon. Since she can't be outside communing with nature, explorer's guides offer an interesting alternative.

The #4 MAN in the next aisle is on a mission; he wants a specific computer-programming book so he can set up his own system and avoid buying costly software.

Overhearing his questions, #7 admires his precise approach, knows just what #4 needs, and offers to help. Ordinarily reserved, she is at her best socially when the subject interests her. Together they peruse every book in the computer section: #4 categorizes according to their suitability for his project, and #7 subcategorizes according to the table of contents and index. Appreciative of her advice, serious #4 is delighted to meet someone as thorough as he is.

Since it's nearly closing time when they finish, #4 thinks it's only fair to compensate the #7 WOMAN for her assistance by offering a glass of wine. As they walk to the bar she's suggested, he decides that if it goes well he might spring for a spaghetti dinner. Discovering that her life is far from an open book, #4 finds himself answering all her questions. His patience is tested at the same time his interest is piqued. At the end of their first evening together, he knows #7 holds her wine well, eats spaghetti like a lady, and likes him well enough to divulge her phone number.

A cozy pairing in the romance category, #4 and #7 make a devoted couple. Able to stir her feelings with his tender loving care, sentimental #4 discovers the hidden content of his #7

WOMAN when he turns the right pages. Uninhibited in the extreme when she trusts her partner, #7 reads like a torrid novel in response to dependable #4. The kind who finishes what she starts, #7 rewards his endurance with actions that speak louder than words.

Planners of the highest caliber, neither one is impulsive. Thrifty #4 and discriminating #7 spend their money and time wisely. On a Friday night they're quite content to stay at home; she helps him research the latest budget programs and he devises a catalog for her rock collection.

Behind closed doors they may disagree, especially when #7 wants to be alone or #4 becomes too fixed in his schedule. Comfortable in their predictable routines, neither wants to disrupt life for long over a disagreement that can be settled efficiently. Their reconciliations are as undramatic as their fights. Sentimental #4 may choose a quiet spaghetti dinner for two, while #7 suggests a trip to #4's favorite bookstore.

THE NAME #4 WOMAN AND THE NAME #7 MAN

The new salesman at the sporting goods store has been on the job for only two weeks, and already he feels like a failure. The #4 WOMAN is asking him a million questions about sleeping bags while the #7 MAN walks by and chimes in. Perfect strangers, they double-team the salesman on backpacks, tents, and stoves; if she doesn't think to ask about pounds per square inch, he will.

They read every word of the guarantees and talk prices like a couple of serious buyers. With "Thanks, I'll think about it" and "I want to look around," they walk out together without making one purchase.

It isn't that #4 and #7 have trouble making up their minds, it's just that they need proof that a product will perform the way it's supposed to before they buy. Immediately aware of their common interests, they retire to the nearest restaurant to read the free brochures #4 collected.

She admires his meticulous table manners and the way he carefully considers his comments. #7 likes #4's practical approach to buying equipment and her attention to detail. When he asks if she'd like to take in another store, she says yes, and not just because she likes sales. Practical and pretty #4's making a conquest of nature-loving #7.

Fanning the spark generated in the sporting goods store, they turn their relationship into a roaring fire. Wooing her with words of wisdom rather than lavish gifts, #7 discovers a partner who's as disciplined and orderly as he is. He admires the way she makes lists and stays within her budget. Agreeing with his taste in books and movies, she's glad that he's so discriminating.

Not the most active members of the social circuit, these two are content with home entertainment. When he wants to go over his topographical maps, she's only too happy to clean out a few drawers or iron his underwear.

Perfectionist #4 loves to plan romantic backpacking trips, weighing every portion of trail mix and carefully packing their new equipment. On the trail, he explains the geological origin of each rock formation and she catalogs their discoveries. In camp, she lays out the position of their tent and admires the precise way in which he pounds in the stakes. Now that #7 trusts his dependable #4, he's free to reveal the kinky side of his nature. Snug in their double down bag, they get back to basics with only the bare necessities.

Often reluctant to express their true feelings, this pair can experience a breakdown in communication. If she tries to rush him or asks too many questions, he may withdraw. The price he pays for his silence is cold-shoulder treatment from stubborn #4. It will take them a while to warm up, since #4, who likes to have business as usual, will pick up and go on, while #7 continues to feel misunderstood.

The secret of their consuming love is that they are loyal and dependable. A couple of camping trips each year and a down comforter at home will keep their romance aglow.

THE NAME #4 MAN
AND THE NAME #8 WOMAN

While the other car-wash customers browse in the gift shop, the #4 MAN uses his calculator to figure his mileage and expense record. Soon joined by the #8 WOMAN, who immediately pulls out her briefcase, he approves of her industrious manner and her well-heeled appearance.

While she points out a grease spot on the fender of her shiny new sports car, he finds black marks on the whitewalls of his classic. Their eyes meet as the two cars are whisked away to be washed again. He admires the way she took control of the situation, and she applauds his desire for perfection.

When they discover they are neighbors with a shared interest in exercise and fitness, she assumes his invitation to jog means the roof of the exclusive, local health club. To her surprise he stops at the park across the street and produces a cooler of mineral water and two beautiful red apples for after their run. The Ritz it isn't, but at least he's thought of everything.

As their courtship progresses, frugal #4 must make a conscious decision to invest in a few extravagant evenings if he's going to hang on to luxury-loving #8. The perfectionist in him is completely taken by her clear vision of what she wants in life and her organized approach to achieving success.

Their love life probably starts when determined #8 persuades her conservative #4 to straighten a crooked picture in her bedroom. Patiently waiting for the right moment to make her move, #8 discovers that dignified #4 makes a sentimental lover capable of spending long hours to achieve complete satisfaction for his partner. Nowhere is his slow, steady approach more appreciated than in the bedroom. Not content merely to fix her pictures, he's willing to perform any other handyman's services she requires.

The #4 MAN is amazed by the amount of money the #8 WOMAN spends on status symbols. It's incredible—she turns in her sports car for a new one every year. Even a tenacious #4 is no match for a strong-willed #8, who can cite all the logical reasons for maintaining her image in the community. Overcoming all his objections, she will persuade him to see things her way. In an effort to be reasonable he may relent, but only because she's convinced him her move is not irresponsible.

As long as they agree on their goals and work together, they should have a happy, successful future. Her visions of grandeur are just what he needs to get out of his rut. She can keep things exciting by seeing to it that #4 is properly rewarded for all his hard work. Who knows, he might even get used to her new red sports car, as long as she pulls up to the self-serve pump when he's along for the ride.

THE NAME #4 WOMAN
AND THE NAME #8 MAN

Faced with the prospect of entertaining ten-year-old nephews for the weekend, the #8 MAN and the #4 WOMAN find themselves touring the Museum of Science and Industry. She wants to impart the work ethic to her spoiled charge, while he wants to inspire his future tycoon with stories of great inventors. Drawn together by their serious mission, #4 and #8 soon join forces while the boys make faces at each other.

Marveling at #4's patience, #8 also appreciates the systematic way she slowly but surely works her way through the entire exhibit. It's easy to see that the boys are getting bored, so #8 takes charge with a lively lecture on the material success achieved by each inventor. Determined to make the most of the encounter, #8 whisks them all off to a restaurant #4 insisted was much too formal for the boys. Overcoming her objections, he orders steaks all around and she's impressed by his generosity.

Attracted by her affectionate, down-to-earth manner, #8 decides she has the makings of a wonderful helpmate. Their courtship is a whirlwind of expensive dates designed to impress #4, who never stops telling #8 it isn't necessary. Persuading her to accept his luxurious way of life is just the kind of challenge #8 enjoys.

Carrying the struggle into bed is the ultimate thrill for #8 as he discovers the depth of her warmth. Once they've established a routine for their intimate encounters, they find how compatible they really are. She's inspired by the intensity of his desires, and welcomes the obligation to satisfy his needs. With a loyal and loving mate behind him, #8 is assured of reaching the heights of personal satisfaction as well as material success.

To the delight of busy #8, self-sufficient #4 doesn't require much hand holding; she happily assumes total responsibility for their home, keeping them well cared for and solvent. Eventually she comes to appreciate #8's reasons for upgrading their surroundings and her wardrobe to reflect more positively on his business image.

In his desire to maintain control during arguments, #8 may become emotional, while #4 digs in her heels. In the end, #8 always wins by appealing to reason and stressing the just solution. Loyal to her man, #4 comes around after she's had a chance to think about it.

This industrious pair will build a strong bond over the years. Although they both enjoy working, they must remember how to play with each other. An active sport is the perfect outlet for them both. She will enjoy tracking their steady improvement and tangible results of their efforts, while he covets the competitive aspect and their trophies.

THE NAME #4 MAN
AND THE NAME #9 WOMAN

An early morning regular at garage and rummage sales, the #4 MAN possesses a good eye for design and value. He's often found treasures, but never one as outstanding as the #9 WOMAN running this sale.

Gathering her many friends to help, she has worked herself to a frazzle. When #4 asks for a price on a beautiful, yet infinitely practical, pewter mug, she admires his taste and generously quotes him a low price. Snapping up the bargain, he decides to repay her by offering to lend a hand; it would give him first crack at hidden treasures and allow him to become better acquainted with #9.

Sentimental #4 sometimes finds it difficult to express his emotions. Watching #9 move happily among her friends, he suddenly wants some of her warmth to come his way. He's bothered by a few of the more eccentric helpers and longs to have #9 all to himself. His patience and perseverance are rewarded when he asks her to lunch, and she accepts, leaving her faithful followers behind to tend the sale.

Responding to his steady, endearing manner, #9 yields to his constant attention and they settle into a dating pattern of his design. He balks at the price of her charity balls until she cajoles him and appeals to his lofty ideals. In return, he helps her become more realistic about the results of her free-handed spending.

Tempering her financial extravagance, he does nothing to dampen her romantic generosity. She touches his heart with the sincerity of her love; in return, he patiently fulfills her desires. Accepting his regular donations, she continues to come up with new ways to stimulate and repay his generosity.

Easily influenced by others, #9 often squanders her energies. Conflict arises when his patience wears thin and he wants her to be more circumspect. Telling him that he doesn't understand, #9 finds him narrow-minded and overly conservative. In the heat of debate, she becomes very emotional while he clings stubbornly to his opinion. Sympathetic #9 will always be the first to forgive and forget; #4 will chew on an issue for days.

While he protects #9 from her own gullibility, she can help him understand a more universal point of view. Rummaging around together, they can renew their intimate commitment as well as maintain their charitable responsibilities.

THE NAME #4 WOMAN AND THE NAME #9 MAN

If history is made at the polls, the #9 MAN and the #4 WOMAN will be able to trace their beginnings to the precinct where she is in charge and he's manning the ballot box. Attracted by her sense of responsibility and organizational skills, #9 admires how hard she works to keep track of details. A true humanitarian, he introduces her to neighbors she's never met, and by the day's end she feels a new sense of belonging in the community. Offering to drive his attractive precinct captain to the collection center to turn in the ballots, #9 feels more than rewarded for his service; her presence has made his day.

As their relationship develops, she often cooks him healthy little dinners at home to offset the lavish restaurant meals he seems to prefer. Quietly tending to his welfare, #4 loves to hear about his travels and interesting friends. She's a practical helpmate who can organize #9's most grandiose plans into workable action.

Believing in the value of hard work, she objects when he's so ready with a handout. When he's overly trusting, she reminds him to ask for credentials; when he's overly generous with his time and money, she revamps his schedule and makes him get receipts for tax purposes.

Although not likely to share political views, they are in the same party when it comes to their intimate domestic policy. Giving is a way of life for #9, while #4 loves to be of service. She's ready to nominate him as her favorite candidate for lover because of the way he touches her heart. His persuasive appeals always sway her opinion, and she can attest to the way he fulfills his campaign promises.

A popular candidate, #9 may neglect #4 in his bid to reach the masses. In addition to their conflict over money, his public mission is the next major point of contention; he feels unappreciated at home and she feels abandoned. Stubborn #4 will wait for an apology; fortunately, #9 is able to forgive and forget and will keep trying.

Accepting the steadying influence she has on his life, prudent #4 will be kept happy if #9 abides restrictions she places on his extravagant ways. She will reward him with the love and admiration he desires.

THE NAME #5 MAN AND THE NAME #5 WOMAN

Traffic school is a likely spot to start a new romance for a pair of #5s. Lead-footed risk takers, they were bound to come to the attention of the local police. She made an impulsive U-turn; he was caught speeding to an appointment.

Immediately attracted to one another, freedom-loving #5s share the fidgets in class. Curious to the point of being nosy, they pass notes back and forth to determine the nature of the offending behavior that resulted in this 8-hour confinement in class. By the end of the day, they've become partners in crime.

Except between their answering machines, friendship may not blossom into romance for a while since restless #5s are seldom at home. (They already know what's happening there and it's usually day-old dishes and undusted tables.) When they do get together, they'll do just about anything for excitement. Not a pair to make cleaning house a priority, they're better off meeting at a restaurant.

They court each other in a manner as unique as they are fearless and unconventional. He won't think to bring her flowers, nor could she find a vase if he did. Talking in shorthand and finishing each other's sentences, they're a couple of clever mind readers.

Their intimate moments are as highly charged as the rest of their lives. Not a pair to stay in low gear for long, they're impatient and full of sexual energy. #5 lovers never take the same route twice. They make love often but rarely replay the same scene or repeat a performance.

A constant source of conflict is their disorganized lifestyle. Each expects the other to do the laundry and pay bills, tasks too mundane for a #5. Even though they value each other's sense of adventure, they soon become fed up with the serious lack of follow-through. Hitting a red light once too often in their domestic struggle, they'll end up in the street yelling at each other until the light turns green again. Fight forgotten, easily distracted #5s are able to shift gears and get on with life.

Since they both thrive on sudden change, they need only keep an eye on each other's turn indicators to keep things interesting. Impromptu rendezvous and frequent changes of scenery will keep them in high gear. So long as they give each other good directions and keep their motors in working order, they'll avoid a collision course. Never out of energy, even though they may forget to gas up, these two are enthusiastic travelers on the road to happiness.

THE NAME #5 MAN
AND THE NAME #6 WOMAN

#6 has invited some neighbors to try out her new hot tub. To her delight they've brought along a new man, and she wonders where they've been hiding him all these months. Busy making the rounds of her guests with snacks and drinks, #6 wants everyone to be comfortable, especially #5. He's tired and sore from a day on the tennis courts; but now that her tender care has restored his original vigor, he's eager to schedule a private therapy session.

Their romance is an interesting blend of his restlessness and her serenity. #5 is used to an active social life; home-loving #6 likes nothing better than to putter around in the kitchen, preparing a delicious dinner for two. Exhausted by his whirlwind tours of night spots, she quickly learns to vary the menu and her hot-tub attire to keep him coming back for more.

When romantic #6 convinces him to slow down and pay attention to what he's doing, he slips into her comfortable style. Her calming influence may even mellow him a bit and reduce his wanderlust. At the same time he challenges her ability to adjust to others. She will learn to keep up with him when he's on a roll (and sneak in a nap when he's not looking).

The surest way to lose him is to pin him down or to be heavy-handed with advice. Arguments bring out his impatience; anticipating her next words, #5 is impulsive in his replies and may hurt well-meaning #6. Nonetheless, he's good at negotiating a settlement—anything to get off a sore subject and on to something more exciting. Since she hates to argue, #6 makes every effort to adjust all wrongs, even if they are her own. Unless she's fighting for a principle, she will usually be the first one to call off the fight.

#5 can take care of keeping things exciting while #6 keeps the home fires burning. The best of both worlds is theirs for the asking.

THE NAME #5 WOMAN AND THE NAME #6 MAN

Spotting the #5 WOMAN stranded on a dark road near her disabled car, the responsible #6 MAN rescues her. Ordinarily polite, he forgoes formal introductions until they reach the gas station. Instead he lectures her fervently on the dangerous consequences of her foolhardy behavior. A real hero, he's just the kind of man she's been looking for, and she does her best to dazzle him on the return trip to the car. The first sparks of romance threaten to ignite the gallon can of gas as he fills her empty tank.

Despite her devil-may-care attitude, #6 admires her effervescent personality. Obviously she needs some help with practical details and he's just the one to take on that responsibility. Courting her in first-class style, he showers her with quality tokens of his esteem and home-cooked meals. He prefers romantic dinners in the comfort of his luxurious home to frenzied meals in crowded restaurants.

She meets his family and friends and is charmed by the variety of evenings he plans with her in mind. Adapting to her love of excitement, he is a willing participant when she comes up with a last-minute suggestion. Given more to adventure, she works in hang gliding and hot-air ballooning between his cozy dinners.

They keep each other's sensual batteries charged, and he doesn't need to worry about her running out of gas. Teasing her about how high her motor idles, #6 works his therapeutic magic so that #5 continues to run well without a single miss.

Under his good influence, she even learns to cook, though following a recipe still seems like a lot of trouble. He has to admit that her beef Bourguignon is as unconventional as she is, but just as tasty.

Trouble along their road to romance develops when she doesn't follow his advice; well-meaning #6 can be a heavy-handed counselor and #5 can tune out. Settling on whether to stay in for #6's kind of evening or to go out on the town #5-style can also cause friction. Though he's got a short fuse, #5 is quick to forget; anxious to head off an unpleasant exchange, #6 usually adjusts to #5 before the argument becomes heated.

Willing to assume responsibility for both, #6 learns to keep #5's tank filled. They should consider moving several times to give her a change of scenery and to allow him the pleasure of designing an even more luxurious and comfortable home.

THE NAME #5 MAN
AND THE NAME #7 WOMAN

Tacking and trimming every weekend with the Lake Sailing Club, the #5 MAN loves the days when the water is rough and the wind changes. The #7 WOMAN enjoys the tranquility of a calm day with a steady wind. With such different requirements it's a wonder they ever meet. She notices when he breezes in late for the meetings, and marvels at all the questions he asks about club business. He finally notices her when she reads the historian's report; her in-depth analysis of the year's activities makes him stop and think about all the exciting things the club has done.

Asking around among the members, he finds out she's a knowledgeable sailor who remains cool in a crisis. To satisfy his curiosity, he asks her to crew for him. Manning the tiller, he keeps her busy on the jib as they come about. She counters his incessant queries with as little personal information as she can supply and still be gracious.

Undaunted by her evasive manner, he changes his tack and chases her as he chases the breeze. Amazed at his versatility, she can't fault him for pressing her; in fact, she's flattered. Agreeing to a dinner date, she figures there's no point in taking the wind out of his sails until she finds out just exactly how he behaves on land.

Despite their differences, they make a well-balanced pair. She counters his impulsive behavior by making plans; he's fearless, she follows her intuition. While she may know all about his past—at least what he remembers to tell her—she will never be able to predict his future. He, on the other hand, will know only what she chooses to reveal. This sense of mystery will keep their relationship exciting.

When he's off exploring new seas, #7 enjoys her much-needed time alone. She loves to analyze the information he brings home, and he appreciates the way she can make sense of the world they live in.

A sensual pair, they don't waste much time before embarking on a voyage to explore the mysteries of love. Beneath her calm surface lie strong sexual currents. She has only to guide #5 through the high swells and into her safe harbor.

Stormy seas are whipped up when she weighs her words too carefully and too long before speaking. If impatient #5 tries to finish her sentences, she becomes even more reluctant to share her thoughts. Resorting to signal flags or Morse code to improve their communication, they still can't eliminate the times he forgets appointments.

She fights with her silence while he impulsively tells her off and forgets. Distracted by a new adventure, #5 will wonder why #7 is still angry. When she's had a chance to resolve all the issues, #7 will make up with #5.

He can sail happily on her still waters for many years rediscovering the mystery of their depths, while she can count on him to make some interesting waves.

THE NAME #5 WOMAN
AND THE NAME #7 MAN

Engrossed in the complicated plot of the movie, the #7 MAN is suddenly confronted with a lap full of hot buttered popcorn.

Arriving in the middle, the #5 WOMAN has just spilled herself (and her kernels) into the last seat in the house. He can't tell what she looks like, but during her ten-minute apology he can feel her retrieving the popcorn. His dignity preserved by the darkness, he thoroughly enjoys the experience, in spite of the fact that he completely loses all track of the plot.

In the light of the lobby, she looks terrific, but the butter-spotted pants obviously need attention. When he refuses her offer to pay for the cleaning, she impulsively suggests that she treat him to a potentially less damaging snack for the second showing of the movie. She wants to see the beginning, and he wants to understand the last half.

Thanks to her he doesn't get a chance. They hold hands while feeding each other melt-in-your-mouth-not-in-your-hand candies when she becomes restless. Analyzing the situation, #7 decides she's much more interesting than the movie. Hungry for more substantial information about him, she accepts his invitation for supper.

After many movies he knows all about her; but like a good mystery, he reveals only clues about himself. She is eager to explore his interests in the great outdoors and books in order to satisfy her curiosity about his secretive nature.

Their intimate moments are never second-rate reruns. Their lovemaking tends toward fantasies and exciting climaxes. A starring role on location is just the ticket, and she loves it when her meticulous #7 director decides to reshoot from a different angle.

Independent #5 is willing to do things on her own, allowing #7 plenty of time for quiet contemplation. Easily distracted, she sometimes forgets to come home. What she considers a simple slip of the hour hand becomes a major misunderstanding to him. While he's still trying to write a script to accurately express his anger, she'll dash in the door with a casual apology and miss the whole point. Long after she's dismissed the incident, introspective #7 will still be replaying it in his mind.

Communication is the key to improving this relationship. She has to slow down and focus her concern for a few close-ups and stills so she can understand him better, while he has to make the big leap from silent films to talkies so he can express his feelings.

Keeping the plot exciting is her department, while unraveling the mystery is his. As long as she remembers to keep the popcorn kernels on her side when they're watching movies in bed, their relationship will become a classic.

THE NAME #5 MAN AND THE NAME #8 WOMAN

Customers at the same auto body shop, the #5 MAN and the #8 WOMAN meet over a paint chip. An impulsive driver, he's there to have the dings and scrapes repaired, while her classic car is there to be restored. He notices that her sleek lines match those of the car and her outfit is as classy as the leather interior.

Both of these people are used to going after what they want without a second thought. He's curious about the source of her obvious prosperity and decides to make her his adventure for today. Without wasting time or mincing words, she's already asked him for a drink. They're off to a promising start, conducting their romance in the noisiest, most popular places in town. She loves to be in control, and rarely lets an opportunity slip by. #5 is just the kind of challenge she likes; his schedule is as busy, but more erratic than hers.

Excited by this strong-willed, powerful woman, he enjoys mingling with her influential friends. She loves to go to all the best places; he simply loves to go. Happy to accept her luxurious tastes, #5 is content to play her game as long as the money holds out.

Their lovemaking is a little like his driving, dangerously exciting and fast-paced. He lets her sit in the driver's seat because he loves the way she toots his horn. Equally as energetic but less conventional, he wants to stay on the move all the time, but not the same route every day. Unlike his organized #8, flexible #5 thinks nothing of an unscheduled, romantic detour down a strange road.

Accepting each other's independence, they pursue busy schedules without guilt over a lonely partner. The collision between her strong will and his free spirit will certainly center around the times #5 shows up late. He thinks schedules are fine for other people; she runs by the clock. Desperate to pin him down, she may resort to giving orders. The ensuing crash will be noisy and spectacular as they dispute who had the right of way. Once the dust settles, they will wheel and deal to hammer out an agreement. No damage will remain and their relationship will go on as if nothing ever happened.

The relationship can be improved if she will loosen up and enjoy his more unconventional ways. It won't take much effort on #5's part to please his #8 WOMAN; knowing that she cares about what others think, he can switch from the latest fad in velvet tuxedos to something more acceptable. Meeting in the middle can be safely accomplished if they both have their brakes in good working order; he can help her stop short of being a workaholic and she can teach him to avoid fender benders by planning ahead and focusing on one task.

Two such highly charged individuals can't help but maintain nonstop excitement. With their combined energy and talents, their romance will never screech to a halt.

THE NAME #5 WOMAN AND THE NAME #8 MAN

Down to his last $100 in cash, the #8 MAN stops at the automatic teller machine to replenish his bankroll. Caught short again, the impatient #5 WOMAN needs money to claim her car from the parking lot and joins the line with her customary flourish.

Attracted by her energetic arrival, #8 also notices her up-to-the-minute outfit and bright smile. He uses the time in line to engage her in conversation, and ends up offering her his jacket when she fidgets to keep warm. In spite of her first refusal (which is so creative he hardly feels rejected), he insists and she changes her mind.

Wrapped up in the jacket of his $800 suit, she has a chance to check out his well-exercised body. When he tells her that if she were his lady she'd have a fur coat for visits to the cash machine, she replies that, naturally, she has a full-length sable in the car. Delighted by her quick response, he launches a plan to pursue her.

From one "in" spot to another they make a highly visible team. Soon she is joining him on business trips. Never at a loss for ways to entertain herself, #5 is a good partner for #8, who tends to work long hours. He appreciates her independence and flexibility when his plans require unexpected changes.

Always a credit to him, #5 likes to cash in on the time they have together. Like the automatic teller, she's available on a moment's notice and can provide a variety of transactions. She doesn't care how many withdrawals he makes as long as he balances her account with deposits. No matter what button he pushes, she functions because he knows her secret code.

Her impulsive whims are in direct contrast to his careful planning. Though he loves to spend, he wants to know where the money is going and isn't too thrilled when she fails to fill in the stubs of their joint checking account. To control this fast-moving #5, #8 is likely to issue strict orders about her banking habits and their calendar. Each time she's late he may wonder if the diamond watch he bought her was a good investment.

His orders often infringe upon her personal freedom. Her response is to put him in his place and declare she can live without him if he's going to be so high-handed. She's a formidable adversary even for a logical #8. If she stays around to finish the fight, he'll inevitably win, because he's willing to struggle and forge his way to a victory.

Making up takes on the character of a high-level negotiating session. #8 must make his points in short order before #5 loses interest. Quick to forget, she is happy as long as there's a change for the better.

Too busy to get bored, #8 and #5 will compound their interest daily by relying on his ability to bring high-powered excitement into their lives and her ability to provide constant change.

THE NAME #5 MAN
AND THE NAME #9 WOMAN

A long line in the passport office is not the best place for a restless #5, who is trying to cram a week's worth of appointments into one day. Glancing around for a phone, he's attracted to the friendly smile of the #9 WOMAN ahead of him helping a couple of people with their applications. #5 is relieved when she agrees to hold his place in line while he makes a quick call.

Sympathetic to his frustration, she spends the next hour helping him pass the time. Just before they approach the window she gives him the names of several restaurants in the foreign cities he plans to visit. Suddenly realizing he'll never see her again, #5 impulsively asks her to lunch; taken by his enthusiasm and appreciation for her attention, #9 accepts.

Seeing each other between trips, they establish an easygoing relationship in which #5 is free to pursue his many interests and #9 has time for her philanthropic projects. Curious #5 is fascinated by her wide assortment of friends and enjoys participating in her hectic schedule.

Inveterate travelers, they could be happy indefinitely on the move. While #5 is satisfied with the sights, sounds, and smells of each new destination, #9's interest goes deeper into the history and present condition of the people. She will buy a wood carving to help the artisans, while #5 buys one because he loves the way it feels in his hand.

Their time alone is very precious. Energetic #5 responds to #9's intense, romantic nature during sexy siestas in Spain and nooners in Nice. He's happiest when he can renew their passports to pleasure.

Ruled by her heart, #9 may be so generous with her time and money that #5 gets short-changed. Relatively undemanding, he may nevertheless resent #9's eagerness to spread herself thin. When they fight, impatient #5 may go off on his own rather than stay home to listen to #9's emotional outbursts. Willing to drop the whole thing for the thrill of a loving reconciliation, #5 finds an understanding partner in tolerant #9, who is able to forgive and forget.

To keep things exciting, she will continue to introduce interesting new people into their social circle, and he will keep their suitcases packed for any unexpected opportunity to change the scene. Though they often have different goals, they can travel happily down the same road.

THE NAME #5 WOMAN AND THE NAME #9 MAN

Feeding quarters into the washing machines, the #9 MAN is doing an extra load for a sick friend. Trailing sheets and spilling soap, the #5 WOMAN disrupts the calm of the Laundromat with her energetic arrival. Once she's tossed her laundry into the machine, she digs in her purse for quarters and comes up empty-handed. Taking pity on her, #9 gives #5 his last two coins and retrieves her stray sock from the floor. When she dashes out the door with a promise to return shortly, #9 amuses himself by thinking about her while he folds his laundry as well as hers.

Breezing in, she hugs him impulsively as she refunds his quarters. When she sees the neatly folded clothes, she showers #9 with praise; he laps it up and offers to help her out to her car.

Feeling needed and appreciated, #9 decides to pursue free-spirited #5 into the coffee shop next door, where they discover a mutual love of people and travel. A gypsy herself, #5 is curious to know more about #9 and his wanderlust.

Delighted with #9's wide variety of friends, #5 is unconventional enough to fit in with the ex-convict or the symphony conductor. Good at character analysis, she's able to help him detect the freeloaders who, although fascinating, may take advantage of #9's kindness.

Both #5 and #9 are good at discarding what is no longer useful in their lives. When he feels as if it's time to move on, she can cope easily with the unexpected because she regards change as a positive force.

A romantic at heart, demonstrative #9 is a perfectionist when it comes to planning their intimate moments. A selfless lover, he will try anything to please energetic, impulsive #5. With an appetite for freedom and variety, she's delighted that he's broad-minded enough to play at sex to please her.

Knowing how much #5 hates routine, tolerant #9 will put up

with her late arrivals and missed appointments. Ruled by his emotions, he will tell her off at times, only to beg her immediate forgiveness. There is little that #5 will stop long enough to argue about. #9 is so loving and so willing to give #5 her freedom that she can't complain.

To make their relationship better, they need to synchronize their movements. Giving each other the freedom they both want will work only if they are there for each other, when generous #9 is worn out from his humanitarian endeavors and #5 is finally exhausted by her frantic pace.

THE NAME #6 MAN AND THE NAME #6 WOMAN

Fumbling for her lace hanky, the #6 WOMAN can feel the tears welling up in her eyes. A handsome #6 MAN sitting across the aisle gestures to her with his monogrammed linen handkerchief, and by the end of the wedding ceremony, she's smiling at the possibility of a new romance.

When they meet later at the buffet table, he decides she's his kind of woman, beautifully dressed and well-groomed. Even before they catch the bouquet and the garter, he'd like to sweep her off her feet. And he's just the sort of man she'd like to cuddle; she loves his nice manners and the way he sees to her every need. Clever with people, they out-clever each other into meeting the next day. They court each other with romantic dinners at home and extravagant gifts.

Now that they've divided their time between her place and his, their biggest problem is deciding which house to keep. Judging from all the friends and family they entertain, they choose the bigger of the two houses and make plans to fill it quickly with the sounds of little feet.

On a perpetual honeymoon, these two lovebirds can't do enough for each other. No gift is too good, no massage too long nor favor too great. Intimate moments turn into intimate hours as they both aim to please. As adept at catching suggestions as she is at catching bouquets, she has the bubble bath drawn before he's undressed. Surrounded by luxury, they move from fluffy towels to satin sheets and feather pillows.

Automatically adjusting to any situation, they try hard to be fair and avoid arguments at all costs. So anxious to see the good in each other, they ignore their faults. Harsh words make them physically ill, so pillow fights are about as combative as they get.

To improve their idyllic relationship these sociable #6s should plan for more time alone. And even though expressing true feelings may threaten their happy home, they must risk telling each other the truth so that little problems don't become big ones.

It's easy for them to keep things exciting. They take such good care of each other and exchange such sentimental gifts, the honeymoon should last forever.

THE NAME #6 MAN AND THE NAME #7 WOMAN

Waiting to pick up her dog at the vet, the #7 WOMAN watches the #6 MAN dash in with an injured stray. From his conversation with the receptionist, she's impressed to learn that he runs a regular rescue operation. By the time he returns to the waiting room, the discriminating #7 WOMAN has agreed to an introduction from the receptionist, who assures her that #6 is a very responsible, single gentleman with a gorgeous home in her neighborhood.

Starting with dinner at a fine restaurant chosen by #6, their courtship moves from one refined date to the next. Thankful that the receptionist allowed him to penetrate #7's aloof shell, #6 is impressed with her serenity and analytical mind. He appreciates her charming notes and thoughtful gifts. She finds #6 a good conversationalist and loves the way he indulges her.

When #6 proves by his words and deeds that he can be a devoted, dependable lover, sensual #7 drops her guard to reveal an imaginative sex kitten. She loves to rub up against his well-cared for body and luxuriate in the beauty of his surroundings. In return, he pets her until she purrs with satisfaction.

This devoted pair are always honest with each other. Problems arise over their differing attitudes toward other people; #6 surrounds himself with needy friends and family, while #7 prefers solitude to a crowd. With his strong advice to be more outgoing, #6 may overpower #7. Both tend to get moody; she feels misunderstood while he magnifies both joys and sorrows.

In order to prevent a fight, #6 may question #7 about her melancholy and only succeed in driving her farther away. Since she hates to be questioned, #7 is best left alone until she can sort things out. Meanwhile, #6 suffers as he tries to keep peace by adapting to her wishes.

When she has analyzed their differences and understands the cause of their fight, she will respond to his call for a truce. Knowing how willing #6 is to be fair and keep his word, #7 is less likely to withhold her feelings.

#6 must give #7 her privacy and make sure she feels understood. In return, she must realize that even though he has lots of friends, #6 wants her as the center of his life. #7 can keep their relationship exciting by flattering #6. He should always encourage her active imagination in the bedroom.

THE NAME #6 WOMAN AND THE NAME #7 MAN

The #7 MAN is so fastidious that the least little spot sends him dashing for help. His latest mishap is a blob of pen ink on his shirt and he's distraught to find that the dry cleaner's spotter has already gone for the night. In comes #6 with her handy home remedies to save the day. She takes him to her car, whips out the hair spray, and removes most of the spot within minutes.

Impressed by her concern for his problem and her ability to solve it, #7 takes a second look and likes what he sees. Her assortment of elegant silk dresses tells him she's a woman of quality, and he quickly calculates that she must be fairly successful to support her taste in clothes.

Attracted by his poise and sincere appreciation for her efforts, she is happy to answer his questions about her cleaning techniques. While she expounds on lemon and salt for copper pots, he is planning how to ask her for a date. Encouraged by her warmhearted response, he suggests a concert and is delighted to find out they share a fondness for music.

At home in her luxurious surroundings, he discovers her high standards of cooking are consistent with his discriminating palate. She realizes how much he values his privacy, and is flattered to be asked to his home.

More expressive on the written page, #7 sends love letters that answer her need to be the center of his life. In private moments she discovers the hidden depths of his feelings and the extent of his erotic imagination. Bathing in bubbles until they are squeaky clean puts them both in a lather. Not only does she know how to take care of his special spots, but he knows just how much starch she likes.

Arguments will seldom spoil their happy home. He's so quiet and she's so adaptable. If she's heavy-handed with advice or allows her friends free access to their home, his glum mood signals that he dislikes any invasion of privacy. Quick to sense his displeasure, she learns not to ask too many questions. Once they reach an understanding, #7 can trust #6 to keep her promises.

Their relationship can be improved through communication. If he remembers to compliment her, #6 will keep coming back for more. She'll please him by avoiding the trouble spots and providing a happy, tranquil home.

THE NAME #6 MAN
AND THE NAME #8 WOMAN

The #8 WOMAN received an unusually large bonus for completing a large project, so she is planning to reward herself with an important piece of jewelry. Perched on a plush stool in front of the glass case, she looks as elegant as any of the gleaming rings in the velvet tray. Seated next to her, the #6 MAN carefully examines the workmanship of the sterling silver gifts he is choosing for his staff.

Attracted by his impeccable grooming and tasteful choice of clothes, #8 decides he's her type. With an eye for quality, #6 has arrived at a similar conclusion.

Taking control of the situation, she asks him if he knows anything about rings in general and diamonds in particular. Taking into consideration her perfect manicure and costly watch, he realizes she wants the best and isn't surprised when she decides on an expensive-looking dinner ring.

Given the obvious opening, he quickly asks her to dinner so she'll have a chance to wear her new acquisition. She dazzles him with a designer gown that matches the caliber of the bauble, and he's donned a custom-tailored suit. No diamonds in the rough, they make a polished pair.

From dinners at the finest restaurants to evenings at the club, their romance sparkles. Tied to responsible jobs, they enjoy working together afterhours; strong-willed #8 makes sure #6 keeps his promise to leave her alone until she completes her tasks. Filling the time when she's at work with his numerous friends and family, he patiently waits until she's ready to put her business aside.

Expert at making her comfortable in luxurious surroundings, #6 knows his #8 WOMAN is satisfied with only the best; exchanging extravagant gifts, they come to a point in their relationship when he offers her his family jewels and she happily places them in her satin-lined vault. From then on he agrees to let her have them whenever she wants them as long as she gives him her combination.

From #8's point of view, the only flaw in their happy home is #6's intrusive advice. Used to giving directions, #8 hates to take them. To maintain harmony, #6 will have to do most of the adjusting while #8 maintains her vision for them both and cleverly gets her way.

To keep the sparkle in their relationship, they need to reserve time for private moments. #8 must pull herself away from work while #6 pulls himself away from friends.

THE NAME #6 WOMAN AND THE NAME #8 MAN

Riding a state-of-the-art titanium bike nearly twenty miles to the harbor may seem extreme, but to the #8 MAN it's an exhilarating experience that provides balance to his demanding job.

The fish vendor stalls at the wharf are part of her Saturday ritual. Appreciating the difference in quality, she settles for only the freshest selections.

Standouts in their designer sportswear, this classy pair attract each other's attention, and it's love at first sight. Luring him with her inviting smile, #6 is flattered by his obvious interest. As he dodges crab pots and crates of iced flounder to reach her side, #8 tells her he's all hers if she'll just say the word. Taking control of the situation, he whisks her off for an alfresco lunch of champagne and lobster. Conversing with him easily, she realizes he has everything that money can buy.

While he loads his bike in her car, she picks out fresh oysters and plans exactly what else she'll give him for dinner. Her dream of a luxurious home full of love could be possible with this dynamic man. Attending to his every need, #6 makes him so comfortable he never wants to leave. Happily trapped in her net, #8 still thinks he's in control and is determined to make their arrangement permanent. Offering no resistance, #6 goes for the extravagant gifts he uses as bait. An eager fish, she wiggles just enough to keep him interested and give him the challenge he likes.

Willing to adapt to his lifestyle, she adds biking clothes to her wardrobe and waits patiently while he works long hours. A first-class hostess for his business entertaining, she creates a beautiful home that fits his image. Always there to indulge him after a busy day at the office, #6 is his little fish in a safe harbor.

Sharing a highly developed sense of responsibility and a desire for luxury, they are rarely in conflict over major issues. Fortunately for #8, who likes to give orders, #6 will go along to keep the peace. It's #8 who won't budge when #6 comes on too strong with her helpful advice. In her spare time she may be able to counsel her many friends, but her #8 MAN runs the show.

A fight between them is over before it begins. It's a forgone conclusion that #8's masterful approach will prevail and that #6 will make every effort to calm troubled waters. Reminding her of big plans that include her, #8 overcomes any objections she may have with persuasive logic and a lavish gift.

To maintain balance in a relationship with powerful #8, #6 should continue to be her own person. By assuming the responsibility for righting all wrongs for their friends and their children, she will gain #8's undying respect. He, in turn, will ensure her love and devotion if he reserves quality time for her away from his demanding business interests.

To keep things exciting, he can lure her with expensive bait, and she can make certain that he always comes up with a good catch when he casts in her direction.

THE NAME #6 MAN
AND THE NAME #9 WOMAN

When the community-minded #9 WOMAN decides to run for office, her supporters encourage her to consider the #6 MAN as a campaign manager. He's earned a reputation for being honest and highly principled—just the man she needs.

Meeting him at a coffee hour arranged by her friends, she isn't quite prepared for what she sees. Handsome and perfectly dressed, he reminds her more of a corporate president than a shirt-sleeves political manager. Attracted by his air of quality and faultless manners, she contemplates another campaign to win his heart.

The #6 MAN is taken by her sincerity. He gives her his vote of confidence and looks forward to a close association. Overcome by the desire to protect her, he offers the comfort of his luxurious home for their late-night strategy sessions. #9 gives him lavish gifts to express her appreciation; he has to remind her not to show her affection so openly in public, although he encourages her when they are alone.

In the moments stolen from the election they spend more time raising their passions than funds. Too honest to stuff her ballot box, he's only too happy to give her a strong vote of confidence when she calls for it.

Even though she knows he means well and takes his role as protector very seriously, the emotional #9 WOMAN may overreact to his firm advice. Willing to forgive and forget, she doesn't stay angry very long. In the interest of keeping things peaceful and upholding his promise to take care of her, he adapts to whatever she wants.

Their dedication to worthy causes keeps the relationship exciting, but #6 and #9 must make sure they have enough time for each other. Although he admires her desire to make her constituents' lives easier, he constantly reminds her not to sacrifice herself in the process. By continually registering their personal party affiliations, they can count on a winning ticket through all their future campaigns.

THE NAME #6 WOMAN
AND THE NAME #9 MAN

Patrons of the arts, #6 and #9 finally meet at a champagne reception before a concert. Each surrounded by an admiring throng, they have heard about one another through mutual friends but have never been introduced. Known for his generous contributions to the community, #9 is aware that #6 has a reputation for being supportive and compassionate. Though unable to detach himself from his fans, #9 catches her eye with a winning smile and a gallant bow that leaves her weak in the knees.

Carried away by the extravagance of his romantic gesture, she doesn't see him sitting behind her. In full control of his faculties, he can't wait for intermission to waylay her. Paying more attention to the tender curve of her neck and the luxurious folds of her satin blouse than the music, #9 resists the temptation to tap her on the shoulder and starts mapping out his pursuit. By the end of the first movement he knows exactly which four-star restaurant would provide a proper setting for elegant #6. By the time the lights come up, he has chosen their honeymoon destination.

Hearing bells as he says her name, #6 comes under the spell of this classy, charismatic #9 MAN. Making excuses to her seat mates, she moves with him to another area where he has arranged for two seats together.

As harmonious as the music of that first night, their relationship develops so quickly that they become a standard duet at cultural events. The consummate hostess, #6 sets the stage for #9's philanthropic endeavors with fabulous parties. Their guests range from visiting ambassadors to struggling artists. Between his humanitarian efforts and her nurturing ways, their home is on its way to becoming both halfway house and mini–United Nations.

Not averse to receiving applause for his generosity, #9 is gratified to see #6 leading the standing ovation. Making his home comfortable and inviting, she polishes his trophies and keeps him fit as a fiddle. Able to adjust to his public persona, she accepts the fact that he belongs to the world and concentrates on his home and family.

She greets him with open arms and guards their precious intimate moments carefully. Theirs is a harmonious love song, especially when he plucks her strings.

Conflicts may arise when he wants to travel and she wants to stay home. Although their arguments never reach a fortissimo, even a minor disagreement unnerves them. Emotional #9 would give it all up for #6, who looks after him so well. Begging her forgiveness with an extravagant memento of every trip, #9 arranges it so #6 can furnish their home exquisitely.

Providing the money holds out for her redecorating budget and his travel and charity expenses, they should continue making beautiful music together.

THE NAME #7 MAN AND THE NAME #7 WOMAN

While most of the contestants are using the sand-castle competition as an excuse for a beach party, the two #7s take the contest seriously. Working alone from elaborate designs, they both seek perfection.

Too engrossed to notice each other, the #7s don't meet until the afternoon judging. They're both awarded prizes in small-scale designs and are pushed together by a photographer. The #7 MAN notices the poise with which the #7 WOMAN accepts her award, and she is taken by the dignified way he responds to the reporter's inane questions.

Granted a tour of her castle, he is impressed that she used her knowledge of the tides and winds to select a good spot to build. As they move to his château, they both agree that the beach is a perfect place to commune with nature. Soon they are strolling along the shore in silence, an occasion to be repeated many times in the course of their relationship.

Communicating intuitively, they are quick to observe each other's habits and please accordingly. Fussy about their possessions, they respect each other's belongings. If they garden in her yard, he's careful to clean and oil the trowels and shovels before he puts them away. In his kitchen she always uses a wooden cutting board so as not to dull the knives.

They choose the perfect gifts for one another's discriminating tastes. He introduces her to quiet restaurants, she takes him to her favorite bookstore, and together they discover the rare record shop.

Withholding their innermost feelings at first, they respect one another's privacy. Only after they develop a mutual trust do they allow their considerable passion to take over. His lyrical love letters arouse her to share a fantasy that sends them off on an endless romantic adventure. Limited only by their unbounded imaginations, the #7 MAN and #7 WOMAN shed their dignified public images for a decidedly erotic relationship.

Happy to wile away the hours by themselves, neither one has the urge to entertain constantly or go out on the town. Left to their own devices, however, they may occasionally feel lonely and misunderstood. Too proud to give in, they tend to overanalyze a predicament and become moody or depressed. They could both build up a tidal wave of emotion that would destroy their castle in the sand. Sometimes the lengthy process of reconciliation between two analytical #7s is hastened by their strong sexual attraction.

By keeping the lines of communication open, two #7s will maintain a relationship as deep and as constant as the ocean.

THE NAME #7 MAN AND THE NAME #8 WOMAN

The #8 WOMAN is condo-sitting for friends and can't wait to jump in the pool. Her splashy dive startles the #7 MAN, who was floating serenely on his raft. Hanging on for dear life, he survives the tidal wave, paddles to the pool's edge, and gets out.

Dignified and unflappable, #7 is not quick to anger; in fact, he finds the whole incident rather amusing. This offending swimmer must be one of those former college champions. When she makes a spectacular exit from the pool in a revealing racing suit he is delighted by her cheery hello.

Now that his peace has been shattered, he finds her an interesting diversion. She's a little more flashy and assertive than he's used to, but her simple gold jewelry and monogrammed towel indicate a woman of substance and quality.

Intrigued by his polite reserve, she finds him attractive in an understated way. He's quite inquisitive about her swimming times, but the only personal data he's provided is his name. Always ready to set a new record, she's determined to break through his shell in a matter of seconds.

#8 lands her first date easily by asking him to recommend a fine restaurant or two. She thinks she's in control, but #7 knows exactly what she's doing. Enjoying all her maneuvers, he realizes she can be spurred on if he plays hard to get.

Fascinated by her competitive nature, #7 spends many long evenings trying to understand her drive for success and status. Content to walk in the park, #7 knows that she always wants to jog a certain number of laps or test her mettle on the fitness course.

They don't see much of each other because she is always busy and often works late. Their differences in philosophy don't keep them apart; somewhat limited in options for late-night entertainment, they find they are very compatible. She's just as formidable in bed as she is in her athletic and business pursuits. Challenged again, she has the stamina to keep up with his bizarre ideas. Late-night skinny-dipping with a little competitive breaststroke suits her fine, once he says he'll give her the prize if she can do it without splashing.

Their problems arise when he is unable to put up with the hours she keeps to further her career. Used to being in control, she may become angry when he won't play her games. Without meaning to, she's able to hurt the feelings of moody #7, who retreats for some much-needed solitude. Understanding what makes her tick much better than she understands him, he'll figure out what happened about the same time #8 decides she'll do anything to overcome their problem. She may have to turn on her charm to persuade him to put aside his pride. Swimming in each other's lane now and then will give them the perspective they need to finish the race together.

THE NAME #7 WOMAN AND THE NAME #8 MAN

The #7 WOMAN is keeping the car salesman on his toes with an onslaught of questions. She's read every brochure and is quoting from magazine articles. More interested in safety features and miles per gallon than color or luxury options, she's obviously analyzing her purchase carefully. When the #8 MAN bursts into the showroom and heads straight to the top-of-the-line model, the salesman breathes a sigh of relief.

Fascinated by #8's take-charge style, she gives in when he asks whether he could place an order with her salesman. Impressed by her refined manner and intelligent comments, #8 quickly orders the luxury model with all the trim options plus undercoating and a heavy-duty battery—thanks to #7's consumer assistance.

When the salesman asks if she's ready to place an order, #7 says no but accepts #8's kind offer to further discuss her purchase over a cup of coffee. She's impressed by his successful image and is curious to know what makes him tick. He wants to know what she's like under her attractive yet businesslike exterior. Proud to be seen with her, he has a feeling she doesn't accept coffee dates with just anyone; only an up-scale café in the right part of town is appropriate.

By the time she finally buys a new car they are an established twosome. He's challenged by her good mind and the mysterious way she maintains her privacy. She doesn't seem to mind when he has to work long hours because she likes plenty of time alone. With his intensely competitive style and her more introspective, low-key approach, they bring an interesting balance to each other's lives.

Nowhere do they perform their balancing act better than in bed. Not satisfied until he has discovered the hidden emotions beneath her dignified exterior, #8 discovers the action of a race car under her conservatively designed hood. Able to gain her trust, he finds her only too happy to match him cylinder for cylinder in sexual performance. A lesser man would run out of gas, but not a well-conditioned #8.

#8's tendency to dominate causes problems with #7, who prefers to come to her own conclusions. Even though she's delighted that he's so bright and successful, she objects when he tries to run her life. She may also begin to wonder whether he's actually at work after hours. Wanting proof of his love, she won't be easily bought off by his extravagant gifts. If she feels he has lied, #7 may become silent or nurse a grudge for quite a while.

#8 wants to win arguments, so he'll use logic and the power of persuasion to overcome her objections. If he feels he's been fair, he won't understand why she's still angry; after all, he's ready to get on with their lives.

Provided he makes the time to maintain their relationship, #8's drive to improve his position is cheered on by supportive #7. Always a bit of the mystery woman, she can keep things exciting by occasionally leaving him in the dark.

THE NAME #7 MAN AND THE NAME #9 WOMAN

Now that the reserved #7 MAN has been introduced by friends to the warm, outgoing #9 WOMAN he decides a second date is in order. Knowing she is adventurous and loves to travel, #7 chooses an intimate Japanese restaurant. He pictures himself sitting on the floor next to her behind the shoji screens. Carefully dividing the evening into stages of an elaborately planned seduction, he is willing to put up with the exotic food and chopsticks in return for the privacy they will have.

Delighted by his choice, #9 gives him a big hug in front of the restaurant. Once inside, she asks the kimono-clad waitress to leave the screens open so they can absorb the total atmosphere more fully. Adept at dealing with many kinds of people, she befriends all the help; even the chef pays his respects before the evening is over.

#7 looks so dignified in his button-down shirt and tie that #9 has no idea of his romantic intentions. Based on her public display of affection, his plan for the evening holds the promise of a more private finale.

By the time the sukiyaki is served, he's holding her hand and playing footsie under the low table; by dessert he's convinced her to have the screens closed so they can eat their green tea ice cream in seclusion.

Within a week the #7 MAN has his #9 geisha eating out of his hand; her romantic heart melts over his poetry accompanied by cherry blossoms. In return, she greets him at her door in a flowing silk kimono and plies him with saki before she bathes him herself. Soaked and scrubbed in her voluminous tub, sensual #7 loves it when she pats him dry and rubs him with exotic oils. Better than his wildest dreams, the seduction is momentarily in her generous hands. Having researched the customs, he knows enough to kiss the nape of her neck before unwrapping her obi. Finishing what he started, #7 finally has what he wants: #9 all to himself and completely undone.

It takes all the ingenuity #7 can muster to keep #9 all to himself. Even on the quiet nature walks #7 plans, a motley assortment of old and new friends threatens to keep them apart. From ne'er-do-wells to national figures, their happy home is a gathering spot. Overly generous with both her energy and her friends, #9 has a tendency to squander her resources; to #7's dismay there is often little of her left for him.

Their arguments are emotional on her part and quiet on his. He wants proof of her love and will tolerate no lies. True to her selfless ways, she will be the first one to give in. While he's still trying to analyze the fight, understanding #9 will forgive and forget. It's hard for him to stay angry when she's so willing to keep trying.

To improve their relationship, #7 must show his appreciation for her benevolence; she must respect his need for tranquil surroundings and her undivided attention. To keep their private world exciting, they can spend a lifetime exploring the intimate customs of many cultures.

THE NAME #7 WOMAN
AND THE NAME #9 MAN

Eagerly accepting the invitation to an exclusive wine tasting, the #7 WOMAN has been thinking about joining the Wine Society. A connoisseur of sorts, she has read about wine, collected a book of labels, and taken notes on her personal favorites.

The #9 MAN is a vintage veteran. He's traveled widely and experienced the grapes both in the field and in the glass. Welcoming her warmly, he tries to draw her out with more questions than she is comfortable answering. But he is so nice about it that normally reserved #7 doesn't mind.

Although his worldly experience impresses her, she distrusts the terms bandied about by the so-called experts. #7 has decided to trust her own discriminating palate until someone can offer a better system. Intrigued by her knowledge of wine, #9 admires her intelligent, though amateur, approach.

She isn't sure whether it is the wine or his attentive behavior that makes her feel giddy. Inspired by his trustworthy manner, #7 finds herself uncharacteristically acting on an impulse to sit next to him. When he punctuates his sentences with an expressive pat on her shoulder or slips his arm around her waist, she surprises herself and enjoys it.

The next day a bottle of the wine she had liked at the tasting arrives with a note asking her to tour a local winery. In addition to sharing his knowledge of the wine-making process, he makes it very clear he is interested in her by answering all her questions and ushering her through the tour most attentively.

Wondering what's behind her reserve and serious approach, #9 decides to stage a private tasting. His original estimation of their romance developing over time like full-bodied red wine is off by a mile; he realizes he's uncorked a fruity young wine in the #7 WOMAN and longs to experience her aroma.

Fascinated by the differences in her public and private selves, he learns by her example to be more discriminating. She is encouraged by his behavior to be more generous and outgoing.

When conflicts arise over his need to save the world and her need to retreat from it, he may become emotional and she may become silent. His tendency to apologize with an extravagant gift will have a negative effect on #7, who has conservative tastes. Fortunately, #9 will keep trying until he gets it right. What #7 wants most is to be understood, and #9 has the empathy to see her point of view.

To keep things exciting, they need to uncork some tasty new experiences. But they should also let the world take a few turns without them while they savor the flavor of their relationship. It's sure to mellow with the years.

THE NAME #8 MAN AND THE NAME #8 WOMAN

The auction is fairly sedate until Marie Antoinette's armoire comes up for bid. Intent on buying, the #8 WOMAN has attracted the attention of the #8 MAN. He noticed her at the preview the day before, and today she's dressed like a million. He likes the fact that his wasn't the only head that turned when she walked in.

The bidding is lively thanks to both #8s. Soon they are the only two left in the competition, driving the price higher and higher. Challenged by her energy and determination, he thoroughly enjoys the struggle. With a final bid calculated to break her bank and win his prize, he figures he'll get the armoire—or set his sights on the impressive new owner and secure visitation rights.

At the payment desk, the #8 MAN launches his plan to possess them both with the hint of an offer she can't refuse. Charmed by his sporting attitude and still excited from winning in such a competitive exchange, she accepts an invitation to celebrate at his private club. Feeling particularly elegant, she makes a stunning impression on him. And when a few of his friends stop by their well-situated table, he thoroughly enjoys showing her off.

From do-or-die caliber tennis matches to the finest night spots, he's willing to spend any amount of money to impress her. She glories in the luxury of it all, taking note of the first-class restaurants where he's known by name.

He's delighted to find a woman who shares his vision of power and success, who obviously appreciates what money can buy. Of one mind when it comes to status symbols, they drive the same kind of car and go to the same first-rate hair stylist.

Not only does the #8 MAN acquire the right to visit the armoire, he takes up residence with it. His game plan has paid off because she had the same goal in mind. Made for each other, they lose no time in making the arrangement permanent.

Living at the same prestigious address doesn't mean these two workaholics will see very much of each other—unless they install a home gym and computer terminals. A few relaxing stretches lead to the kind of homework that will bring them together in no time.

Because they are used to giving orders and making power plays, two executive #8s continually try to take control of their relationship. Alternating between high-level emotional exchanges and logical debates, their fights represent the struggle they both love. A contest of wills is usually settled fair and square because they both see the big picture and value their commitment. Saving enough energy to do a proper job of making up, these two enjoy the intensity of their battles and use them to keep their lives exciting.

THE NAME #8 MAN
AND THE NAME #9 WOMAN

Used to competitive sports, the #8 MAN reserves Sunday afternoon for endurance rides on the park's hilly bikeways. But now
that he's spotted the #9 WOMAN, who's just set up her easel to
paint a landscape, his concentration is broken.

Noticing her on his third lap, he observes her more carefully
each time he passes. Giving her appearance and talent a superior
rating, he startles her on his next pass by getting off his bike.
Having no idea who he is or where he came from, #9 laughs at
the helmeted, goggled stranger who is hopping around, trying to
pull up his warm-up pants as he introduces himself. Her warm,
sympathetic smile and readiness to chat puts #8 at ease while he
regains his balance. He asks where she's studied, where her work
is exhibited, and where she'd like to have a cold drink. Impressed
by his serious interest in her, she packs up her materials for the
day. Adjourning to a sidewalk café, they discover their mutual interest in a group of well-known local painters.

Usually scheduled to the minute, he doesn't mind whiling away
a few hours in the company of this obviously gifted and charming
woman. Although his goal has been to acquire signed originals of
promising new artists, he now wants to possess more than this
painter's signature. Plying her with a mahogany easel and sable
brushes, he quickly becomes her favorite patron. Her friends in
the arts and his business contacts mix well, so they fall into an
easy round of cultural and philanthropic events.

As direct in bed as he was in the park, #8 matches his athletic
endurance with his prowess in the most intimate contact sport.
Understanding of his need to dominate, #9 is delighted to let
him take the lead.

#8 and #9 provide good emotional balance for each other.
While he pursues power and success, she unselfishly supports him
and applauds his efforts. When she takes on too many charitable
projects, he helps her to become more selective in her choice of organizations. If he works too hard and gets too bossy, she can help
him refocus on friends and exercise his cooperative muscles.

Ruled by her heart, #9 will express her feelings in an argument, while #8 uses logic to overcome her objections. If he be-

comes forceful and competitive, she may wind up in tears one moment, only to forgive and forget the next. Always willing to be fair, she usually gives in first.

Their relationship will be a success if she remembers to let him win and caters to his love of luxury. All he has to do is say "thank you" to his generous, romantic #9 to keep her truly happy.

THE NAME #8 WOMAN AND THE NAME #9 MAN

The #9 MAN's committee is painting the boy's club rec room next weekend and he wants to surprise them with new flooring as well. He's trying to choose the right carpet to donate when the stylish #8 WOMAN enters the store with accent pillows and fabric swatches.

Since he's impressed by her systematic search for the perfect color rug, #9 asks if she would mind giving him some advice. Touched by his generosity, she offers to coordinate the whole project and launches a whirlwind shopping spree to buy the paint, carpet, and light fixtures. Exhausted by her pace, but exhilarated by her enthusiasm, he offers to buy her dinner at a restaurant as classy as she is.

#9's humanitarian spirit and genuine warmth intrigue the #8 WOMAN. She accepts his first invitation and many more, after the project is finished. Happy to fit him into her already busy schedule, she assists in his other charity projects, enhancing his image with high-powered, corporate donors.

She frequently calls him on the carpet for spending too much time away from her. Shutting out the world, she persuades him to make a personal donation to her cause. When she teases him by saying their first meeting was all her idea, he gives in to her every desire.

As generous to others as he is to her, #9 may run into problems with #8, who thinks he does too much. If he donates his business expertise when he could be getting a consultant's fee, she will take over and curtail his benevolence. She absolutely draws the line when he takes pity on down-and-out friends and wants to include them in her exclusive circle of successful associates.

Fights are one-sided: #8 wins. Selfless #9 is no match for her strong-willed determination. It doesn't take much effort on her part to overcome his objections with her brand of logic. Hurt for the moment, he will forgive her and forget the incident. If she tries to keep him from making the contribution he wants to make to the world, he will keep looking for a way around her.

To improve their relationship, #8 must accept their differences and channel his humanitarian spirit into a productive project that satisfies them both.

THE NAME #9 MAN AND THE NAME #9 WOMAN

Seated next to the #9 WOMAN at the head table of a community-service award dinner, the #9 MAN is being careful to mind his manners. Impressed by her credentials, he had no idea she was so glamorous and so warm. Feeling more like a schoolboy than a community leader, he wishes he had replaced his outdated tuxedo for the occasion.

She loves the recognition but is nervous at the thought of meeting such a wonderful man in front of the town's most prominent citizens. Taken aback by his charm, she feels like an idiot exchanging social pleasantries. She'd really like him to ask her to dance so they could have a small measure of privacy.

He manages to get her number before they are both whisked away by their friends. Sending her a huge bouquet the next day, he restates his congratulations and suggests lunch in a place less conspicuous than the speaker's platform. Lunches turn into dinners, and dinners into long evenings, during which they continue to sing each other's praises. As they work together on projects, their romance blossoms along with the showy flowers he gets in the habit of sending each week.

Understanding each other's philanthropic involvements, they accept the endless hours they put in on behalf of their pet charities, and savor the precious moments alone. Their intimate interludes are the ultimate expression of their generous natures. All over each other with tender loving touches, they give new meaning to the word "share." Each feels the other's needs and desires are as important as his or her own.

The picture of understanding and patience, they may both come up short when tired from giving to a good cause. If one of them falls for a phony cause or allows someone to take advantage, the other may become very angry. Seeing their faults in each other may also cause conflict. Fights will be brief; expressive #9s get it all out, then forgive and forget.

Keeping their lives interesting is a fairly easy task with the whole world as their major interest. Since they love to travel, they often combine their good works with some marvelous trips.

To enrich the relationship, #9s need to find time alone. Sustaining one another with well-deserved praise in private will mean more than all their trips to the speaker's platform for public service awards.

LESSON
NUMBERS

Your LESSON NUMBER is
determined by adding the month,
day, and year you were born. It
describes what you must learn in
life in order to take advantage of
your greatest opportunities.
Instructions for calculating your
LESSON NUMBER begin on page 23.

LESSON #1

■ Learn to believe in yourself and value your individuality.

■ Develop your own point of view and speak up for yourself in a nice way; have the courage of your convictions.

■ Take control of your life by making decisions without taking advice from others.

■ Build on what makes you unique and put your personal stamp on everything you do.

LESSON #2

■ Learn to listen and read between the lines. Fine tune your antennae so you can collect impressions as well as facts.

■ Cultivate patience and refrain from forcing issues.

■ Learn to use tact and diplomacy.

■ Practice both the give and take of cooperation to prevent people from taking advantage of your kindness.

■ Take criticism in stride and don't take things personally.

LESSON #3

■ Learn to express yourself by using words effectively.

■ Develop your imagination and unlock your creativity.

■ Cultivate your sense of humor and use it to entertain others.

■ Learn to enjoy the spotlight and to handle attention with humility.

■ Overcome your tendency to be shy and develop your social skills.

■ Learn to project the positive, optimistic side of yourself.

LESSON #4

■ Master detail by learning to develop practical systems; use your logic to divide big jobs into smaller, more manageable tasks.

■ Develop the habit of building a firm foundation when you undertake a new project.

■ Be patient and finish what you start.

■ Organize your time and make the most of it.

■ Learn to curb your spending habits and be sure to get your money's worth.

LESSON #5

■ Open yourself to new ideas and welcome change as a positive force in your life.

■ Learn to adapt yourself to each situation as it presents itself.

■ Be an opportunist who's willing to jump on the most promising bandwagon.

■ Learn to listen patiently and curb your tendency to finish other people's sentences.

LESSON #6

■ Learn to be more loving and responsible toward family and friends.

■ Develop your ability to advise people, keeping in mind that what's right for you isn't always right for others.

■ Be a harmonizer. When others aren't getting along, be the one to smooth ruffled feathers.

■ Don't borrow trouble; solve only those problems which concern you and for which you have the necessary expertise.

■ Learn to keep your word and deal fairly with others.

LESSON #7

■ Discover how to enjoy the quiet side of life and appreciate nature.

■ Learn to be alone without being lonely.

■ Don't take things at face value; develop the skill to ask probing questions and learn to evaluate the answers.

■ Cultivate a detached point of view and keep your emotions from clouding the issue.

■ Learn to appreciate the value of silence and how to keep a secret.

LESSON #8

■ Develop the ability to handle money, power, and success.

■ Learn to organize every aspect of your life and balance your emotions.

■ Pay attention to good health, diet, and exercise habits.

■ Learn to recognize good ideas and execute plans.

■ Become a master at managing and delegating responsibility.

LESSON #9

■ Learn to concentrate on the big picture and leave the details to others.

■ Learn to love by letting go.

■ Consider the welfare of others before your own.

■ Give generously without thought of receiving.

■ Put aside prejudices and focus on people's strengths.

PERSONAL YEAR NUMBERS

Your PERSONAL YEAR NUMBER is determined by your birthday. It describes what you can expect during any year and suggests appropriate activities. Instructions for calculating your PERSONAL YEAR NUMBER begin on page 25.

PERSONAL YEAR #1

■ The slate is wiped clean. This is a time of new beginnings—the fresh start for which you have been waiting.

■ Now's the time to cultivate a new attitude for a new lease on life.

■ Have the courage to make the changes you have been contemplating.

■ This is a year for action. Be ambitious and take the initiative. Do what you have been putting off.

■ Believe in yourself. Listen to the voice within and don't be swayed by others.

■ Visualize what you want. Formulate a plan. Whatever you can hold in your mind you can hold in your hand.

■ Set goals: Don't just talk about your ideas, accomplish them.

PERSONAL YEAR #2

■ Be patient; this is a waiting time. You may feel as if you are taking one step forward and two back.

■ Togetherness and partnership are on your mind.

■ Use tact and diplomacy to cooperate with others.

■ Be sensitive to other people's feelings, but don't take things personally.

■ Study a subject that interests you.

■ Collect the facts and consider all sides carefully. Avoid making hasty decisions.

■ Don't dwell on your fears this year.

■ Attend to details. Do the little things this year.

PERSONAL YEAR #3

■ Reap what you have sown. Something planted and nurtured in the last two years will come to fruition.

- Use words to communicate your ideas in spoken or written form.

- Socialize. Enjoy family and friends in addition to cultivating business contacts.

- You will be busy and moving at a fast pace; avoid scattering your energy.

- Use your imagination and develop your creativity.

- Be optimistic and spontaneous.

- Look forward to a year of expansion and good fortune.

PERSONAL YEAR #4

- Build firm foundations for the future. Solidify your business relationships and cultivate lasting personal relationships.

- Be practical and logical as you face a great deal of detailed work.

- Concentrate and be patient. Your efforts will pay off in the near future.

- Keep busy to avoid feeling bored and restricted.

- Plan for adequate rest.

- Don't overextend yourself financially.

- Learn from past mistakes.

PERSONAL YEAR #5

- Change is in the air. Welcome it as a positive force in your life.

- Look for ways to vary the monotony in your routine; be more flexible.

- Be open to new opportunities and make the most of them.

- Capitalize on your restlessness and curiosity to lead you in new directions.

- This is a great year to travel; keep your suitcase packed and expect the unexpected.

- Plan to be extremely busy and have fun.

- Remodel or move; you're in the mood for a change.

PERSONAL YEAR #6

- Love, home, and family will be on your mind this year.

- Do your fair share when responsibilities increase.

- Cater to the needs of others to create a harmonious atmosphere.

- Make necessary adjustments to right all wrongs.

- Beautify yourself or your surroundings.

- Be just and keep your word.

- Give freely of your advice when asked. Remember, what's right for you isn't necessarily right for others.

PERSONAL YEAR #7

- Take time for yourself; this is a sabbatical year.

- Analyze where you have been and where you are going. Instead of brooding over the past, look forward to the future.

- Opportunities will present themselves if you don't go out looking for them. Don't force issues.

- Enjoy the restorative powers of nature or the company of a good book if you are feeling misunderstood.

- Dig deeply for the answers to all your questions and rely on your intuition.

- Concentrate on what you do want, not what you don't want.

PERSONAL YEAR #8

- Money, power, and success will be on your mind this year.

- Get organized and capitalize on your lucrative business ideas.

- Get your finances in order.

■ Be efficient and make every moment count. Direct others to take care of the details.

■ Be energetic and enthusiastic.

■ Attend to matters of health, diet, and exercise. This is a good year to reach your ideal weight.

■ Keep your emotions on an even keel.

PERSONAL YEAR #9

■ As a nine-year cycle comes to a close, this year points toward a new beginning.

■ Complete projects and tie up loose ends.

■ Take inventory and discard what is no longer useful.

■ Be loving and generous; put the interests of others ahead of your own.

■ Be tolerant and compassionate. Forgive and forget. Put the past in the past.

■ Broaden your horizons by traveling.

■ Practice the golden rule. Life is a boomerang—what goes around comes around.

PERSONAL MONTH NUMBERS

Your PERSONAL MONTH NUMBER is
determined by your birthdate. It
describes what you can expect
during any month and suggests
appropriate activities. Instructions
for calculating your PERSONAL
MONTH NUMBER begin on page 30.

PERSONAL MONTH #1

- Renew your purpose and direction with ambition.

- See an old problem in a new light and think of an innovative solution.

- Get off the fence and be more decisive.

- Be independent and stand up for yourself. Don't be swayed by the opinions of others.

- Don't just talk about your plans; execute them.

PERSONAL MONTH #2

- Your mind is like a sponge; learn something new.

- Weigh all the facts before making decisions.

- Be a good listener; resist the urge to preach or give ultimatums.

- Be patient; don't force issues.

- Use tact and diplomacy to help others cooperate and reach compromises.

- Be sensitive to other's feelings, but don't take things personally.

- Inspire others by sharing your knowledge.

PERSONAL MONTH #3

- Put creativity into everything you do; express your talents.

- Be optimistic; refuse to worry.

- Develop your communication skills.

- Be spontaneous.

- Don't take things too seriously.

- Entertain and accept invitations; be the life of the party.

- If things don't go your way, resist the temptation to whine or pout; use your charm to get what you want.

- Avoid extravagant expenditures.

PERSONAL MONTH #4

- Reorder your priorities and get organized.

- Make a schedule that allows for rest and stick to it.

- Be practical and think logically; use good judgment.

- Get your life and your finances in order.

- Pay attention to details; read the fine print before signing agreements.

- Lay good foundations.

- Use patience and perseverance to tackle the chores you have been avoiding.

PERSONAL MONTH #5

- Be adventurous and seize new opportunities.

- Throw routine out the window and welcome change.

- Follow up on your curiosity.

- Keep an open mind and be flexible.

- Make as many contacts as possible.

- Try making some beneficial changes in the way you operate.

PERSONAL MONTH #6

- Be responsible and meet your obligations.

- Attract new friends and business contacts.

- Spend time with loved ones.

- Make necessary adjustments to create a harmonious atmosphere.

- When asked, give freely of your advice and assistance.

- See duty as a pleasure: write thank you notes, repay social obligations, and fulfill promises.

- Update your wardrobe and revamp your appearance.

PERSONAL MONTH #7

■ Spend quality time with your loved ones.

■ Stay calm, cool, and collected. Don't allow any person, place, or thing to upset you.

■ Refuse to be a party to petty gossip. Resist the temptation to reveal secrets.

■ Examine your goals and analyze your position to determine how to improve it.

■ Play super sleuth; dig deeply and ask the right questions. Then follow your hunches.

■ Analyze the causes behind the effects.

PERSONAL MONTH #8

■ Focus on what you want; take control of the situation and do something constructive to achieve your goal.

■ Channel your energy. Don't limit yourself; you have what it takes to succeed on a large scale.

■ Work efficiently; organize your time.

■ Motivate others to deal with the details.

■ Be fair in your dealings and maintain your emotional balance.

■ Monitor your diet and exercise regularly.

PERSONAL MONTH #9

■ Tie up loose ends and complete projects.

■ Forgive and forget.

■ Release what is no longer useful.

■ Extend a helping hand; be generous with time and energy.

■ Give credit where credit is due; express your appreciation.

■ Project your positive image to the public.

■ Use caution and play by the rules. What goes around, comes around.

■ Look at the big picture and avoid being petty.

PERSONAL DAY NUMBERS

Your PERSONAL DAY NUMBER is determined by your birth date. It describes what you can expect on any day and suggests appropriate activities. Instructions for calculating your PERSONAL DAY NUMBER begin on page 32.

PERSONAL DAY #1

- Be original.
- Start a new project.
- Be self-sufficient.
- Take the lead.
- Be ambitious.
- Keep your goals in mind.
- Be determined, but don't be stubborn.

PERSONAL DAY #2

- Contact a friend.
- Be polite and agreeable.
- Listen more than you talk.
- Be a follower instead of a leader.
- Straighten out a misunderstanding.
- Put people at ease.
- Be considerate of others' feelings.
- Attend a class or lecture to increase your knowledge.
- Don't take things personally.

PERSONAL DAY #3

- Be sociable with friends and associates.
- Express your viewpoint, but don't insist on getting your way.
- Be positive and optimistic.
- Look your best.
- Call someone or write a letter.
- Refuse to worry.
- Concentrate; don't scatter your energies.
- Live for *now*. Play today. Rest tomorrow.

■ Let your inner light shine.

PERSONAL DAY #4

■ Adhere to your budget and don't overspend.

■ Keep your nose to the grindstone.

■ Pay attention to details and correct errors.

■ Make a list and check off your accomplishments.

■ Aim for perfection.

■ Finish what you start.

■ Get a good night's rest.

PERSONAL DAY #5

■ Take a new route to work.

■ Vary your schedule.

■ Meet someone new.

■ Channel your restless energy by getting out to do errands.

■ Be physically active.

■ Take a short trip; get a change of scene.

■ Say yes to a new opportunity.

■ Enjoy your freedom.

PERSONAL DAY #6

■ Be loving.

■ Keep your word.

■ Be even-tempered.

■ Clear up a misunderstanding.

■ Look your best.

■ Help someone.

■ Be good to yourself.

■ Be an attentive host or hostess.

PERSONAL DAY #7

- Take time out for yourself.
- Enjoy nature.
- Avoid worry.
- Listen and think before you speak.
- Remain calm and poised.
- Relax with a good book.
- Let opportunity come to you.

PERSONAL DAY #8

- Be enthusiastic.
- Stay on schedule.
- Make every minute count.
- Be ambitious.
- Accomplish what you set out to do.
- Exercise and eat properly.
- Keep your emotions under control.
- Be a leader, not a follower.

PERSONAL DAY #9

- Be sympathetic and understanding.
- Finish a project.
- Give away what you don't need.
- Be generous.
- Put others first.
- Count your blessings.
- Do a favor for someone special.
- Get on your soapbox.

HOT
TIPS

ALPHA NUMBER CHART

1	2	3	4	5	6	7	8	9
A	B	C	D	E	F	G	H	I
J	K	L	M	N	O	P	Q	R
S	T	U	V	W	X	Y	Z	

THE MINI-MEMORY COURSE

The HOT NUMBERS mini-memory course is designed to help you remember the letters and their corresponding numbers.

1	is strong, active, and can get out of *jams*.	**J A S**
2	is a collector who needs a *basket*.	**B K T**
3	uses words to give us *clues*.	**C L U**
4	gives us order, rules, and regulations, like the *D*epartment of *M*otor *V*ehicles.	**D M V**
5	loves freedom and is always ready for a *new* adventure.	**N E W**
6	loves nice clothes and dresses like a *fox*.	**F O X**
7	is an analyzer who would recognize a *gyp*.	**G Y P**
8	is drawn to money and power; has *h*igh *q*uotient *z*eal.	**H Q Z**
9	is a humanitarian, interested in *i*nternational *r*elations.	**I R**

SUPER SHORTCUT METHOD

Do you like the sound of applause and standing ovations? This method is for you! Your friends will be amazed at how quickly you add up their numbers. By casting out 9s, you can simplify the HOT NUMBERS addition.

Let's take the name RUTH RODMAN RULE. First, let me add up the name using the Shortcut Slash Method.

R U T H   R O D M A N   R U L E

9 3 2 8   9 6 4 4 1 5   9 3 3 5

22/4   29/11/2   20/2

4   +   2   +   2 =

8

Now let me show you the Super Shortcut Method. We'll eliminate, or "cast out" 9s, or any combination of numbers that add to 9. However, do not cast out the final 9. You are never suddenly reduced from a 9 to a 0!

R U T H   R O D M A N   R U L E

9̶ 3 2 8   9̶ 6 4̶ 4 1 5̶   9̶ 3 3 5

13/4   +   11/2   +   11/2 =

8

Step 1   Start with the first name. Are there 9s, or any group of numbers that add to 9? Put a line through them, or "cast out."

Step 2   Add the remaining numbers in the first name, and reduce.

Step 3 Check the middle name. Put a line through any 9 or any combination of numbers that add to 9.

Step 4 Add the remaining numbers in the middle name and reduce to a single digit.

Step 5 Take the last name. Put a line through any 9s or any combination of numbers that add to 9.

Step 6 Add the remaining numbers in the last name and reduce to a single digit.

Step 7 Add the single digit from the first, middle, and last names for the grand total of the NAME NUMBER. You did it!

As you can see, RUTH RODMAN RULE added to 8, no matter which method was used.

Casting out 9s is definitely faster, but feel free to use whichever HOT NUMBERS addition method you prefer.

HOT NUMBERS FORMULAS

NAME # Add the numeric values (according to the ALPHA NUMBER CHART) of ALL THE LETTERS in your name as it appears on your birth certificate. Reduce to a single digit. Complete instructions may be found on page 6.

PERSONALITY # Add the numeric values of the CONSONANTS in your name as it appears on your birth certificate. Reduce to a single digit. Complete instructions may be found on page 13.

HEART # Add the numeric value of the VOWELS in your name as it appears on your birth certificate. Reduce to a single digit. Complete instructions may be found on page 18.

LESSON # Add the numbers of the MONTH, DAY, and YEAR of your birth date. Reduce to a single digit. Complete instructions may be found on page 23.

PERSONAL YEAR # Add the number for the MONTH and DAY of your birthday and the YEAR OF YOUR LAST BIRTHDAY. Reduce to a single digit. Complete instructions may be found on page 25.

PERSONAL MONTH # Add the number of the MONTH in consideration to the number of your PERSONAL YEAR. Reduce to a single digit. Complete instructions may be found on page 29.

PERSONAL DAY # Add the numbers for the MONTH and DAY in consideration to the number of your PERSONAL YEAR. Complete instructions may be found on page 32.

ACKNOWLEDGMENTS

Helena Davis, who introduced me to numerology and who inspired me to help others.

Earl Miller, who shared his knowledge of the numbers, his common sense, and his good humor with me.

Jim Simpson, who encouraged me to live up to my potential, and to follow my true love—numerology.

Jamie, Brooke, and Chelsea, my precious daughters and most honest critics, who willingly screened my calls, did the shopping, and ran the errands while I was writing this book.

Gregg Hackethal, my devoted confidant and staunchest supporter, who was always there and who did everything humanly possible to help me succeed.

Gilbert Kohatsu, who introduced me to my literary agent.

Sherry Robb, who recognized the potential of this book and, with her endless energy and enthusiasm, helped me to launch it. You've opened many doors, my friend.

Libby Walker, my tireless and dedicated assistant, who laughed with me until we cried and who continually encouraged me by saying, "If you can think it and say it, you can think it and write it."

Barbara Grossman, my brilliant and articulate editor, whose vision, expertise, and commitment were invaluable in the development of this project.

Everyone at Crown Publishers, Inc., for the professionalism, interest, and enthusiasm shown toward me.

Debbie Russell Miller, my talented sister, whose wonderfully wacky imagination saved the day!

Michael Wallach, my personal manager extraordinaire, whose wisdom, intuition, and business acumen have been vital to the protection and promotion of my best interests.

Ken Bostic, who believed in the book and made things happen.

Sidney Liebowitz, Roger Zissu, and Mary Donovan of Cowan, Liebowitz and Latman, my trademark attorneys, for their expert legal advice.

The countless thousands of people who have shared their most precious possessions (their names and birthdays) and allowed me to read their numbers.

ALPHA NUMBER CHART

1	2	3	4	5	6	7	8	9
A	B	C	D	E	F	G	H	I
J	K	L	M	N	O	P	Q	R
S	T	U	V	W	X	Y	Z	